Praise for Clarina Nichols and *Revolutionary Heart*

D0596408

Revolutionary
Heart

Revolutionary Heart

The Life of
Clarina Nichols
and the
Pioneering Crusade for
Women's Rights

Diane Eickhoff

Quindaro Press

AUTHOR'S NOTE: This book is a work of nonfiction. All quotations have been taken from historical sources. The reader will clearly know where discrepancies or gaps in the public record required me to engage in scene-setting or conjecture.

—

Revolutionary Heart: The Life of Clarina I.H. Nichols and the Pioneering Crusade for Women's Rights

Quindaro Press
P.O. Box 3463
Kansas City, Kansas 66103
quindaropress.com

Printed in United States of America

Library of Congress Control Number: 2005909927
ISBN-13 (paper): 978-0-9764434-4-5

Photo credit for preceding page and cover: Kansas State Historical Society

Cover and book design: Aaron Barnhart

In memory
of my sister
Myrna Irene Lewis

Contents

ONE Frontier Justice 3

TWO A Vermont Childhood 11

THREE New York Trials 24

FOUR In Print and in Love 36

FIVE The Road to Worcester 48

SIX 'On the Responsibilities of Woman' 58

SEVEN Bloomers and Trousers 67

EIGHT 'The World Is on the Move' 74

NINE Winning Wisconsin 83

TEN A Country Divided 92

ELEVEN Mush and Molasses 100

TWELVE Life and Death on the Prairie 108

THIRTEEN Bleeding Kansas 121

FOURTEEN Quindaro 134

FIFTEEN Woman on a Mission 144

SIXTEEN 'A Vast Army of Widows and Orphans' 156

SEVENTEEN With Liberty and Suffrage for All 169

EIGHTEEN 'Grant! Grant! Grant!' 182

NINETEEN Third Class to California 193

TWENTY 'The Heart of a Loving Woman' 201

Epilogue 213

Acknowledgments 217

Appendix A
The Antebellum Women's Rights Movement 223

Appendix B
Preamble and Constitution of the
Moneka Women's Rights Association 229

Appendix C
'The Birds' 232

Appendix D
Mrs. Nichols v. Rev. Blachly:
An Imagined Debate 234

Appendix E
The Family of Clarina I. H. Nichols 236

Notes 239

Index 269

List of Illustrations

Clarina Nichols, circa 1843   iv

Early Quindaro, Kansas   5

Clarina Howard at age three   13

Chapin and Birsha Smith Howard   15

The Howard home in Townshend   18

Clarina Howard as a young woman   21

Packet boat on the Erie Canal   27

"Poor Drunkard's Wife"   31

Brattleboro, Vermont in the 1850s   41

George W. Nichols, George B. Nichols   45

Elizabeth Cady Stanton, Lucretia Mott   52

Paulina Wright Davis, Abby Kelley Foster   53

Cartoon of woman's rights speaker   60

"Responsibilities of Woman" excerpt   65

Susan B. Anthony   68

Woman in bloomers   70

Broadway Tabernacle   80

Phrenology diagram   84

Man and woman farming in Wisconsin   89

Windham County Democrat excerpt   94

Map of slave and free states in 1860   97

Early Lawrence, Kansas   104

Cartoon satirizing Kansas border election   112

Clarina Nichols, circa 1854   117

"Liberty, the Fair Maid of Kansas"   123

John Brown   128

A.O., Howard, and Birsha Carpenter   136

Quindaro Chindowan masthead   141

Wyandotte Constitution site   148

"Lady Clerks Leaving the Treasury
Department"   168

Hutchinson Family Singers   173

Lucy Stone   178

Birsha Carpenter Davis   185

Ulysses S. Grant cartoon   187

George B. Nichols, Birney Nichols,
Katherine H. Nichols, Helen C. Nichols
197

Clarina Nichols engraving   208

Grace Carpenter Hudson   214

Alphonso Taft   215

Lady Liberty presented with Wollstonecraft's
Vindication of the Rights of Woman   222

Abigail Adams, Frances Wright   223

Ernestine Rose, William Lloyd Garrison   224

Amelia Bloomer, Elizabeth Cady Stanton   225

Sojourner Truth, Susan B. Anthony   226

Antoinette Brown Blackwell, Lucy Stone   227

Frances Willard, Alice Paul   228

Personal effects of Clarina Nichols
on display at Grace Hudson Museum
237

———

"Many daughters have done virtuously, but
thou excellest them all. Favour is deceitful,
and beauty is vain: but a woman that feareth
the Lord, she shall be praised. Give her of
the fruit of her hands; and let her own works
praise her in the gates."

Proverbs 31:29–31

———

ONE

Frontier Justice

In 1860 I was arrested with several of my neighbors, among them a Congregational clergyman and his wife, his deacon and wife, a Notary Public, and an ex-Probate judge, for kidnapping neighbor D's children. As a matter of fact, we had aided the mother in recovering her little ones from the clutch of a husband who had lived for years on the earnings of her needle, beaten her once to death's door, finally choked her to insensibility, and thrust her out of doors, throwing her clothes after her.

The whole tale was absurd, outrageous, and tragic, which is probably why she loved to tell it. On the eve of the Civil War, one of the most respected women in Kansas Territory, a New England expatriate of excellent pedigree, a newspaper editor, and one of the country's best-known lecturers — Clarina

I. H. Nichols — had been hauled into court to answer charges filed by a known wife beater and one of the town's leading scoundrels.

Her crime, it seemed, was befriending a young woman whom she had met on her daily stroll through Quindaro, a frontier outpost on the west bank of the Missouri River. Three years earlier, Quindaro had been one of the most desirable destinations in Kansas Territory. By 1860, however, it had gone bust, a victim of the economic and political reversals that ruined many a Western town in the nineteenth century. Scattered among Quindaro's dwellings were half-finished or abandoned shops, mercantile stores, and homes, their vacant windows staring out onto dirt streets and a landscape littered with tree stumps, rock piles, and debris. Only the town's hardiest residents remained, many of them holding on in the hope that they could recoup their investments.

Lydia Peck had been through too much to be discouraged by the dismal sight that greeted her as she stepped off the steamboat and started up the road to the town hotel. Since her marriage to James Peck, she had known little but hardship. For years she had supported her family, earning a modest living through diligent sewing and clever handiwork. But James was an abusive and a vengeful husband. When she asked him for a divorce, he threw her out of the house, converted their assets into cash, and fled with the children, Alma and Liberty, to parts unknown. Not knowing where they had gone, lacking the means to find them, Lydia Peck sought work in a New England cotton mill where she skimped and saved until she had $400 in gold. Then she set out, determined to find her children and take them back home with her.

The trail led to Quindaro, where James Peck was said to be living under an assumed name. Within hours, Lydia Peck had chanced upon the one person in town best prepared to help her. Clarina Nichols recognized the man Lydia was describing to her. He was none other than James Dimond —

This painting by Charles Goslin shows the free-state port of Quindaro with the steamship *Lightfoot* approaching. The Missouri town of Parkville is visible on the opposite bank. *(Courtesy Ed Shutt)*

"neighbor D," as she would refer to him in newspaper accounts — a ne'er-do-well who lived with two young children in a rundown shack just down the road.

Nichols quickly assembled a circle of allies from among the leading citizens of Quindaro. On hearing of Lydia's plight, they were ready to dispense with the law and take immediate action. "The gentlemen advised that I with several other women should go with the mother and take the children by force, and they would go with and protect us from violence," she would later write.

Her instincts, however, told her to avoid a confrontation with James Peck, a man known for his vile temper. It had also occurred to Nichols that Lydia's plight could serve a larger purpose. For her husband's actions, while extreme, were not illegal. Domestic abuse was not a crime in 1860, and his absconding with Alma and Liberty was tolerated as well, since the ordinary legal assumption of the day was that they were his children, not hers.

Laws making spousal abuse a crime were still years away from passage, but in progressive states across the Union, legislatures had started to level the field in custody cases. Nichols herself had recently lobbied the territorial legislature in Kansas, and at her urging it had passed a bill that, in theory at least, ended the automatic right of fathers to their children in a divorce. "Neighbor D," Nichols realized, could serve as an ideal test of the new law. After all, this father's idea of custodianship was well known throughout Quindaro. Nichols and others had seen Alma and Liberty begging scraps of food from neighbors, and the home he provided for them was, in Nichols's words, "a hovel." Challenging James Peck in court had something else in its favor: it would be the easiest way to wrest these two children from their father, who did not strike anyone as being the negotiating kind.

After some discussion, the group agreed that Nichols should travel to the territorial capital and seek a divorce, with full custody rights, for Lydia Peck. Packing her "knitting work and reputation," Nichols headed for the legislature.

For a month she stayed on, finding work as a legislative clerk to support her efforts as she helped the divorce bill wend its way through subcommittees and both houses. While this was going on, several of the lawmakers asked her to educate them as to why a woman might need protection from her own husband, and Nichols helped enlarge their understanding. Though James Peck's attorneys challenged the bill, they could not prevail on the lawmakers. The divorce was signed by the territorial governor on February 27, 1860, winning freedom for Lydia and stripping James of custody over the children.

That should have been the end of the matter, but Clarina Nichols knew that things were not always as they seemed in Kansas Territory. At that time in its history, the territory was, in her words, "intensely political in every fibre." In that uncharted wilderness, the personal, the political, and the criminal intersected as they rarely have in United States history. Large numbers of fugitive slaves were crossing from Missouri, where slavery was legal, into Kansas Territory, where it was not. Some living in the border towns were ready to aid escaping slaves, but others were just as ready to hunt them down and sell them back to their Missouri masters for one hundred dollars a head.

Nichols felt contempt for "conspiring Kansas officials" who actively aided the bounty hunters. She also knew that if they felt no pangs of conscience about profiting from the fugitive slave trade, they would scoff at a Kansas law granting Lydia Peck custody of her children. They would surely aid her ex-husband instead.

But with the law firmly on her side, Nichols was ready to take the direct action she had been reluctant to try earlier. She recruited a friend with a fast horse to race back to Quindaro and tell the local sheriff to be on the lookout for James Peck making a run for the border. Sure enough, he was soon spotted with a rifle on his shoulder and his children in tow, trying to sneak out of town after being served the divorce papers. The sheriff arrested and detained him, and Alma and Liberty were put in the care of a neighbor. This gave Nichols the opportunity she needed to recover the children without having to deal with their ill-tempered father.

The children, however, were almost as much trouble. It turned out that James Peck had told them that the reason he had taken them from their mother was that she was trying to poison them. Nichols wrote that the youngsters had to be dragged from the neighbor's house "screaming, biting, and scratching their captors." Finally, around midnight, Mrs. Peck, Alma, and Liberty were spirited out of Quindaro using the escape routes of the local underground railroad.

The next day, Nichols began staging an elaborate charade to convince James Peck that his children were hidden somewhere in the village. For three days she and her co-conspirators darted about Quindaro, meeting in the shadows, exchanging notes, looking for all the world like they were up to something. By the time Peck realized he had been tricked, his former family was halfway across the country. Not willing to let go of the matter, he convinced (or paid) local officials to have Nichols and several others arrested. They were charged with "wilfully, maliciously, forcibly and fraudulently enticing, leading, carrying away and detaining" Peck's children.

Throughout the weeks that followed, Nichols kept the newspaper readers of northeastern Kansas entertained by her accounts of the courtroom shenanigans. Writing under the pen name "Quindaro" for the Lawrence *Republican*, she described the case as though writing a drama review, with each update serving as a new scene. "The curtain is about to rise on scene fifth," she wrote as the case was nearing conclusion. She recalled how, earlier, Peck's lawyers had entered the courtroom with a "flourish of trumpets," parading their "wonderful legal acumen" before the grand jury. But the prosecution's case had quickly unraveled, and now there was nothing to sustain it but the claims of James Peck. The judge threw the case out, and afterward, Nichols joked, Peck's lawyers beat such a hasty retreat that "it is not known certainly whether they are alive."

By then she had received a letter from Lydia Peck, who was back in New England, beginning a new chapter in her life. Nichols reported that each night Lydia went to bed with "a little sunny head on each arm, because neither [child] was willing to be separated from her."

Two decades later, Clarina Nichols was still telling that story. A lengthy account of the case appeared in a San Francisco newspaper in 1878, and another account was sent to her longtime friend and comrade, Susan B. Anthony. It is likely

that Lydia Peck's story became a staple in the speeches that
Nichols gave over the years, for it served as a graphic reminder
of the need for laws that gave the so-called "second sex" the
same basic rights and protections that men had.

During her long and productive career as a lecturer, activ-
ist, and journalist, Nichols collected stories of wives, widows,
divorceés, and children who were put in harm's way because of
a legal system that failed to protect them. Whenever she spoke
before a group or wrote an article for a newspaper, Nichols
included stories that illustrated injustice. The widow sent to
the poorhouse because the laws of her state did not permit her
to collect her husband's estate. The wife helpless to stop her
spouse from spending all she earned on drink. The little boy
left orphaned and penniless because his dying mother could
not leave him an inheritance.

Stories, she discovered, touched hearts, and she used them
to animate the cases of injustice she brought to light. Like
a mother encouraging her children to include an ignored or
picked-upon playmate, Nichols, in her calm and genteel way,
helped both men and women respond to the plight of women
in untenable situations.

There was one story, however, that Clarina Nichols never
told — her own. Few of the women who poured out their souls
to her would ever know it, but she had once suffered the same
fate as they had. She knew how it felt to be betrayed by the person she had promised to love beyond all others, and she knew
what it was like to come home and find her children missing.
She rarely spoke of these formative years, however, and she
kept a full decade of her life cloaked in secrecy. Unlike many
who served in the early women's rights movement, she did not
write a memoir. Perhaps Nichols wished to avoid reliving those
painful memories, or she may simply have wanted to deny her
opponents any chance to dredge up details of her past. Whatever the reason, she rarely discussed those early experiences
that had shaped and strengthened her for the struggle ahead.

And strengthen they did. Though she did not attend the historic Seneca Falls Convention of 1848, Clarina Nichols was one of the early leaders of the first organized movement in the United States for women's civil rights. Other sisters in the struggle eventually would grow weary or get married and leave the movement behind. But Nichols devoted herself wholeheartedly to the cause of women's rights until the end of her life.

———

Since her death in 1885, her name has faded almost entirely from the annals of history. Her two-page entry in the landmark 1971 encyclopedia, *Notable American Women*, brought her accomplishments to light, and two years later the first partial collection of her papers was published. Anyone reading those letters and articles can see that this was an unjustly overlooked pioneer of the women's movement. Little was known, however, about her motivations. Why, for instance, did she close down her newspaper in Vermont and set out — at the age of forty-four — to make her dream of equality come true on the tough, unforgiving soil of the American frontier?

In the past six years, new documents by and about Nichols have been discovered. They shed light on both her public career and the forces that impelled her to follow the westward expansion of the United States, from Vermont to Kansas to California. They reveal a sociable but solitary woman who remained optimistic and productive in the face of constant adversity. And they provide greater insight into why Nichols identified so closely with women trapped in poverty and abusive relationships, and why they occupied a tender place in her heart.

It is time to tell that story.

TWO

A Vermont Childhood

Clarina Irene Howard was born January 25, 1810, in West Townshend, a small farming village tucked into the Green Mountains of southern Vermont. If she were alive today, she would easily recognize the countryside where she grew up — the bend in the river, the valley, the mountains that wrap themselves around the little town like a giant's protective arm.

Clarina Howard's earliest American ancestor was William Hayward, a young Puritan who at eighteen set sail from England in the mid-1630s, married an adventurous shipmate two years his senior, fathered four sons, and died at sea in 1653. In fact, both sides of her family had pedigrees intertwined with the farmers, merchants, soldiers and statesmen who formed New England in its early days. After her grandfathers fought in the Revolutionary War, they "packed their brides on horseback, with feather beds strapped on behind and blazed tracks from

Connecticut, Massachusetts, and Rhode Island to the green hills and fertile valleys of the Green Mountain State." Though Vermont was an isolated, uncultivated wilderness at that time, there were opportunities for people willing to work hard for the chance to improve their fortunes — which Clarina's grand-parents did to a remarkable degree.

Chapin Howard, her father, operated the town's tannery, a business that turned raw animal skins into leather for sturdy shoes and stout harnesses. An ambitious, public-spirited, likable man, Chapin later owned a hotel, served three terms in the state legislature, helped organize and finance a Baptist seminary in Townshend, and made a fortune with his son Aurelius buying and selling land in territorial Michigan. By the time Clarina Howard was grown, her father was one of the wealthiest men in town, but because he was generous, tactful, and didn't put on airs, Mr. Howard was respected by rich and poor alike.

Her mother, Birsha Smith Howard, expected her daughters to work hard, even though the family was wealthy enough to employ servants. Mrs. Howard wanted to make sure her five daughters could run their own households, with or without servants. As she grew up, young Clarina learned how to cook delicate pastries and roast gourmet cuts of beef, but she also learned how to milk cows, churn butter, and take care of veg-etables from planting to pickling. Though every female was expected to develop some level of proficiency in the sewing arts, Mrs. Howard's eldest daughter excelled at any type of handwork. After she had solved a vexing sewing problem with a bit of collar ribbon, her mother declared, "That is Clarina all over — so ingenious!" She became expert at fine embroidery, could spin and weave, sew and knit, and construct every article of clothing from dainty bonnets to thick wool stockings. She was especially apt at knitting, which would become a trademark occupation for her later in life. "We always knit while we read," she would one day tell the reformer Amelia Bloomer, "and can

Clarina Howard, age three, in an 1813 painting.
(Grace Hudson Museum, Ukiah, California)

think so much better to the click of the needles."

Despite being well-to-do, the Howards were not extravagant and didn't spend money unnecessarily. Clarina Nichols recalled having "a handsome suit for summer and another for winter." The following year her Sunday dress became her everyday dress, and her everyday dress became her petticoat. Old petticoats were used for quilts and hooked rugs. After that they could still be used for patches and rags. She liked to quote her grandmother Smith's words: "There is nothing like economy in a family."

Mrs. Howard was a good republican mother who understood the need for an educated citizenry. All her children —the five girls as well as the three boys — received good basic educations.

She expected them to do well in school, and she meant business. Clarina Nichols recalled being spanked once because she was unable to spell the word "cider." She needed little incentive after that: "I took to learning like a duck to water."

The summer after she turned eight, a religious revival swept into West Townshend, sending ripples of excitement into the countryside and adjoining communities. Spiritual fervor had been building in New England for a decade. It was further fueled by an enormous volcanic eruption in 1815 in Indonesia that dramatically affected the weather in the northeastern United States for several years. Record low temperatures led to massive crop failures, and 1816 became known as "the year without a summer." At a time when the public had little understanding of how natural disasters could alter the climate, the suffering caused by crop failure was widely interpreted as a sign that the world was coming to an end.

Whenever a powerful preacher came to town, word quickly spread and crowds gathered. Camp meetings sometimes went on for upwards of a week. In a secluded meadow outside town, people sat round a blazing bonfire on hard benches for hours at a time, all eyes fixed on the itinerant preacher in their midst, his face lit up like the noonday sun. In one hand he held a worn leather Bible, which he played with the other like a virtuoso, ranging from one passage to the next until he reached the climax of his sermon — an invitation to his flock to come forward, repent, confess, and accept Christ.

Clarina Howard and her parents answered that call in 1818. They were baptized and became lifelong members of the Baptist church. Baptists were a minority in New England and viewed with suspicion by members of the dominant Congregational church, but they were increasing their numbers in Windham County and gaining influence. In time Baptists came to reject Calvinist doctrines of predestination in favor of a belief that salvation was obtained through an act of free will and the

Chapin and Birsha Smith Howard. *(courtesy Grace Hudson Museum, Ukiah, California)*

grace of God. The Howards' church was less radical than the Free Will Baptists, who supported both abolition and women's rights, but it did recognize its female congregants, which many churches at that time did not. On the church roster of 1818, the name of Clarina Howard appears right after her father's. She was eight years old.

The young believer took her religion seriously. She read the Bible through many times, studied it intensively, memorized great portions of it, and became familiar with even its most obscure passages. That would serve her well in later years when ministers challenged her stand on women's rights and told her the Bible commanded females to be submissive and silent.

Like most churches of that time, Baptists had a strict code of conduct for their members. They opposed drinking, playing musical instruments in church, and dancing. Because of church policy, Clarina never learned to dance. "Only the devil inspired the violin," she recalled, "and to keep step to its music was the march of death."

The larger community she grew up in had a settled quality to it and a rich mixture of families and neighbors who had known each other a long time. There were many children. In their free hours they played on the streets and explored the fields and meadows surrounding West Townshend. In winter they sledded and skated, went sleigh-riding, played parlor games, carved apple and pumpkin rings, and concocted maple syrup treats. She recalled a particular October evening when a visiting cousin was telling the Howard sisters ghost stories around the fire. Suddenly, loud popping noises made the girls "rush screaming from the room." A merry Clarina called them back and explained that the "exploded ghosts" were only acorns that she had secretly buried in the embers.

Throughout a good portion of the year, the Howard family spent their evening hours assembled in front of the large open hearth, the only source of warmth in the house. Out came the workbaskets filled with the family's knitting and mending. While Mrs. Howard and the older girls patched and sewed, the children of both sexes played games or knit mittens and socks, while Mr. Howard and the older boys whittled or repaired small tools and implements. To pass the time they took turns reading aloud the week's newspapers, the Bible, or chapters from a book. They talked about what they read and what was happening in the broader world. Clarina Nichols would remember the "animated discussions that filled our happy evenings." Later in her life, she would declare central heating to be the bane of family life, because a house whose rooms were evenly heated allowed individuals to go off by themselves instead of gathering together before a cozy fire.

On some of those cool evenings, her Grandfather Smith told his grandchildren stories about his narrow escapes during the Revolutionary War. Years later, when she herself was fighting for freedom on the Western frontier, Clarina Nichols remembered her grandfather's words:

"Oh, my children, you can't know what your liberty cost."

———————

As the hardships of Revolutionary times eased, and the blurred lines that allowed women to do "men's work" during a time of national emergency hardened, people fell into a division of roles by sex.

Men were the undisputed heads of their households, in charge of all affairs outside the home. They made the important decisions and controlled the family property and purse-strings. Building, planting crops, caring for the larger animals and tools — these were men's jobs. Almost exclusively, men practiced the higher-paying trades and higher-status professions, such as tanner, blacksmith, carpenter, cobbler, doctor, lawyer, and preacher.

Everything connected to the home, vegetable garden, farmyard, and child-rearing was woman's work. Without her hard work, thriftiness, and intelligent planning, the family would not survive. She made the garden, preserved food for the winter, spent long hours cooking over an open hearth, spun and wove clothing for each member of the family, cared for the chickens, milked cows, and often taught her children their first lessons and prayers. Women worked in the field when necessary, and men helped in the home, especially if the woman of the house was ill or absent for some reason, but these were not their primary responsibilities, and everyone knew that. As the Industrial Revolution gained momentum, and more and more of the nation's paid labor was performed away from the family farm or homestead, this notion of separate "spheres" gained currency. The idea of a public domain that men dominated and a domestic realm where women's "natural instincts" could

Chapin and Birsha Howard's home still stands
on the village green in Townshend, Vermont.

find full expression helped explain the world. In their weekly
preaching, religious leaders reinforced a view of separate
spheres and discrete roles for men and women, with God
overseeing the division of roles and pronouncing it good.

As the oldest child, and a daughter besides, Clarina was
expected to shoulder a great deal of responsibility in the family.
She was only two years old when her mother told her to mind
the new baby: "Be a little woman and rock the cradle, and let
Mama wash [clothes]." Children as young as two or three were
expected to help out wherever they could — gathering wood
chips for the fire, scattering feed for the chickens, and taking
care of children even younger than themselves.

—————

She had seven younger brothers and sisters: Aurelius,
Catherine, Ormando, Mary, Laurinda, Ellen, and Bainbridge,

all of whom survived into adulthood. In later years Nichols painted an idyllic picture of her childhood and of her well-ordered, loving family.

Even though Chapin and Birsha Howard trained their children in boys' and girls' roles, there are signs that they valued their children equally. They gave each one an education and an equal inheritance. They gifted their eldest daughter with a wooden laptop writing desk for her twelfth birthday — a sign that they appreciated her mind as well as her skill with a needle. Unlike other early women's rights advocates, Nichols never reported her father saying that he wished she had been a boy. Nor did he try to shelter her from the harsh realities of life.

Among his other duties, Chapin served for many years as one of West Townshend's selectmen and at times acted as its "overseer of the poor." New England villages were governed by "pauper laws" that required them to provide for the destitute persons in their midst. But there were strict residential restrictions to make sure the burden of caring for paupers did not overwhelm a town's resources. The hardest part of Mr. Howard's job was turning away people he could not help. Recalling her early years, Nichols said she had "frequent opportunities" to observe her father's interactions with the poor who came to him for aid:

> While I sat in the quiet corner, an indignant and silent listener to revelations from the quivering lips of the poor, and the heartless contrivances of men to evade the paupers' support, I saw my father's moistened eye and heard his regretful replies to the oft-recurring tales of sorrow — 'I can't help it. I am only the agent of the town to do its bidding' and 'the law allows it' — until I learned first to despise such laws, and second, to doubt the wisdom of the men who could make them.

This was Clarina Howard's legal awakening to the problems of the poor and especially the problems that impoverished women faced. She concluded that the politicians who made laws and the lawyers and judges who interpreted them did not care about helping widows, orphans, abused and abandoned wives, or any other person in need. This, in turn, steeled her resolve: "I would shrink from myself as less than human, and an anomaly of womanhood, if I could have seen all this and not resolve to *be* that I might *do*."

As an adult, her knowledge of the legal system would distinguish her in the women's rights movement, leading one of its founders to observe that Clarina Nichols was "as conversant with the laws of her state as any judge or lawyer in it."

Chapin Howard encouraged her further explorations, not just by letting her overhear his dealings with destitute women but by agreeing to pay for a year of private education. She said she had told her father that if he had to choose between giving her a fine dowry or an education, she wanted more schooling. Chapin, who by this time had plenty of money for both, sent her at age seventeen to Timothy Cressy's Select School in West Townshend. Beyond district (elementary) school, this was her only year of advanced study, but it was more education than the average person, male or female, received.

In November of 1828, the students at Timothy Cressy's Select School put on an "exhibition" to show the community what they had learned during their year of intensive study. The opening address by James Phelps was delivered entirely in Latin. Other "gentlemen" gave talks on mathematics, business, politics, and the pressing social issues of the day: the Indian situation, slavery, and temperance. An all-male cast presented two Biblical dramas, including one based on the story of Daniel in the lion's den.

By contrast, a much smaller representation of the "misses" appeared in the program. Their topics pertained to moral uplift and self-improvement:

A portrait of Clarina Howard painted in
her teens. *(Courtesy Janice Parker)*

Mental Improvement a Source of Happiness
Reflection a Source of Improvement
Benevolence a Source of Personal Happiness
Love of Immortality
Moral Influence of Novels
Moral Influence of Balls
Moral Influence of Slander
Hopes of Immortality

The one exception to this litany of virtuous feminine striv-
ing was Clarina Howard, who gave a dissertation titled,
"Comparative of a Scientific and an Ornamental Education
to Females." The text for that talk has not survived, but the
title would have been self-explanatory to those who attended
the exhibition.

At that time in history one of the questions society was

puzzling over was how to educate girls. There was general agreement that they needed some facility with the three R's of reading, 'riting, and 'rithmetic, but middle- and upper-class families wanted something more for their daughters. An "ornamental" education included the reading and writing of poetry, singing and piano lessons, and enough French to make young women sound cultured and refined. In addition, they were taught embroidery and fine needlework, art, and manners. The curriculum was designed to turn them into ladies — with improved marriage prospects. A "scientific" education, on the other hand, prepared young men for the university and professional careers. The subjects included science, mathematics, history, English, Latin, Greek, rhetoric, and philosophy.

Though Cressy's school appears to have taught students of both sexes the same academic curriculum, the popular belief at the time was that girls could not learn "scientific" subjects with any facility. Girls' brains, it was believed, were too small and underdeveloped to handle such complex information, and even attempting to do so might be harmful to them. Anyway, "scientific" education was deemed worthless to females, since they would not be going to college. In 1828 not a single public university in the country admitted women.

Clarina Howard may not have begrudged her first cousin and classmate, Alphonso Taft, his educational opportunities, but surely she felt at least a twinge of envy. The Taft family had less money than the Howards, yet there was no question that Alphonso would go on to higher education and train for a profession. Indeed, he would go on to become Townshend's most distinguished son. After attending Yale, he became a career diplomat in the Grant administration and the father of the Taft dynasty in Ohio. His son, William Howard Taft, became the twenty-seventh President of the United States.

As Clarina crossed the stage to begin speaking, she probably worried about what people were thinking of her. She once confessed to being "very sensitive to the sensation my face —

when at rest — generally creates." She lacked the pert nose, bow mouth, dimpled cheeks, and diminutive figure of those girls who were considered pretty.

"I never desired beauty," she once said, "but always lamented that I was not handsome enough to dispel the prejudices it was my mission to combat." She was striking in her own way — tall with a long face, high forehead, prominent nose, and wide, full lips. She had a deep dimple in the cleft of her chin, and a steady gaze through intelligent blue-gray eyes. It is not hard to imagine those features relaxing and coming to life before an audience. But beneath the surface of the self-controlled young woman who looks out from her portrait, she burned with intellectual curiosity. At age eighteen she had already begun to face a hard truth. It didn't matter how clever she was or how hard she worked; in the United States, the land of opportunity, a female would never be more than a second-class citizen.

After graduation Clarina Howard taught school around Windham County. "I had a longing desire to do good," she later recalled, "but the teacher's desk was the only sphere that opened before me."

THREE

New York
Trials

Marriage, not employment, was foremost in Clarina Howard's mind in 1830. Before she went off to Timothy Cressy's
school she had commenced writing poetry, copying the verses
into a journal in a generous hand, with flourishing loops and
high-crossed *t*'s that flowed across the page like banners.
The dedicatory poem in her album, which she began in 1827,
gushes with radiant optimism about the future:

> I go, I go to regions of song
> And I'll bring thee rich bouquets
>   of friendships ere long;
> In the springtime of life
>   All pure blooms the flow'r
> Unsullied by interests
>   Unshackled by power!

To the garden of romance I'll hie;
In the green bowers of fancy
Rich blossoms I spy;
Undim'd is their beauty
Uncanker'd by care
No grief has assailed them
No sorrow is there!

Alas, the man she was about to marry would never come close to fulfilling these dreams of eternal romance.

———————

In April of 1830, when Clarina was twenty years old, she married Justin Carpenter. Her new husband came from a family of devout Baptists with a distinguished New England lineage; his grandfather was one of Vermont's founding fathers. Justin, who was ten years older than her, had just completed law studies at Union College. There he belonged to the Adelphic Society, whose purpose was to promote "three great objects: Literature, Friendship, and Morality." Though he had studied law, Justin was uncertain about what he wanted to do next. The one thing he knew was that he didn't want to spend the rest of his life in small-town Vermont.

As for his new bride, her speech at her high school graduation showed a young woman who already saw the world differently than did most of her peers in West Townshend. It is easy to imagine this literate, ambitious couple planning their new life together on the other side of the Green Mountains. Many people were moving west at this time. Justin and Clarina Carpenter decided to join them.

In 1830 "the West" meant western New York state. The 300–mile journey from Vermont would take many days, but thanks to the Erie Canal that trip was easier than ever before. Instead of an uncomfortable, bumpy stagecoach ride over rough roads, travelers could glide through the canals on brightly-colored packet boats. A team of horses or mules walked along the shore, pulling the packet boats along at a steady four miles per hour.

The Erie Canal cut across the heart of New York state, from the Hudson River in the east to Lake Erie in the west. The canal had become the stimulus for new towns that sprang up all along its twisted spine. Roads connected inns, businesses, factories, and storehouses with the Erie Canal, which in turn linked sellers and buyers up and down its route. Western New York, with its immense fields of gleaming wheat, was fast becoming the nation's breadbasket and an important center of commerce.

Justin and Clarina headed for Brockport, a boomtown taking shape just west of Rochester. They were eager to put down roots and find their niche in the rapidly growing town, for they were already expecting their first child. On March 8, 1831, Clarina Carpenter gave birth to a little girl, whom they named Birsha after the baby's maternal grandmother.

It was a common belief that someone living in Brockport needed more drive, more ambition, more "push" than a person "back east" did. Justin and his business partner, J. M. Davis, seemed to have the right spirit. They put together a lending library and organized a private school, the Brockport Academy, where Clarina taught. She also launched a small literary magazine and filled its pages with poetry and writings solicited from members of the community.

———◆———

The young couple had arrived in western New York State just as another force was sweeping through it, one more powerful than even the mighty economic engine of the Erie Canal. In tent revivals and standing-room-only prayer meetings throughout the area, growing throngs of believers were dedicating their lives to Christ and to moral improvement. Clarina Carpenter was living in the crucible of the Second

The Erie Canal made long-distance travel possible and brought thousands of emigrants to western New York. Notice horse-drawn packet boat at left. *(Carl Rakeman Collection, Federal Highway Administration)*

Great Awakening, led by preachers such as Charles Finney and Theodore Dwight Weld, whose path would cross with hers years later. The religious enthusiasm stoked by Finney, Weld and others would soon fan out across the United States and help launch reform movements such as the young nation had not seen before.

The Second Great Awakening fueled the rise of the temperance movement, with thousands of societies forming in the 1820s and 1830s, comprised of Christian men and women — often the most educated and refined members of their community — who opposed the consumption and, in some cases, the sale of alcohol. The Temperance Society of Brockport formed May 1, 1830, and Justin and Clarina both threw themselves into the cause.

As Baptists, they had always opposed drinking, but people of all faiths were now supporting temperance. This was not surprising given the per capita consumption of alcohol in post-

Colonial America. The average adult of that time consumed
three times as much alcohol as the typical American does today. Ale and hard cider flowed as freely as water through the
daily lives of most people. Female drinkers must have been
less problematic, less numerous, or more hidden than male
drinkers, for temperance supporters focused their attention
on men. Temperance advocates claimed alcoholic husbands
drank up their wages and deprived their families of food and
the other necessities of life. They linked domestic abuse and
every known vice to liquor, from Sabbath-breaking to de-
bauchery. For Clarina Carpenter, however, married men were
at the heart of the problem. She had heard enough stories in
her father's house to know that saving one man from the bottle
might spare a whole family from heartbreak.

The newlyweds signed their names to a temperance pledge
in which they promised not to touch strong drink, except for
medicinal purposes, for the rest of their lives. By the December meeting, 214 men and women had joined the Brockport
Temperance Society, and Justin Carpenter had been elected
one of its four directors.

By its first anniversary the society had grown to four hundred members, many of whom eagerly spread the word about
the sorrows of intemperance and the joys of sobriety. They
often talked of "a good time coming," a phrase that would
endure for decades in reform circles as an expression of hope
and a belief that one day the evils of society would cease. And
while alcohol was the first priority for many reformers, over the
years the list would grow to include slavery, poverty, war, and
injustice of every kind, including the oppression of women.

As the Fourth of July, 1831, approached, the Brockport
Friends of Temperance saw an outstanding opportunity to
make its message heard. By then the nation's anniversary
had become an excuse for a daylong drinking party. Patriots,
soaked to the gills with "good old democratic whisky," fired
pistols into the air, got into fistfights, and generally raised hell.

For those who wanted to have their alcohol and eat it too, there were recipes for crowd-pleasing Independence Day cakes that featured a quart each of wine and brandy.

To counter this, a small committee which included Justin organized and promoted a "Cold Water Celebration." At ten in the morning of July 4, 1831, a large group lined up in front of Wales' Coffee House in downtown Brockport. The men wore their best suits and stood at the front of the line. Neatly attired in snow-white dresses, the women lined up behind, followed by town officials. A corps of wizened veterans from the Revolutionary War brought up the rear.

With a marching band playing patriotic music, they paraded up Main Street to the Presbyterian Church where they sang, prayed, and listened to long speeches under large, open-air tents. Someone recited the familiar words of the Declaration of Independence: "When in the course of human events, it becomes necessary for one people to dissolve the political bonds...."

Then dinner was served "with coffee, tea, and pure, cold water," wrote the *Brockport Free Press*, a solidly pro-temperance newspaper. The paper's editor declared the march a success and praised the Cold Water Celebration as "the most pleasing and heart-cheering commemoration of our National Independence that we ever participated in, or ever witnessed."

———◆———

For the Carpenters, the Cold Water Celebration may have been the high point of their marriage. Despite his fine education and impressive credentials, Justin struggled both professionally and personally. Few details were ever revealed outside the closed circle of their marriage, but by 1832 Justin's life had begun to follow a tragic arc. Clarina did not keep a diary because, she said later, her years with her first husband were too painful to record.

Justin's partnership with J. M. Davis was dissolved "by

mutual consent," read a terse announcement in the *Brockport Free Press*. Though he tried to carry on alone, he was soon forced to close down his school. The *Western Star*, a newspaper he published, lasted only a year, and despite his fine education, he never got a law practice going in Brockport.

Justin became a burden to his wife, who later wrote that her "flourishing female boarding school" was forced to close down after an unexplained incident involving her husband. At times she took in boarders to earn cash. To save money, she did all the work herself — while pretending to be only the "intelligent mistress" of the house. When all else failed, she took in sewing, for she had always been an expert seamstress. In a letter written to her parents in July, 1833, she referred to Brockport as "this scene of past sorrows, vexations, and disappointments."

By 1834, Justin and Clarina were living in New York City. At that time thousands of European immigrants, especially from Ireland and Germany, were streaming through New York's harbors. The new immigrants, whether skilled or un-skilled, were willing to work at anything that would feed their families and get them started on the road to a better life.

Justin may have thought he would improve his chances of success in the city, but failure followed him to New York. Once again he tried to establish a law practice and a publish-ing firm, but in a short time he was "burned out and lost all," according to a note in his college record.

Like so many other newcomers, Clarina Carpenter did what was necessary to survive. She used every thrifty lesson her mother had taught her. Still, she had a hard time making ends meet on "women's wages," one-third to one-half what men received for comparable work. In New York City she kept a roof over their heads by doing French crimping — tiny rows of fine decorative stitching — which she contracted on a piecework basis for a hat-making establishment. She was learning to be a woman alone in the world, supporting a family

Clarina Nichols shared a widely held nineteenth-
century view, reflected in this sheet music cover,
that intemperance was the major cause of poverty in
American families. *(Courtesy Amaranth Publishing)*

on a meager income.

Though their marriage was a rocky one, the Carpenters had
two more children. Chapin Howard, named for his maternal
grandfather, was born on August 11, 1834. His mother called
him Howard to distinguish him from his grandfather Chapin.
Two years later, on November 27, 1836, a second son was
born. He was named Aurelius Ormando after his mother's two
brothers, but she called him Relie. Neither boy was named for
Justin. Perhaps she knew, at some level of consciousness, that
their difficult father would not be on the scene much longer.

She had returned to her parents' home in Townshend for the
births of her sons. This in itself was not an unusual decision;
many more women died in childbirth than do today, and going
home to a trusted midwife and female relatives probably felt

safer to Clarina than giving birth in a strange city.

Relie was a good-natured "lovely babe," his mother wrote, a "treasure sent to check grief's hidden tide." She believed the joy he brought to her was divine compensation for the hardship of being yoked to a troublesome husband.

For the next several years she lived a somewhat vagabond existence, going back and forth from New York to Townshend and for a brief time settling in Herkimer, New York, where she founded a female seminary (school for girls). The economic hardships brought on by the Panic of 1837 likely forced families in Herkimer to trim nonessential items from their budgets, including education for their girls. Near the end of the decade her letters to the family were sent from Meriden, Connecticut, though it is unclear what she was doing there. What little is known of this period comes from an account twenty years later, which she wrote in the third person under a pen name, so that she could express her feelings candidly without revealing her identity:

> When her recreant husband failed to provide — too resolute and independent to ask or receive aid from friends — she resolved to support her family with her own labor. *And she did it.*

Even with her best efforts, there were times when she had no alternative but to "farm out" her children to the relatives. For a proud, independent woman, that must have been heartbreaking. The low point came when Justin ran off with their children in what she called "a malevolent desire to wound her." She was finally forced to turn to Justin's family for help. With her father-in-law's aid, she tracked down her husband and recovered her children, but that experience severed the last shred of trust and allegiance.

During parts of the 1830s, letters were the threads that connected Clarina Carpenter and her children. No amount of written communication, however, could have filled the void left by an absent mother during their early years. Birsha, who was seven years old in 1839, when her mother wrote from Meriden, was deeply affected by the upheavals and separations within the family. Clarina learned later that her daughter would "sit and weep" when her mother's letters were read to her. Clarina must have hoped the occasional poems she sent to her children would give them something special to hold onto until she could reunite the family. The poem below was addressed to three-year-old Aurelius but includes references to his siblings as well:

> Aurelius, my son, when day is done
> And the moon is up in the sky so high
> When the shining stars like laughing eyes
> Are hung around in the deep blue sky—
> Go look on the moon as the clouds sweep by
> And look at the stars that gem the sky
> The eye of your mother shall turn to them too
> And she'll think of Howard and Birsha and you—
> And send from far
> Through the evening star
> On a ray of light, a fond "good night"
> "Good Night."
> Then send to me through the gentle moon
> A sweet, sweet kiss
> And I'll see you soon.
> *Ah, soon!*

Her children were not the only recipients of her poetry. She composed verses for all kinds of family occasions — birthdays, marriages, deaths, and anniversaries. She wrote poems about nature, faith, honeybees, and Vermont. But a good number of the poems during this period were about lost love, spurned love, grief and sorrow. "I cannot love another," begins one,

"Why do I weep?" a second, and "Days of Sorrow! Nights of Anguish!" yet a third. While most of her poetry would be considered overly sentimental today, it performed a valuable service during this bleak period. Poetry gave her an outlet for expressing her hopes, fears, and anxieties; it also gave her a way to unite with the optimistic spirit of the age. Better times were coming. Joy follows mourning. Endure to the end and receive a crown of life. All these were recurring themes. She filled a thick notebook with her poems.

"I had not a drunken husband," Nichols would later reveal in a letter to Susan B. Anthony after they became acquainted in the early 1850s. However, she confessed that her marriage to Justin had resulted in the same sad fate that befell the drunkard's wife: "defeated purposes, one-sided love, and no support."

The tumult in her life made Nichols especially sensitive to the problems other women were facing. On one of her trips up the Erie Canal she came across a scene that made her heartsick. "I saw a middle-aged, stalwart Methodist clergyman spanking with his brawny hand a two-month old baby," she recalled years later. While the minister spanked the child, he scolded his wife for not following the strict feeding schedule that he had set up for the infant.

"I have less nourishment for the baby than I had at home, and it cries with hunger," said the baby's mother, who pleaded with her husband to stop hitting the child.

"The poor mother's eyes were kept swollen with weeping," Nichols remembered. "Every time the baby cried, he spanked it."

Finally she and another female passenger decided they had to step in. Approaching the father, they told him the baby was too little to understand his discipline and that spanking such a small baby could injure it.

The minister flew into a rage and told the women they

had no right to interfere with a father's right to discipline his child.

Indeed, the weight of law was on his side. A father in those days had absolute authority over both his children and his wife. He could discipline either in any way he saw fit. He could even brag, as did another minister of that day, that he horse-whipped his wife every week just to keep her in line.

———

By 1840 the shining star of one of Townshend's most prominent families was back home. There is no indication that Justin stayed in touch with his children or tried to win back his estranged wife. A few years later Justin Carpenter died of typhus in New York City.

FOUR

In Print
and in Love

Clarina Carpenter moved back into her parents' spacious home on the village green in Townshend. She joined the local church and sent her children to school. She described herself during this time as "a wounded dove in the maternal nest." If that was the case, however, she apparently didn't lick her wounds for long. Free of worry about Justin and no longer needing to patch a relationship badly riddled by distrust and unkindness, she could concentrate on the road ahead. At age thirty she had already traveled — often without an escort —farther than many of her fellow townspeople would travel in their lifetimes. She had walked the streets of New York City and ridden the length of the Erie Canal. And though she may not have been fully aware of it, she was being pulled toward a new way of thinking by the reform spirit of the day.

During the last decade she had started schools, run boarding houses, and supported herself with sewing, but none of those pursuits held any lasting appeal. Professional opportunities for women were extremely limited, so when she realized that newspapers would publish her poetry, she saw a way to move forward. Some of her poems had already been published in local papers, but she began composing and selling short articles as well. The themes of these early articles are similar to the ones her female schoolmates had expounded upon in Timothy Cressy's Select School graduation exercises: hope, faith, piety, virtue, benevolence — all acceptable topics for females to ruminate on. The *Vermont Phoenix* in nearby Brattleboro published a number of her articles on moral uplift and positive thinking in 1840. Poetry had helped her survive the hard times. Now prose helped her put the past into perspective and begin thinking about the future:

> It is when disappointment first lays its withering hand on fond and cherished hopes, — the first sigh of deep regret having been rendered, — the first tear for blighted expectations having been dried, — we turn to glean from the past a lesson for present use — a surer foundation for the expected good of futurity.

Though the past ten years had been difficult, she began to see them as the prelude to a life of "heroic sacrifices." She had not known domestic happiness, but she had been tested in sorrow's kitchen, and she knew her own strength.

> The calm monotony of domestic peace and prosperity trains no master genius — nerves no deep fount of feeling to thrilling resolves and heroic sacrifices; — but let disappointment curdle the very springs of the soul, — let the canker of undervalued affection, — the chilling glance of selfish indifference blast the confidence that distills sweetness, and the whole character undergoes a change.

She ended this article with two prescient questions. Public opinion said a woman's place was in the home, but what if that home was inhospitable? Might not such an experience transform a sweet, home-loving woman into a reformer, someone who longed to work for "universal benevolence"? Might not such an experience justify a woman's entering the "theatre of public action"?

> What but lacerated sympathies ever drew the retiring, affectionate woman, from her deep devotion to the unobtrusive joys of domestic life, to a theatre of public action? What but the pang of heartless indifference from those in whom her heart is garnered, could so effectually turn the tide of her affections and nerve the energies of her soul for the channels of universal benevolence?

From the first day of her marriage, she had never been a simple homemaker. Her difficult domestic life, the necessity of earning a living, and her own ambition kept her out of the home as often as in it. She seized every opportunity that came her way and actively pursued new sources of employment or revenue. When necessary, she parceled out her children so that she could continue to earn a living. For most of her life she was a self-supporting, independent woman, yet her public persona became — and remained — that of a domestic homebody who had been forced by circumstances to articulate positions that she would have happily left to others. It's fairly clear, however, that Clarina Carpenter enjoyed being part of the public conversation — in print at first.

She began writing for the *Windham County Democrat,* a weekly newspaper also based in Brattleboro. Her association with the *Democrat* no doubt grew out of her articles for the rival *Phoenix.* The editor of the *Windham County Democrat* was George Washington Nichols, a widower with six grown daughters. Quiet, shy, intelligent, and progressive, he liked women who were frank and outspoken. Three of his daughters were unmarried and supported themselves as printers.

The letters between Clarina and George became friendly and then cautiously romantic. Since he considered himself shy, and she considered herself homely, letter-writing had its advantages. According to George, she made the first move. He was wary of the twenty-eight-year age difference between them, but she brushed it aside. He was discerning, dependable, and kind — a good man, she decided. The only document that has survived that captures the passion between these two New Englanders is an 1841 letter, written by George to Clarina, two years before their marriage. They had evidently still not met in person, despite their frequent correspondence. George refers to a previous letter, in which Clarina has warned him that she is a "plain person" in looks. He replies, "Personal beauty, if I can judge from my own experience and observation, has no lasting influence upon the affections. A jewelry box is not valued for itself, but for the jewels it enfolds."

Even here, there are references to the professional relationship that was also developing between them. "You must bear with me," he writes, "if your articles do not appear so immediately as you could wish."

Before she could marry George Nichols, Clarina would have to formally dissolve her previous union. On February 16, 1843, she was granted a divorce from Justin Carpenter on the basis of "cruelty, unkindness, and intolerable severity." Though divorce was not unheard of in those days and was more easily obtained in Vermont than in many other states, it was still uncommon enough to raise eyebrows in most locales. Many people looked down on someone — especially a woman — who obtained a divorce for whatever reason.

Justin had ignored three court summonses in the divorce suit, and his own father and brother testified against him. The Carpenter family lived nearby and "without exception," she claimed, "sustained me against all reproach," She returned their loyalty with discretion, but she had other reasons for keeping the divorce quiet. She wanted to protect her children from public censure. Over the years she wrote little about her first marriage and never talked about her divorce in public. It is also likely that as she entered the political arena, she wanted to deflect any opportunities her opponents might use to shame her about her divorce. By cultivating a respectable, maternal public image, she would make any attempts to paint her as the enemy of marriage and motherhood seem ridiculous. Strangers assumed that her first husband had died, and she did not bother to add that he had died *after* she had divorced him.

On March 6, 1843, Clarina married George Nichols in the parlor of her parents' home in Townshend, then moved seventeen miles down the road to join George at his home.

Located in the southeastern corner of Vermont, Brattleboro was a picturesque, forward-looking town of neat cottages and grand homes, of towering elm trees, flower gardens, and terraces planted with spicy pinks, eglantine, love-lies-bleeding, and sweet William. Churches flourished, and civic organizations like the Brattleboro Book Club, the Shade Tree Association, and the Thief-Detecting Society held regular meetings. Reed organs were manufactured here, as were fine violins and cellos crafted of old-growth spruce from the nearby forests.

Opposite the *Democrat*'s offices was the Stage House, where the stagecoach lines left Brattleboro each morning. Some headed north toward the mountains that border the town, some crossed the river into New Hampshire, and some set out on the 130-mile journey to Boston. Shortly after Clarina Nichols arrived, the city began attracting visitors from all over the country. They were drawn by the growing fame of Brattleboro's "water cure." Patients of the water cure paid handsomely to be awakened at 4 A.M., wrapped tightly in hot wool cloths until they were sweating profusely, then stripped

Main Street of Brattleboro, circa 1854.
(Used with permission of the authors of Before Our Time: A
Pictorial Memoir of Brattleboro, Vermont*)*

and plunged into ice cold water. Advocates of the water cure claimed the hot-cold treatments purified the body and revived the spirit. In addition to the wakeup plunge, treatments included other types of hot, cold, and tepid baths, rubbing baths, a regimen of simple food, and outdoor exercise. The water cure was said to improve any condition from bad nerves to weak kidneys.

In the spring of 1846, nearly four hundred patients came to Brattleboro, many of them accompanied by their families, to partake of the water cure. They were generally wealthy and well-educated; two-thirds of the patients were women who found hydropathy, as it was called, preferable to the mercury treatments and bloodletting that were commonly used in everyday medicine.

Their presence added to the cosmopolitan flavor of the city

while straining its hotel accommodations. Residents often opened their homes to the overflow. One summer the famed poet Henry Wadsworth Longfellow and his family boarded with Clarina and George Nichols. The Longfellows and Nicholses opposed slavery and shared progressive views on health. Frances Longfellow was among the first women in the United States to use anesthesia in childbirth (over the objections of clergymen who cited the book of Genesis as proof that women should suffer during childbirth).

Clarina had become a vegetarian after reading health advocates like Sylvester Graham and John Harvey Kellogg sing the praises of the graham cracker and whole-grained cereals. She even lent her endorsement to a patent medicine in an advertisement that appeared in the *Semi-Weekly Eagle*, which was published in the office next door to the *Democrat*:

> I most cheerfully certify to the exceedingly curative properties of the Green Mountain Vegetable Liquid manufactured by Robert Pender, having used it in my family in a case of poison by ivy. Its application gave immediate relief, reducing the inflammation, and in a few days healing the flesh. — C. I. H. NICHOLS.

She felt better than she had in years. The terrible backaches she'd had while married to Justin had vanished, and she was pregnant again with her fourth child. Little George was born in 1844 when her older children were eight, ten, and twelve.

But just as her health and spirits improved, and she had settled into a much happier domestic situation, her husband's health took a turn for the worse. Shortly after their marriage, George Nichols became ill with a chronic lung disease that left him a semi-invalid. He no longer had the energy and stamina to run the newspaper on a day-to-day basis, though he kept his interest in politics and retained his title of publisher on the newspaper's masthead. For the first time in Clarina Nichols's life, a misfortune opened, rather than closed, a door of opportunity.

———————

The *Windham County Democrat*, which had been established in the 1830s under a different owner, began as a conventional Jacksonian newspaper. It remained so for a time after George Nichols purchased it in 1837. Now — without fanfare or so much as an announcement in its pages — Mrs. C. I. H. Nichols began running the newspaper. With her husband's backing and encouragement, she monitored its business affairs, served as editor, and wrote many of its articles, adding a literary flair to its pages.

Under her leadership the *Democrat* began a decade-long political shift. The newspaper reflected a growing disenchantment many Northern Democrats felt toward their party, which was on the verge of splitting over the issue of slavery. By the 1840s the country was deeply divided over the slave question. A better word might be "splintered." Abolitionists believed in ending slavery immediately, but they were in the minority, considered "ultras," even in New England. Others were antislavery but not in favor of immediate emancipation; they argued that the practice should be gradually phased out and that owners should be compensated for "loss of property" if their slaves were freed.

The great majority of Southerners did not own slaves, but most supported the right of whites to enslave blacks, especially if slaveowners treated their human chattel as well as livestock and promoted Christianity among them. Slaveholders claimed that they took better care of their slaves than Northern factory owners did of their workers. Still others saw slavery as evil but believed that integrating large numbers of free blacks into white society would cause havoc. They favored colonization, sending slaves back to Africa. And yet another splinter thought the best policy was to let slavery die of its own weight in its own time.

On one subject those opposed to slavery were united. "The bounds of slavery must be set," Clarina's cousin Harley Smith wrote to her in 1847, "beyond which it shall not pass." Slavery was already firmly rooted throughout the South, but large plantation owners were starting to feel crowded and restless to expand into Western lands. The problem was that their "property" reproduced and outgrew the land, so that new territory was deemed necessary for success.

———◆———

In the early 1840s, however, Clarina Nichols was less concerned with an evil that she abhorred in the abstract than with an injustice she observed every day. From the time she was a youth through her marriage and divorce to Justin Carpenter, she had seen first-hand that the law treated women unfairly. After becoming an editor, she had more opportunities to learn what others were saying on the subject, through exchanges with newspapers across the region. She stacked these papers in piles in her parlor and read them until late in the night by her solar lamp, a heavy oil-burning lamp that was found in many of the finer homes of the day.

She would eventually be reading other newspapers edited or written by female journalists: Amelia Bloomer, Lydia Jane Pierson, and Jane Swisshelm. "It will cheer them," she said, "to know that they contribute largely to our social and intellectual enjoyment and our ability to do and dare for the cause of humanity."

Women in trouble sensed that she was sympathetic. They approached her in public and in long letters poured out the details of their difficult lives. "I am a walking storehouse of facts on the subject of woman's wrongs," she said in a letter to a friend. Nichols had no trouble identifying with women in desperate circumstances. She had learned firsthand what it was like to lie awake at night worrying about how to put

George Washington Nichols with
George Bainbridge Nichols, circa 1847.
(Grace Hudson Museum, Ukiah, California)

bread on the table.

Once a woman said "I do," she may as well have added, "I do hand over to my husband my property, my money, and all my earthly possessions. He may do with them as he wishes." The quilt her mother made for her, the horse her father gave her, the wedding dress she bought with her own earnings —all these now belonged, legally, to her husband. He could sell, gamble, or give them away, as he chose, and his wife could not object, for she was under her husband's legal control. In the eyes of the law she did not exist.

American civil law, based on English common law, adhered to the principle of *coverture* for married women. A wife was subsumed into her husband's identity. Nothing showed that more clearly than the legal status of her name. A married woman was no longer Mary White, but Mrs. Henry Jones.

Her husband was bound by law to protect and support her; in return, she was obliged to obey him and follow his leadership. Fortunate wives had kind, wise, loving husbands. Wives who had chosen poorly, or whose husbands changed for the worse after marriage, had few options. If a wife could not convince her husband with reason, tears, anger, affection, deceit, flattery, or coaxing, she was out of luck. A husband had the legal right to have his way, to demand sex, and to discipline his wife if she didn't carry out his wishes or please him in some way he deemed vital. For most men, male authority was a source of pride and satisfaction, for even the least worthy man could claim to be lord of his own castle.

Gradually, Nichols came to believe that married women could never achieve security for themselves and their children unless they had economic rights — the legal right to own and control their own property and wages. Many people at this time were talking about the need to revise property rights laws. Some men liked the idea because they saw its potential: all they had to do was register property in their wives' names, and no creditor would be able to touch it. But other men and women were genuinely interested in how new laws could protect women and give them some control over their lives.

Clarina Nichols was probably inspired by the work of Ernestine Rose, a trailblazer for women's rights in New York, who had doggedly conducted petition drives on behalf of married women's property rights for twelve years. For Nichols, who had not even openly identified herself as the editor of her own newspaper, thinking about that much exposure to public scrutiny probably gave her pause. And so she inched her way along at first, testing her own strength and gauging the strength of the resistance.

She began writing on the subject of property rights in the editorial pages of the *Democrat*. One of her readers was so impressed by what she wrote that he brought her ideas to his colleagues in the state legislature. They passed Vermont's first married women's property rights bill in 1847.

The new law did not cover all kinds of property, but it was a start. Nichols called it "the first breath" of life for married women in Vermont. At her urging, a legislative ally tried to get a stronger law passed, but his bill was defeated and ridiculed by fellow lawmakers. In their opinion, the women of the Granite State already had all the rights they could possibly desire.

At this point Nichols realized she could not rely on men for full and consistent support. She had enjoyed working for reform behind the shield of anonymity in Brattleboro. Now, though, she realized that if Vermont women were to gain more rights, someone of her own sex would need to step forward and demand them.

FIVE

The Road
to Worcester

On a snowy day in late February of 1849 all of Brattleboro turned out to witness a great event — the train was coming. Men, women, and children crowded onto the grounds around the depot. They filled the surrounding banks and lined the tracks leading into town. For two and a half hours they waited with cold noses and high spirits to see the inaugural run of the Vermont and Massachusetts Railroad into Brattleboro. At about two-thirty, when the great, black hulk of an engine appeared in the distance, the cheering began. Fifteen hundred passengers riding the train's sixteen cars returned the cheers. *"Viva! Viva!"* they shouted as they hung out windows and dangled off the ends of the cars. Cannon were fired, a band struck up a sprightly tune, and church bells pealed all across town.

The arriving passengers eagerly shared every exciting

detail about their pioneering journey. The town celebrated the coming of the railroad with six barrels of strong, black coffee and a gala dinner dance into the early hours of the next morning. Every hotel room in Brattleboro was booked. Those without rooms bedded down under snug buffalo robes on the pews of the Congregational Church.

Over the next decade Clarina Nichols would log thousands of miles on the train, often traveling alone. The railroads rapidly displaced the canals as the transport of choice in the Northeast, and soon its tendrils extended throughout the nation's industrial midsection and westward. The endless reach of steel rails may be the best-known symbol of American expansion in the 1800s, but their arrival in Brattleboro in Nichols's fortieth year also served as a kind of a foreshadowing. The editor of the *Windham County Democrat* would soon be going places, literally and otherwise.

By 1850 she was a seasoned polemicist who relished the parry-and-thrust with her critics and the camaraderie of like-minded editors. She had yet to announce her role in print, however, for the masthead of the *Democrat* still carried her husband's name, and there was no mention anywhere in the paper of her role as editor. That soon changed, after a rival editor at another newspaper published an article revealing her involvement with the *Democrat.* The article, however, belittled her duties, alleging that Mrs. Nichols was merely carrying out the orders of her sick husband. This demanded a reply, and she gave one. An article soon appeared in the *Democrat,* informing its readers that Mrs. Nichols had been in charge of all aspects of the newspaper for many years. Henceforth, George Nichols remained on the masthead, but a line was added to the top of page two that read, "Edited by Mrs. C. I. H. Nichols." Writing to a friend in 1852, she confided, "My husband wanted me to come forward before, but I wanted to make sure that I had gained men's confidence in my abilities to run a political newspaper."

Many readers must have known the secret, especially those who saw her coming and going from the *Democrat's* second-floor office in Brattleboro. Who else but Mrs. Nichols would have invented a character like "Deborah Van Winkle," the salty country woman whose cornpone observations on human nature, society, and male-female relationships occasionally graced the pages of the *Democrat*?

In one article, the fictitious Mrs. Van Winkle went to Washington, D.C., to observe the workings of government:

> They tell about wimin being great talkers and telling all at once; but dear me, I never in all the quiltins and parin-bees and frolics I've been to — and I went to 'em all when I was a young woman — I never did see such a strife of tongues. Why they put a man in the chair to keep 'em in order and to say who shall talk, and what is in order and what is in disorder; and don't you think, they call him Mr. Speaker, jest as if he did the chief of the talkin, when he's the stillest and best behaved man among 'em.

Here and elsewhere, Nichols used her newspaper to poke fun at men who said that women shouldn't meddle in politics because so-called feminine traits made the fairer sex unsuited to the weighty affairs of state. In another column, Mrs. Van Winkle recounted debating a local gentleman over the subject of women's intellectual capacities:

> I know some folks argue that because wimin's fisical powers ain't so strong and won't hold out so long as men's at any bodily labor, her mind can't be that strong. But God and the angels and glorified spirits hain't got no bodies, nor fisical powers at all, and I reckon that's proof enuff that wimin may have as much intellect as good men.

Even most men in the temperance and antislavery movements — the two leading reforms of the day — felt that wom-
en's place was behind men. At the 1840 World Anti-Slavery
Convention in London, the male delegates voted to expel the
female delegates who had undertaken an ocean voyage of
thousands of miles to attend. Denied seats on the convention
floor, the women were sent to the galleries to sit as spectators
behind a black curtain. William Lloyd Garrison, editor of *The
Liberator,* had just gone through a split in his own organization,
the American Anti-Slavery Society, over the role of women.
To show his support for the ousted women, he sat with them
in the galleries.

In the 1840s and '50s women were doing much of the day-
to-day work in the reform movements. They were circulating
petitions, organizing meetings, writing articles, and running
campaigns. A few had become polished public speakers. The
first American women noted for their public speaking tours
were Sarah and Angelina Grimké, two sisters from South
Carolina who disavowed their slaveholding family ties and
began speaking out for the Northern abolitionist cause in the
late 1830s.

Women constituted two-thirds of the membership in most
churches, making them a *de facto* volunteer army with enormous potential strength. There were reform-minded ministers — Thomas Wentworth Higginson, Theodore Dwight
Weld, Samuel May, and Ralph Waldo Emerson, were some
of the best known — who supported equal rights for women
from the beginning, but most men of the cloth were adamantly
opposed. Women in church were supposed to be as silent as
church mice, to listen and learn, but not to express their own
thoughts and ideas. Nichols once described the level of ab-
surdity that could result. In one church meeting where only
women were in attendance, the minister restricted the ladies to
responding with memorized Bible passages and hymn verses.
They were not to use their own words.

Elizabeth Cady Stanton (left) and Lucretia Mott
were prime organizers of the 1848 Seneca Falls
Convention. *(courtesy Elizabeth Cady Stanton Trust)*

Though most women had been trained not to question
such practices, a small but growing minority did. Women on
both sides of the Atlantic were beginning to speak up about
the legal, political, and religious status of women. When they
did, they invariably found other women who were thinking
along the same lines.

Lucretia Mott and Elizabeth Cady Stanton had been
present at the 1840 antislavery convention in London. That
humiliating experience created a strong bond between them,
even though they were as different as two women could be:
Stanton, a young woman, with a flair for both fashion and
language; and Mott, an older, plain-dressing Quaker preacher
revered for her work in the antislavery movement.

In the summer of 1848, Stanton, Mott, her pregnant sister
Martha Wright, and two other women called for the first
women's rights convention ever held in the United States — or
the world. The historic meeting was held inside a sweltering
brick chapel in Seneca Falls, New York, in July. More than
three hundred women and men heard Stanton read a state-

Paulina Wright Davis (left) organized the 1850
National convention; Abby Kelley Foster was
among the veteran speakers there.

ment she called the "Declaration of Sentiments." Modeled on
the Declaration of Independence, it began with words familiar
to everyone in the audience: "We hold these truths to be self-
evident, that all men *and women* are created equal." For two days
the attendees at the meeting discussed women's complaints.
Then they passed a long list of resolutions, including a controversial demand that women be given the right to vote.

Women had been a "submerged continent" for centu-
ries, though there had always been a few women who were
influential within public circles dominated by men. Once the
idea of women's conventions emerged, however, the women
greeted it like an old friend. They knew how to run conventions. This was familiar territory. A second small convention
was held in Rochester, New York, and another in Salem, Ohio.
By 1850, a call was issued for the First National Woman's
Rights Convention. It was to be held in Worcester, Massachusetts.

Worcester was a logical choice for the convention. Its solid
industrial base had made possible a flowering of cultural
institutions funded by the largesse of its leading citizens. En-
trepreneurs built halls and theatres for traveling lecturers and

performers and put up hotels to accommodate out-of-town visitors. Getting to Worcester would be easy, as it was the railroad hub of New England, with twenty-four trains passing through each day.

Worcester had become a hotbed of radical thinking. Many of the country's most reform-minded citizens lived in the area, and they were curious to learn how broad-based the support for women's reform was. In the years before the Civil War, thousands of Americans threw themselves into movements that had been organized to tackle all manner of public ills, from the most diabolical (slavery) to the trivial (ending the delivery of mail on Sundays) and the futile (eliminating profanity in public). Women's rights was a welcome and noble addition, but even its supporters were unsure if it enjoyed the same broad base of support as the temperance and antislavery causes.

The First National Woman's Rights Convention decisively dispelled all doubt. On October 23, 1850, an overflow crowd of reformers and curiosity-seekers poured into Brinley Hall in Worcester. One attendee had come all the way from California. A reporter for the *New York Tribune* observed, "The room was crowded to excess, every seat and aisle and the space around the platform being filled, men and women standing on their feet the whole evening."

The chief organizer of the First National Woman's Rights Convention was a wealthy New Englander named Paulina Wright Davis. She had created a sensation with her lectures on female anatomy, a subject that was deemed unsuitable for proper ladies, who in those days did not even undress for their doctors. Determined to educate women about their bodies, Davis toured the Northeast, teaching female anatomy, pointing out the reproductive organs on a mannequin that she traveled with. She was a confident speaker who lectured widely, despite frequent criticism and threats.

The strong core of women who assembled at Worcester

included Lucretia Mott, Ernestine Rose, Antoinette Brown, Harriot Hunt, Sojourner Truth, Abby Kelley Foster, and Lucy Stone. These women had cut their teeth in the antislavery and temperance movements and had become seasoned speakers not easily intimidated by controversy or challenges. Some, like Foster, had faced down angry proslavery mobs.

In addition to these veteran reformers were a number of women who had never addressed audiences of any magnitude. Throughout the convention they had difficulty being heard across the unamplified hall, and Mott had to repeatedly urge them to speak up. Some of the women later reported being so nervous they trembled as they spoke or became lightheaded. Nonetheless, many who attended would later remark how astonished they were by each speaker's eloquence.

Nichols attended the convention and was deeply interested in all that she heard. In later years she remembered being so worked up at one point that she needed to return to her room and lie down to compose herself. She must have been thrilled to see and hear so many like-minded women assembled in one place, speaking out on issues that resonated deeply within her. Ten years after she had expressed her desire to enter the "theatres of public action," she had arrived in one and was standing just offstage. Her heart may have been racing from the bold ideas she was hearing, but she also must have sensed the implications this convention had for her own life.

Among the speakers at the 1850 convention was Abby Price, who lived in nearby Hopedale with a utopian community that was committed to gender equality. Price captivated the convention with her survey of the indignities suffered by women around the world:

> In many countries we see women reduced to the condition of a slave and compelled to do all the drudgery necessary to her Lord's subsistence In others she is dressed up as a mere plaything for his amusement.

Some women, Price said, were driven into a life of prostitution in order to make a living wage. Even gifted young girls could look forward to nothing better than mindless factory work or half-paid work as seamstresses, hat-makers, or typesetters. "The natural rights of woman are co-equal with those of man," Price declared. "They were both made in the image of God. Dominion was given to both over every other creature, but not over each other." The early advocates of women's rights called this doctrine "co-equality" or "co-sovereignty."

———————

Over the course of two days the members of the First National Woman's Rights Convention of 1850 passed these resolutions:

- Women should have equal access to education and jobs.
- Women should receive equal pay for equal work.
- Married women should be allowed to hold and control property in their own names.
- Mothers should have equal custody rights with fathers.
- Women should be allowed to vote.

The delegates claimed these rights not only for themselves but for "the million and a half of slave women at the South, the most grossly wronged and foully outraged of all women," thus tying the new women's movement to the antislavery movement.

Nichols signed the resolutions along with more than two hundred sixty women and men. As a professional journalist, she was one of the most accomplished women who attended the Worcester gathering. "Women are beginning to have much influence in politics," said Frederick Douglass, the ex-slave abolitionist leader who was present at this and all the early women's rights conventions. He singled out two journalists in particular:

> There are few papers exerting greater influence than the *Saturday Visiter* edited by by Mrs. Swisshelm, and the Brattleboro *Democrat*, edited by Mrs. Nichols ...both of them Free Democracy papers of great force and high intellectual order.

Douglass, a self-professed "women's rights man," observed that many newspapers across the country reprinted articles from both these women's newspapers, greatly expanding the reach of their relatively modest circulations.

Nichols served on two committees at the 1850 convention, and though she did not give a formal speech, she was active behind the scenes, where fellow delegates found her outgoing, witty, and well-informed. They named her one of five vice presidents for the following year's convention.

———

On October 15, 1851, at the Second National Woman's Rights Convention, also held in Worcester, the noted abolitionist Wendell Phillips led Clarina Nichols to the podium. A thousand delegates and newspaper reporters awaited her words as breathlessly as they had awaited the first train. It was the first time she had given a public address since graduating from Timothy Cressy's private school in Vermont.

She must have hesitated, for as she later recounted, Phillips leaned over and whispered to her, "You must speak now, Mrs. Nichols."

SIX

'On the Responsibilities of Woman'

Nichols spoke for one hour. She claimed that she had not prepared her remarks ahead of time, because she wanted to find out what the speakers before her had chosen for topics. Once she began speaking, however, it was obvious that she had planned for this moment very carefully. When she finished, she had delivered one of the most influential speeches of the early women's movement.

She began with a simple story. A woman that she knew was married to a humble farmer. One day the farmer became seriously ill. He was too weak to do all the chores himself and too poor to pay a laborer to help him out. So the farmer's wife went out into the field. She helped her husband move a pile of heavy logs so that they could plant their crops.

The farmer's wife was not doing "woman's work" when she was helping her husband, said Nichols:

[But] my sympathies, which recognized in her act the self-sacrificing love of woman, forbade that I should judge her [as being] out of her sphere. For I felt in my heart that if I were a wife and loved my husband, I too would help him when he needed help...and what true-hearted woman would not do the same?

The story of the farmer's wife, she said, showed how easy it was to talk about "man's sphere" and "woman's sphere" when times were good. When a man fell ill — or was a drunkard, or squandered the family finances — the woman often had to take over the "man's work" for the well-being of the family.

The other important fact about the farmer's wife was that she was "true-hearted." Despite an obvious need to do what would normally be considered "man's work," she kept her womanliness intact. This was a major theme of her speech. "I shall say very little of woman's rights," she told her audience, but "would instead impress upon you woman's responsibilities." It was a shrewd choice of words. Most people in 1851 weren't sure that women needed more rights. But if they saw that women needed rights to carry out their responsibilities, they might be provoked. Clarina believed that Americans disliked nothing so much as the thought of someone being treated unfairly.

So she filled her speech with the stories of women who were treated unfairly under the law. No story was more heartbreaking than the one she told about a self-made woman she knew in West Townshend:

In my native town lived a single woman, of middle age. She had accumulated something, for she was capable in all the handicrafts pursued by women of her class. She married a worthy man, poor in this world's goods, and whose children were all settled in homes of their own. She applied her means, and by the persevering use of her faculties they secured a snug home...he doing what his feeble health

A female speaker was still something of a novelty in 1856, when this cartoon appeared. *(Library of Congress)*

permitted toward the common interest. In the course of years he died, and two-thirds of that estate was divided among his grown-up children; one third remaining to her. No, she could only have the *use* of one third, and must keep it in good repair — the law said so!

When a husband died, his wife received the widow's dower, which gave her temporary use of one-third of their estate. Even if the property had originally belonged to her, it was no longer hers to control. She became, in effect, a squatter in her own home. She could occupy a portion of it (as long as she took good care of her share), but could not sell it or have any say in what the legal heirs did with their two-thirds share.

But that was only part of the story:

The old lady patched and toiled, beautiful in her scru-
pulous cleanliness. The neighbors remembered her, and

many a choice bit found its way to her table....[Later] she was found in her bed paralyzed; and never to the day of her death — three years — could she lift her hand or make known the simplest want....And now, friends, how did the laws support and protect this poor widow? I will tell you: they set her up at auction and struck her off to the man who had a heart to keep her at the cheapest rate! Three years she enjoyed the pauper's support, then died, and when the decent forms of a pauper's burial were over, that third was divided — as had been the other two thirds — among her husband's 'well-to-do' children.

The story had its intended effect. An observer noted a "great sensation" from the audience after hearing the story of the widow. The women in the audience knew such things happened to widows, but Nichols's intimate anecdotes opened their minds to the injustice she was trying to expose. They knew that if the couple's fates had been reversed, and the woman had died first, her husband would have inherited everything.

O men! In the enjoyment of well-secured property rights, you beautify your snug homesteads...and it never occurs to you that no such blissful feeling of security finds rest in the bosom of your wives. The wife of a small householder reflects that if her husband should be taken from her by death, that home must be divided, and a corner in the kitchen, a corner in the garret, and...in the cellar, be set off to her use as if she were a rat!

According to the eyewitness, another "great sensation" went up in the audience.

She gave more examples of how the law, which was supposed to protect families, was often their worst enemy. She even used an example from her own first marriage (although she deftly avoided mentioning how it had ended). By law, she told her audience, her second husband was the sole guardian of her children — even though he was not their father.

> I address myself to you, *fathers*, I appeal to every man who has lived a half century, is the *mother* not the most faithful guardian of her children's interests? If you were going on a long journey, to be absent for years…would you exclude your wives from the care and guardianship of your children? Would you place them and the means for their support in any other hands than the mother's? If you would, *you have married beneath yourselves.*

The audience cheered, then she added:

> I ask you, how it happens that when you die your estates are cut up, and your children and the means for their support consigned to others' guardianship by laws, which yourselves have made or sworn to defend?

She knew George Nichols was a good man and would never do anything to harm her children. But not every woman was so fortunate. As a girl, she had learned this from the women who came to her father for help, and in her first marriage she herself had suffered.

With her audience firmly on her side, she told the story of the young mother. Congress had passed a law the year before making it a crime not to assist slave owners in capturing runaways fleeing from the South into the so-called "free" states. The Fugitive Slave Law had ignited a furor of anger across the North. Knowing this, Nichols used the despised code as an analogy to the plight of abused women, many of whom were in danger of being returned to their "masters" after fleeing untenable circumstances.

She told the story of one such woman whom she had met years before:

> From a love of the social glass, her husband in a few years became a drunkard and a brute; neglected his business, and expended their entire living. She struggled bravely, but in vain. At length, just before the birth of her youngest child, he pawned the clothing which she had provided for herself and babes, sold her only bed, and drove her into the streets to seek from charity aid in her hour of trial. After she recovered she went to service, keeping her children with her. But he pursued her from place to place...collecting her wages by process of law, and taking possession of every garment not on her own or children's persons.

She continued:

> But alas! not yet have I exhausted that fountain of wrongs growing out of the alienation of the wife's property rights....I have a friend who, not long since, procured a divorce from her husband — a [philanderer] and a drunkard — and by the power of the law he wrested from her their only child, a son of tender age. Think of this, fathers, mothers!....If we are the weaker sex, oh, give us, we pray you, equal protection with the stronger sex!

Paulina Wright Davis later recalled that "many eyes, all unused to tears, were moistened as Clarina Nichols described the agony of the mother robbed of her child by the law." Davis herself found "a touching, tender pathos in her stories which went home to the heart."

The speech ended with some words of encouragement. There was "a good time coming," she said, when women would not be cheated out of what was rightfully theirs. Again she spoke of responsibilities. A young woman, she said, had an obligation to develop her mind instead of spending her time fussing over her appearance. But how could she do that if the universities were closed to women? "We can educate ourselves," she told them, and once again she drew on her own experience:

> Beyond a single year's instruction in a High School for young men and women, I have enjoyed no public educational facilities, but the Common School which our Green Mountain State opens to all her sons and daughters....I resorted to books and the study of human nature...[because] the world in which we live and act, and by which we are impressed, is the best school for woman as well as man....I have been accustomed to look within my own heart to learn the springs of human action...and the result has been a fixed resolution, and indomitable courage to do with my might what my hands find to do for God and humanity. And in doing I have best learned my ability to accomplish.

Nichols then challenged the old canard that had bothered her since her school days:

> It may be that you hesitate, from a supposed inferiority of intellect....But I have long since disposed of this question to my own satisfaction, and perhaps my conclusion will inspire you with confidence to attempt equal — I would hope superior — attainments, for man falls short of the intelligence within reach of his powers....Next to God, woman is the creator of the race as it is, and as it shall be. I ask, then, has God created woman man's inferior? If so, He has been false to his wisdom, false to his power, in creating so inferior a being for a superior work!

In closing she issued a challenge to the young women in the audience. Forego the pursuit of superficial beauty. Cultivate

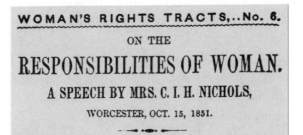

ON THE

RESPONSIBILITIES OF WOMAN.

A SPEECH BY MRS. C. I. H. NICHOLS,

WORCESTER, OCT. 15, 1851.

Mrs. C. I. H. Nichols, of Brattleboro', Vt., then came forward and spoke as follows :—

My friends, I have made no preparation to address you. I left home feeling that if I had anything to do here, I should have the grace given me to do it ; or if there should be any branch of the subject not sufficiently presented, I would present it. And now, friends, in following so many speakers, who have so well occupied the ground, I will come as a gleaner, and be as a Ruth among my fellow-laborers.

I commenced life with the most refined notions of woman's sphere. My pride of womanhood lay within this nicer sphere. I know not

Nichols's speech was included in a series of
Woman's Rights Tracts, first published in 1853.

the mind and soul. Devote yourself to the earnest work of life. This, she said, was the way to a good man's heart:

> Early in life my attention was called to examine the value of beauty....I could not believe that God had created so many homely women, and suffered all to lose their beauty in the very maturity of their powers, and yet made it our duty to spend our best efforts in trying to look pretty. We all desire to be loved; and can it be that we have no more lasting claims to admiration, than that beauty [that] serve[s] us only in the springtime of life?...Cultivate, then, your powers of mind and heart, that you may become necessary to [man's] better and undying sympathies. Aid him in all the earnest work of life. Sell your jewelry, abate your expenditures for show; and appropriate your means

and time spent in idle visiting, to the culture of your souls.
Then will his soul respond to your worth.

Tapping her head, Nichols said, "My education has been not only bread, but an inexhaustible fund of enjoyment in all the past of my life."

She was cheered off the stage.

Of the hundreds of speeches she would deliver over the next two decades, "On the Responsibilities of Woman" would be her best known. It was turned into a tract for women's rights and widely distributed for years.

It was probably not her finest piece of oratory. As a newcomer to public speaking, she was likely more restrained than she would be in later years. She would soon begin to argue for rights not because they grew out of women's responsibilities, but because they were inherent in citizenship. Nonetheless, this speech lays out the agenda that would occupy her for the rest of her life: property rights for married women, control of wages, custody rights, reform of inheritance laws, equal educational and vocational opportunities for females — and in one brief passage, the right of women to vote.

The tone of the Worcester speech was vintage Nichols, with its heartfelt appeal to human decency and traditional values. "On the Responsibilities of Woman" makes rights for women seem as American as apple pie and motherhood. Looking back years later she would say, "I have found my best success in presenting truth ready peeled of burrs if possible."

SEVEN

Bloomers
and Trousers

The year 1852 saw the arrival in the women's rights movement of a thirty-two-year-old former schoolteacher from Rochester, New York. Right from the start, Susan B. Anthony was organizing. She contacted Clarina Nichols to speak at a meeting, but Nichols, by now quite busy with speaking engagements in addition to her full-time newspaper duties, had to decline. But she offered to send Anthony issues of the *Democrat* and a copy of her Worcester speech, and the two struck up a correspondence.

They had much in common. Both women were active in the temperance movement. Both were abolitionists. Each had felt the humiliation of being paid half the wages that men received for teaching. And within months of joining the nascent women's rights movement, each felt it to be a calling. "It is most invigorating to watch the development of a woman in the work

Susan B. Anthony in 1852, the year
that she and Clarina Nichols met.

for humanity," Nichols wrote to Anthony in April 1852. "First,
anxious for the cause and depressed with a sense of her own
inability; next, partial success of timid efforts creating a hope;
next, a faith; and then the fruition of complete self-devotion.
Such will be your history."

The first draft of that history was written in the penny
presses of the day. They recognized the "strong-minded"
women, with their call for equal rights, as just the kind of tit-
illating controversy that sold newspapers and were happy to
spread the message far and wide. A few editorialized in favor
of the women, but most newspapers ridiculed the movement
and its "hen conventions." The more vicious branded the
women's rights advocates as "unsexed" and "freaks of nature."
They suggested the women were "she-men," that they were

anything but true women. Instead of focusing on the issues the women raised, these newspapers made fun of their looks. They printed cartoons that showed the women with bulging muscles and masculine features — square jaws, receding hairlines, beards and moustaches on faces curdled into unladylike expressions of rage.

But what gave the press a heyday with the movement was the introduction of a new fashion — bloomers — one of the most controversial fashion statements in history.

By mid-century women's dresses were dragging in the streets. The skirts were so full and cumbersome they required steel hoops to hold them up. Women complained that the floor-length hems swept the streets and carried germs and grime into their homes. The long, heavy skirts kept their wearers from running, mounting a horse without assistance, or even carrying a basket of laundry up steps without tripping. Nichols believed such oppressive clothing could be hazardous to women's health.

The solution — named for Amelia Bloomer, the reformer whose journal, *The Lily*, promoted the style — was a pair of baggy trousers worn under a knee-length dress. Wearing bloomers made women feel as free as young boys. They were amazed at how comfortable the new fashion was and what a difference it made in how they could move.

Men almost universally hated bloomers. Nichols found their attitude amusing and hypocritical. "The dress — short skirts and full pantalets — has been worn for years by the misses of all nations in Christendom and by all the women of the Turkish nation from time immemorial," she wrote in an article that was reprinted in the *Anti-Slavery Bugle* in Salem, Ohio. If men were concerned with women's feminine modesty, she pointed out, they would be as worried about "inches cut from the tops of ladies' dresses" as they were about inches cut from the hems.

She carried on a debate with a rival newspaper editor about

bloomers that went on for weeks. "We can't understand how shortening women's skirts will cause such dreadful mischief," she wrote in her newspaper. The young men, she charged, were the ones causing the social disturbance. Gangs of them circled any bloomer-wearing woman they saw walking down the street and threatened her safety.

Bloomers

The other editor argued that the Bible was against women wearing trousers and predicted great evil would come from the new fashion. Long skirts, he wrote, made women act like women were supposed to act — modest and refined.

If that was the case, she fired back, perhaps *men* should try wearing long skirts for a while. Maybe that would make men more modest and refined. Then the women who chose to wear bloomers would no longer have to fear "being molested by rowdy and obscene jeers."

Did she wear bloomers in Vermont? A town record later asserted, "Mrs. Nichols and her daughter, in bloomers made of buff calico, walked the streets of Brattleboro to the amazement of the natives." But she herself wrote in 1851 that she had decided against wearing bloomers for fear they might become a "stumbling block," distracting people's attention from more important issues that the women were raising. She may have changed her mind, though, and tried out the fashion after writing that opinion.

At any rate, other women's rights leaders eventually came to the same conclusion Nichols had reached. Bloomers had started to take center stage in the discussion of women's rights, and though they were a political statement in their own way, the women didn't want their wardrobe to dominate the discussion. Regretfully, they went back to wearing long skirts — at least in public. In the West, however, various iterations of the bloomer costume remained in use over the years for the most practical of reasons.

———

Vermont men may not have been ready to see their women in bloomers, but Nichols hoped they might be prepared to allow women to vote in school elections. After all, what could be more womanly than an interest in schools and children? She believed school suffrage might get men used to the idea of women voting and provide an "entering wedge" to full voting rights. Once men saw that the earth did not spin off its axis just because women were voting, she hoped they would be more open-minded. Like all of the early women's rights leaders, she came to believe that women would never be taken seriously until they had the right to vote for the candidates and issues they supported. Nor would they be able to hold onto any rights they secured through the good graces of their male advocates.

In 1852 she gathered two hundred signatures on a petition that she circulated around Brattleboro asking for school voting rights. Her advocacy of women's rights apparently divided the town and led some residents to suggest the *Democrat* be shut down or handed off to someone else. A letter to the editor that she printed October 27, 1852, and signed "Many Citizens," defended her policies and gave her a strong show of support. It referred to the *Democrat* as a "good family paper" that "speaks out fearlessly for good morals and the highest interest of humanity."

It continued:

> Some, it is true, object to having quite so much in it about women's rights; yet passing over all that is said on

that subject, they are willing to allow that what remains
renders it quite superior to many other papers.

———◆———

Earlier that month, Daniel Thompson, a judge and newspaper editor in another town, convinced the state legislators
to invite Mrs. Nichols to come and present her petition in
person. "Come to Montpelier," he said, "and I will stick by
you like a brother."

Clarina discussed with George the idea of speaking before
the legislature. "Shall I go?" she asked. George answered with
a question of his own. "Have you the nerve?"

She had spoken to small groups and to large, friendly wom-
en's rights conventions, but this audience would be skeptical,
maybe even hostile. Some legislators wanted nothing so much
as to see Mrs. Nichols come and make a fool of herself. Said
the chairman of the education committee, "If the lady wants
to make herself ridiculous, let her come and make herself as
ridiculous as possible and as soon as possible."

In the end, she could not pass up such a splendid opportunity. She accepted the invitation and went to Montpelier to
address the Vermont legislature — the first woman to do so.

As she started to speak, she stopped suddenly and rested
her head in her hand. Judge Thompson's wife later said she
feared Mrs. Nichols might faint. But whether she was feigning
fragility to elicit sympathy or was genuinely overcome by the
occasion, Nichols quickly pulled herself together and went on
to deliver the speech.

One of the legislators had planned to present her with a
pair of pants at the end of her speech. Men often complained
that women's rights leaders wanted to "wear the pants in the
family." Giving her a pair of pants was sure to get a laugh.

Before sitting down, she turned to address her staunchest
opponent, the man who was secretly planning to embarrass

her. She said that though she had bought the dress she wore with her own money, her husband by law owned it, not of his own will, but by a "law adopted by bachelors and other women's husbands." She said she didn't think it was fair for men to tease women about wanting to wear men's pants until men had given up their right to own women's skirts.

For a moment there was silence. Then came the "muffled thunder of stamping feet." The legislature was showing appreciation for their quick-witted guest speaker. The trousers were never presented. Later she joked that if men were so concerned with "wearing the pants," perhaps they should make a pair of men's trousers the national symbol instead of the bald eagle.

A crowd of excited women waited for her afterwards. Invited by Judge Thompson, they had listened in the galleries to the first speech on women's rights that they had ever heard. One of them extended a friendly hand to her. "We did not know before what woman's rights were, Mrs. Nichols," she said, smiling broadly, "but we are for woman's rights!"

The legislature did not act on Nichols's petition, but she considered her speech a triumph anyway. She had presented the case for women's rights as logically and thoroughly as she knew how to, and the legislators had been attentive, civil, and respectful. That was as far as she could go for the present.

One newspaper said that in spite of the subject matter, Mrs. Nichols had been unable to "unsex" herself. She appreciated this observation and saw it as evidence that people were beginning to understand that she was a true woman despite her unusual calling.

"Only those who have suffered as I have can have the courage and determination to move steadily forward against such opposition," she said in later years. "And if people like this give up, the work of reform is hopeless."

EIGHT

'The World Is on the Move'

In the fall of 1853 thousands of visitors from home and abroad traveled to New York City, already home to half a million people. Visitors from Europe, South America, Canada, Asia, and all parts of the United States descended on New York City to see the first World's Fair ever held on American soil. The city's ninety-two hotels were booked and its streets jammed with coaches, omnibuses, and hacks. The sidewalks were crowded with fairgoers in a festive mood and vendors selling everything from sausages to old rags.

The main attraction was the Crystal Palace, built especially for the fair to house thousands of industrial exhibits and inventions. An enormous structure of iron and glass designed in the shape of a Greek cross, the Crystal Palace shimmered at night, lit from the inside by hundreds of gas lanterns.

The organizers of the World's Fair had no less a purpose

than advancing world peace. They were not alone; the editors of the two-year-old *New York Times* believed new technology like the telegraph would help unite the world. "The Crystal Palace is a symbol of the might of Man," it editorialized. "Look on, ye Nations, and vow eternal peace and justice."

Clarina Nichols probably visited the Crystal Palace — it was the talk of the town — but she was in New York for other reasons. Two temperance conventions, an antislavery meeting, and a women's rights convention were held in New York that September, all of them covered extensively by the city's eight daily newspapers. Women were excluded from one of the temperance conventions and given places of honor at the other. An unruly mob nearly took over the women's rights convention, while a small number of men repented of past prejudices and asked the women for forgiveness.

In an organizing meeting the previous spring, the World's Temperance Convention had denied Susan B. Anthony a seat on their business committee. If there was one woman qualified to serve on a business committee, it was she. Anthony had a reputation throughout the reform community as a superb organizer and a precise bookkeeper. A majority of men voted not only to keep Anthony off the committee but to bar *all* women from participating — exactly what had happened thirteen years earlier at the World Anti-Slavery Convention in London. (The World's Temperance Convention also refused to admit Dr. James McCune Smith because he was black.)

Outraged, the women and their male allies marched out and organized their own convention. Thus, when the World's Temperance Convention met in September, it was upstaged by a rival gathering — the *Whole* World's Temperance Convention, which excluded no one on the basis of sex, race, creed, or national origin.

America's most progressive men and women turned out in force at the Whole World's Temperance Convention. Anthony was appointed secretary. From her seat on the podium,

Nichols presided over the proceedings with a roster of all-star vice presidents. They included Lucretia Mott; showman P. T. Barnum; and newspaper editors Horace Greeley of the *New York Tribune* and Sherman Booth of the *Milwaukee Free Democrat,* who would earn fame (and a prison sentence) for violating the 1850 Fugitive Slave Law by aiding an escaped slave. The *Tribune* praised "the scarcity of white neck-ties on the platform" and the presence of "such champions of reform and humanity as Antoinette Brown, Lucy Stone, Mrs. Jackson of England and Mrs. C. I. H. Nichols."

The two thousand attendees cheered one speaker after the next. The Amphions, a musical group popular with reformers, entertained the convention with such crowd-pleasers as "The World Is on the Move," "Dawn of the Good Time Coming" and "The Temperance War Song." The delegates were told that the wind was shifting and that victory would be in sight if they stayed the course. The world would soon be free of the effects of alcohol. Sober citizens would abolish slavery; domestic abuse and poverty would cease; and women would take their rightful place in society. It was a glorious vision.

Other papers did not share the *Tribune's* enthusiasm. The *New York Times* described the two-day affair as if it were a perfectly harmless national gathering of pretty schoolgirls:

> It was not speeches, nor the singing — which, too, was very good — that drew the fine houses of yesterday, and bewitched the ladies of the City. It was the marvelous free-and-easy habit of the meetings. Ladies laid off their bonnets, and had a good time generally. Strangers abounded more than citizens even. Everybody wanted to know who everybody else was. Nice little girls from Massachusetts whispered to nice little girls from Missouri, to know which Greeley was; and lasses from Connecticut grew acquainted with prettily attired lasses from Illinois....It was a kind of Ladies' Exchange. Whoever

went there on Monday, wanted to go on Tuesday to see
their new-made friends again.

———◆———

Many speakers declared that temperance could not be separated from abolition and women's rights. Freedom for slaves,
rights for women, and a drug-free world — these were three
strands of one strong cord.

The original goal of the temperance movement had been to
convince people to swear off alcohol. Thousands of Americans
had already signed temperance pledges and done just that.
But now the sons and daughters of temperance wanted a
more thorough way of dealing with the problem. Cut off the
sources of alcohol, they said, and there will be no alcoholism.
Inns and "grog shops" where alcohol was served were threatened or closed down. Barrels of alcohol were dumped in the
streets. Some temperance supporters even went so far as to
chop down apple orchards if they thought the apples would
be made into hard cider or to destroy wheat before it could
be turned into beer.

Amid loud applause, Nichols was introduced to the convention.

> I say that woman is the greatest sufferer because the laws
> of the land have bound her hand and foot and commited
> her soul and body to the protection of her husband, and
> when he fails to protect her through imbecility, misjudg-
> ment, misfortune, or intemperance, she suffers. It is
> because the Mother of Humanity cannot hold in her own
> hand the bread she earns to feed her babes and children.
> It is because of the crimes of her inebriate husband — if
> he be one — that she suffers. It is because the babes
> that she rears are given to the custody of the drunken
> husbands. And, friends, if intemperance did not invade
> our homes, if it did not take from us our clothing, our

bread, and the means for our self-development, and for
the training of our children to respectability and useful-
ness — if it did not take the babes from our bosoms, I
would not stand here.

To protect women and children, she put forth a dramatic
proposal: the delegates should lobby Christian churches to use
their substantial power to enforce temperance. "You may think
me ultra," she told the audience, "but what is the organization of Christianity worth if you cannot bring the force of the
Church to bear on every individual?" The people cheered.

Earlier in the day, Lucy Stone had proposed even more
radical ideas: people who drank one drop of alcohol should not
be allowed to marry or be parents, she declared. Furthermore,
if a spouse became a drinker, the sober spouse should seek an
immediate divorce. Nichols objected: if the drinker reformed,
she argued, wouldn't it be a tragedy if his wife had married
someone else but was still in love with him? It seems unlikely
that Nichols was feeling nostalgic for her first husband, who
was no longer alive to plague her. She obviously was not opposed to divorce, but she saw it as a last resort. Divorce would
separate a woman from the source of her misery, but it might
also separate her from any property she brought with her into
the marriage, and possibly even her children.

Stone and Stanton, who vigorously opposed Nichols on this
issue, argued that drunkenness should be made a reason for
divorce and that anyone married to a drinker had not only a
right but a duty to seek a divorce. Neither had experienced
the emotional, social and financial toll of leaving a marriage,
as Nichols had. Furthermore, Nichols knew that all too often
alcoholic fathers "with a good coat" were awarded custody in
divorce cases. She believed that legal separation — with full
custody and property rights for the wife — was a better solution for families riven by alcohol.

When it was over, Greeley's *New York Tribune* declared the gathering "the most spirited and able Convention on temperance that was ever held. It has already done good, and cannot fail to do more."

———◆———

Nichols had barely finished with one convention before she had another to attend. As it turned out, the women's convention was the wildest of them all. The days were already warm, but the sight of so many "strong-minded" women around New York City raised the temperature several more degrees. Some were wearing bloomers — and being taunted in the streets by bands of young men, who no doubt disdained the women's stance on temperance as well.

On the Sunday before the opening of the women's convention, the Anti-slavery Society held its meeting. That evening Antoinette Brown, the first woman ordained by a mainline Protestant church in the United States, preached a public sermon that attracted five thousand people.

The correspondent for the *New York Herald* was appalled:

> We saw, in broad daylight, in a public hall in the city of New York, a gathering of unsexed women — unsexed in mind all of them, and many in habiliments [clothing, in this case, bloomers] — publicly propounding the doctrine that they should be allowed to step out of their appropriate sphere, and mingle in the busy walks of every-day life, to the neglect of those duties which both human and divine law have assigned to them. We do not stoop to argue against so ridiculous a set of ideas.

Alarmed by both events, those opposed to women's rights went on the counterattack.

The women's convention had an open admission policy. Anyone with twenty-five cents could enter. Between two and

Broadway Tabernacle, site of the "mob convention"
Nichols addressed in 1853. (*Library of Congress*)

three thousand people crowded into the Broadway Tabernacle,
a multi-tiered meeting hall whose balconies looked down unto
a large stage. Every seat on the floor was taken, and the galleries were packed. Scores of young men fanned out through
the audience for the purpose of raising a ruckus. They hung
over the balconies, called out to one another across the hall,
swigged alcohol from flasks concealed in their jackets, and
began to boo, heckle, and harass every speaker who came to
the podium. The women suspected that the young men had
been recruited by older establishment men to do their dirty
work.

Antoinette Brown, who had just given a sermon the preceding Sunday to great acclaim, was now drowned out with
cries of "Shut up!" "Time's up!" and "We don't want to hear
you!"

Ernestine Rose, who took over from Lucretia Mott when
the tumult was at its height, called in the police and demanded
they root out the rowdies and deal with them. "The mayor

promised to see that our meeting should not be disturbed, and I call upon him to keep order," she said. "As citizens of New York we have a right to this protection, for we pay our money for it." She called on the members themselves to help restore order. Greeley and other male delegates tussled with the troublemakers and dragged a few of them out.

Nichols spoke on one of her favorite topics — the wronged widow and the wife whose husband had absconded with the children. During a discussion on religion she said she had noticed that "In the Green Mountain State a great many sermons have lately been preached on the text, 'Wives, submit yourselves to your husbands.'" But what if the husband was a woman's rights man, she asked. What if he wanted her to enjoy the same rights as he enjoyed? "My husband wishes me to vote," she declared, adding that if this was her husband's wish, who could say she was opposing the will of God?

One of the speakers that stood up to the rowdies was Sojourner Truth, an ex-slave who had already shown, at an earlier convention, that she would not be intimidated by anyone. Truth had responded with "power and directness" to a minister who had argued that the Bible ordained the authority of men over women. "Where did your Christ come from?" she asked. "From God and a woman. Man had nothing to do with Him."

Now, Truth pulled herself to her full six-foot height and crossed to the podium. At the sight of this tall, confident black woman, the rowdies increased the volume of their whoops, hollers, and hisses. "You may hiss as much as you like, but it's coming," she declared. "We'll have our rights. See if we don't! And you can't stop us from them — see if you can!"

Both days of the convention ended in total uproar.

The "mob convention," as it came to be called, won sympathy for women and new interest in the women's rights cause. The ungentlemanly behavior of the young rowdies at this convention and their older compatriots at the "Half-World" convention made some men reconsider their opposition.

In *The Liberator* Nichols wrote that "several gentlemen" came to the women's convention and publicly apologized. Isaac C. Pray, a poet and former editor of a leading New York journal, was one of them. He told the women he was sorry for his past attempts to make the women's rights cause look ridiculous and said he now believed their cause "was from God and bound to succeed."

Nichols was pleased with this confession and conversion. As a true woman, there was nothing she liked better than a true man. "His whole appearance and language proved him a *man*, noble enough to appreciate the good and courageous enough to turn from the beaten path of popular approbation when it leads astray from the right." She and the other women gave him heartfelt applause and invited him into their fold.

In one of the resolutions that the delegates managed to pass over the yelling of the rowdies, the delegates declared that women's rights were not for the nation only, but the whole world. What had been in doubt just three years earlier was now stated as fact: Women's rights was one of the greatest reforms of the age.

While Nichols was in New York, Horace Greeley approached her. Would she go to Wisconsin on behalf of the New York State Temperance Society? he asked. They needed a strong speaker to canvass the state in favor of the new temperance law in Wisconsin, and she had already promoted a similar law in Vermont. Most people outside the big Eastern cities had never heard a woman speak at a public meeting. That, in itself, would draw crowds.

NINE

Winning
Wisconsin

"I wish Mr. Nichols could be relieved from so much suffer-ing," a friend wrote to Clarina in the fall of 1853. We can only speculate on the nature of George's "suffering," since its origins are unknown, but what is remarkable is his generous reaction when his wife told him about Greeley's request that she canvass Wisconsin.

"Go," he responded, "you will be doing just the work you love and enjoying a journey which you otherwise could not afford." He had two daughters who could help out while she was away.

She would tour with Lydia Fowler, one of the first female doctors in the United States and the first woman to teach at a medical college. Nichols was happy to have her as a partner in the campaign and a companion during the long journey. The two women worked out a complementary program that would

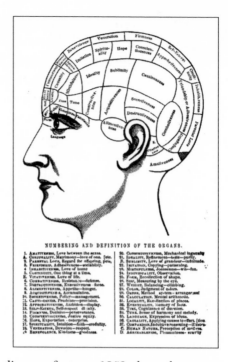

This diagram from an 1859 phrenology manual by O.S. Fowler and L.N. Fowler (the husband of Lydia Fowler) divides the brain into sections such as "Spirituality" and "Mirthfulness."

best present their anti-liquor message. Each night Fowler would lecture on the dangers of alcohol from a medical point of view. Then Nichols would take the stage and follow up with a more personal lecture on the consequences of alcoholism on the family, drawing on her abundant supply of stories. The entrenched liquor interests of the state were sure to make trouble, but the women were confident they could handle that.

In addition to her medical credentials, Fowler was greatly in demand as a phrenologist — someone who specialized in determining people's strengths and weaknesses merely by examining the shape of their heads. She and her husband, Lorenzo Fowler, were responsible for bringing phrenology from Great Britain to the United States, where it quickly became popular among the elites as "the only true science of the mind." Though there is no record of Nichols having her head examined by one of the Fowlers, there is no reason why she would not have. At the core of phrenology was a belief that all people were created equal. Individuals who were found to have deficiencies could improve themselves with a series of simple physical exercises assigned by the phrenologist. This would certainly have been an agreeable outlook to the progressive-minded Americans of that era, which may explain why it flourished among them: Horace Mann, Samuel Morse, Mark Twain, Clara Barton, and even Abraham Lincoln were all said to have had phrenology readings.

The two women traveled north by stagecoach to Niagara Falls, where they admired the suspension bridge that spanned the falls like a delicate spider's web. They marveled at the enormous stone piers that were being built for the coming railroad. After spending a day touring the falls, they boarded a steamer to cross Lake Erie. In their first-class stateroom in the center of the boat, they were spared its heaving and rocking. Nichols reported that there was much "moaning and wretching of passengers in the lower cabins." The two women, however, reclined in their deck chairs, chatting amiably, as they watched the white sails in the distance.

After an overnight train trip and a steamboat ride across Lake Michigan, the two reformers docked in Milwaukee in time for an early tea. The women expected to be welcomed by the temperance community. Instead, they were met by a surly man who was dismayed that the New York Temperance Society had sent a woman to speak for temperance. Even worse, they had sent *two* women, including Mrs. Nichols, the well-known champion of women's rights. These women would disgrace the cause of temperance, he fumed. They would all become laughingstocks. On and on he went, she said, "stooping to the most disgusting depths."

But soon they were in for an even ruder shock. The Wisconsin Temperance League voted to strip the women of their responsibilities and withdraw support in a move similar to what had just happened at the "Half-World" Temperance Convention in New York. Nichols and Fowler had not reckoned on such a reception in a young pioneer state.

News of the rebuff quickly reached the attention of Sherman Booth, the radical abolitionist editor of Milwaukee's *Daily Free Democrat.* He had shared the platform with Nichols at the recent Whole World's Temperance Convention, and he was well aware of strong elements within the temperance community who did not want women giving public lectures to mixed male-female audiences, even for so good a cause as temperance. In the front pages of his newspaper, Booth told his readers how inhospitably the two Eastern reformers had been treated. Wisconsin should "joyfully welcome" these women, he scolded. "We believe that no men can be obtained whose services would be half so efficient in this cause."

He reminded his readers that the state vote on temperance was just five weeks away. "There is no time to be lost. The State must be thoroughly roused," he wrote. "Shall this be done? That is the question."

Nichols, Fowler, and Booth received a hasty invitation to attend the Wisconsin Women's Temperance Convention in Delavan. Here they were welcomed like heroes, listened to in rapt attention, and entertained by the local brass band. The women at the convention agreed that their state was in crisis, awash in alcohol, and vowed not to rest until they had helped reverse the tide. Milwaukee was already something of a hopeless case. As a large influx of German immigrants poured in, breweries sprang up to serve their national beverage. The great majority of Germans were unaware that there was anything wrong with drinking beer or schnapps and bewildered by the idea that they should give it up.

The Wisconsin Women's Temperance Convention voted to appoint and financially support Nichols and Fowler in their canvass of the state. This was no small sacrifice, as the Temperance League had already solicited funds from many of these same individuals, only to renege on supporting the women. The pro-temperance *Milwaukee Daily Free Democrat* reported that the convention delegates were "indignant that these funds must go to sustain an Agent in the field whose conduct toward women they disapprove."

The delegates gave Nichols and Fowler a rousing sendoff, and the president of the convention read a declaration:

> We hereby give notice to the law-makers of Wisconsin, as we have before done, that the Women are *COMING*: that they are fully determined to give them no peace until they pass a law for suppressing the sale of intoxicating liquors throughout the State.

Temperance was the granddaddy of reform movements in the 19th century. It attracted multitudes who believed it was the answer to society's most perplexing problems. Though temperance attracted men and women across the political spectrum, it was also the issue that tipped many women into public action. The antislavery movement had the same effect but involved a smaller number of women. Interest in temperance among some radical women's rights advocates waned after the calamitous events of the 1853 conventions, but throughout much of the country, women continued to support temperance wholeheartedly. Temperance gave women the most socially acceptable avenue to public platforms, but it also gave a broad range of women something they could unite over.

There was often little difference between a temperance and a women's rights meeting in Wisconsin. Mrs. Ostrander, the convention's president, assured the assembled delegates (and readers of the *Free Democrat*, which published her address) that women were not going to neglect their domestic duties just because they spoke up for temperance. Still, she couldn't help throwing in a few jabs at the "Lords of creation" who needed such reassurance.

> I am sick of hearing this canting phrase — 'getting out of our sphere.'...Oh, that some giant intellect among our opposers would define our sphere — as they understand it! — so that we might, at least, see how far we may diverge from our accustomed orbits without danger of flying off to a returnless distance from the great centres of attraction — the 'lords of creation.'

After a few jerks and starts, the campaign took off at full gallop. During October and November of 1853, Nichols and Fowler lectured for four weeks without a day's rest. They spoke in forty-three towns to more than thirty thousand people. In most places standing-room-only crowds gathered to catch a glimpse of them. It was as good a show as the circus. People came in wagons from five to twenty miles to see the unusual sight — two women lecturing to what was then called a "promiscuous" audience, one made up of both men and women.

They traveled nine hundred miles around Wisconsin by horse and wagon or stage. Before starting out, Nichols worried that she might not have the stamina to travel and lecture on a daily basis, but the large turnouts — which were almost always friendly and sympathetic — both surprised and energized her.

Riding through the gently rolling countryside under blue skies in the crisp air of Indian summer, she fell in love with Wisconsin. "Broad prairies, gallant lakes, and noble humanity," she wrote, enumerating the state's best qualities. She observed fine brick houses lining the road, men and women hard at work, signs of progress everywhere. Even the fences in Wisconsin impressed her. The farmers had piled up mud from the prairies

A couple farming "side by side" in Wisconsin, 1866. The woman is wearing a rural version of bloomers. *(Wisconsin Historical Society)*

in two-foot high ridges, then driven split oak rails into the mud at regular intervals. When the mass hardened, it formed a fence as solid as New England stone.

The biggest challenge on the circuit continued to come from the temperance community itself. The League, which had tried to abort the Eastern women's campaign, seemed as interested in discrediting the women as in winning the anti-liquor vote. They raced ahead to the towns Nichols and Fowler were scheduled to lecture in, spread rumors about the women, told people not to attend their lectures, and tried to close off public accommodations to them. Overall, their efforts had little effect and seemed to increase rather than diminish interest in the visiting lecturers.

When the hotels were closed to the women, some sympathetic family was always found who offered to put the women up for the night. If one minister closed his church to the women, another invited them to use his. Told they could not address a large church convention in Madison, the women were invited instead to lecture at a much more prestigious location: the chamber of the state assembly.

At a Congregational Church in Waukesha, they sat in the pews for over an hour while the deacon and another man carried on a long, dry business meeting that appeared to serve no particular purpose. It seemed that the real intent of the "meeting" was to keep the women from speaking. That became obvious when the deacon started gathering up his things and telling everyone to go home. The people who had come to hear the women were irritated. One said he rode his horse twenty miles to get there, while another man said he had walked thirteen miles so that his wife and daughter could ride. They demanded that the women be allowed to speak the next evening.

Rudeness, slights, "mistakes" in scheduling, and printers who tried to undermine the women's message by adding or deleting information from their tracts and handbills — these were tactics that lecturers for unpopular reform causes, including women's rights, were all too familiar with.

What shocked Nichols was that she had recognized the deacon as an old friend from her Brockport days. She had once encouraged him to speak out for temperance at a time when he had been reluctant to do so. In Brockport, she herself had felt it was improper for a woman to speak in public. The only woman doing so at that time was Frances Wright, a radical Scottish reformer who was branded "the Red Harlot" for her boldness in breaking social taboos. In the intervening twenty years Nichols had changed her perception of what was and wasn't appropriate behavior for a woman. "My friend," she observed, "had only stood still."

When it was her turn to speak the following night, she scanned the audience for the deacon and found him sitting in the middle of the audience with no sign of recognition on his face.

She thanked the congregation for asking her and Mrs. Fowler back. She told them it was not the first time she had been refused the podium. Why, there was even a time when an old friend stepped in her path. She and this friend had once been coworkers in the temperance cause back in Brockport, New York. She had encouraged and supported him, but years later he had turned around and tried to prevent her from speaking.

The deacon looked puzzled at first. As she went on with her story, he slowly reddened as he realized who the speaker was and that he was the one she was talking about. After the meeting, he came up and apologized. Even better, he volunteered to secure her an invitation to speak at a county temperance convention. Instead of confronting and embarrassing an old friend, as she had every right to do, she had won an ally to the cause.

The crusade in Wisconsin was a resounding success. The legislature soon passed a law that gave wives control of property and custody of children when their husbands were drunkards.

It also marked a decisive turn in Clarina Nichols's outlook. Deeply impressed by what she had seen in Wisconsin, she now began to entertain the idea that men's and women's roles were less rigid in the West than they were in the East. Other than run-ins with male temperance leaders, she found that Westerners were not as tradition-bound as Easterners were. She recalled the sight of wagons heading for the markets in Milwaukee, with men and tidily dressed women atop mountain-high loads of grain, riding side by side.

When she returned from her trip, George's health had worsened. Clarina thought about Wisconsin, its expansive prairies and open-minded people. She began to seriously ponder the idea that the West might have restorative powers for George and potential for herself.

TEN

A Country Divided

Clarina Nichols returned from Wisconsin on a high note. After a rocky start, her path had been smoothed by new friends who enthusiastically supported her efforts in their state. The entire sequence of events that fall—the raucous conventions in New York, the adventure of traveling to a Western state, and the vigorous campaign that followed—all these boosted her confidence.

In two short years she had transformed herself from a cautious defender of oppressed women to a self-assured advocate of reform. Now she had reached a crossroads. Should she keep the *Democrat* going? Devote herself to lecturing? Move to Wisconsin? George's health had not improved, and her father had become seriously ill also. Every week she took the stagecoach from Brattleboro to Townshend to look in on him and help with his care.

By the end of 1853 she and George decided to close down the *Democrat*. Lecturing would give her more freedom and flexibility than running a weekly newspaper, and she felt sure that her growing reputation would result in as many engagements as she desired. She sent notices to *The Lily* and *The Liberator* informing them of her decision and soliciting lecture dates. The notice in *The Liberator* made reference to her needlework, which had become something of a running joke with her readers:

> Mrs. Nichols has suspended the publication of the newspaper which she has edited, and announces that she will devote herself to lectures on temperance, woman's rights &c., and that while she shall not neglect to 'darn the stockings,' she will not overlook that the men have souls to be darned also.

She resumed her busy schedule of lectures and appearances at lyceums, which many communities formed to educate and entertain their residents. In late December she lectured in Massachusetts. The following month she was invited to Rhode Island for a four-part series with Lucy Stone, Antoinette Brown, and Ernestine Rose. In March she was booked for two nights at the Tremont Temple in Boston.

Her lyceum programs were often structured as debates between all-male and all-female teams. Without this artificially contrived "battle of the sexes," Nichols said, the lyceum debates would have been "too tame" or "no debate at all." She noted with amusement that when members of the clergy were present, they were always selected to speak against woman suffrage. Their wives, however, would be assigned to the affirmative position. It made for a lively evening.

She always allowed the ministers to open and close the debate, but even with that advantage, her opponents generally got the worst of it. Clergymen who expected to sway the

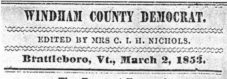

WINDHAM COUNTY DEMOCRAT.

EDITED BY MRS C. I. H. NICHOLS.

Brattleboro, Vt., March 2, 1853.

The Paupers' Removal.

"It isn't a *woman's* vocation to write politics; her sphere is at home," says one and another, and we always say *amen*. 'Astonished' are you, gentle reader! And did you think that Mrs Nichols "meddles with politics" because she finds their details congenial with her tastes, or for any reason but that politics *meddle* with the happiness of home and its most sacred relations, with *woman* and all that is dearest to the affections and hopes of a true woman? If you dreamed that politics have any hold upon our sympathies not strictly belonging to their power over the *homes* of the land for weal or woe—any claim upon our time and efforts not identified with our own home interests, you have done us grievous wrong, dear reader, and we pray you just listen to a brief chapter of state policy which was forced upon our notice, a few days since, and say if women, as the "guardian angels" of the "*sanctity* of home" and the "inviolableness of the home relations," have not a call to *write* politics, to *talk* politics?

"You were waiting, a few days since, at a railroad

This editorial, published in the *Democrat*'s final year, shows Nichols making a familiar argument: that she "meddles with politics" only because "politics meddle with the happiness of home and its most sacred relations."

audience with a few choice pronouncements were upstaged by Nichols's understanding of both Scripture and law. After one such debate, a flustered minister said, "I told you, ladies and gentlemen, that I had given little attention to the subject … and you see that I told the truth."

She was proud of her ability to lay out "clear and convincing" arguments and win over her skeptics without becoming a "masculine brawler." One reporter wrote that "the first tone of her voice" had removed all "impertinent curiosity," for it was "seen that she was both a mother and a lady, with all the graces of education and modesty."

Still, she was not afraid to throw grace and modesty to the wind when the occasion called for it. In January 1854, while riding the train to a speaking event in Templeton, Massachusetts, Nichols confronted two men attempting to take children away from their mother in a disputed custody case.

As she recounted six weeks later in the Brattleboro *Eagle*, she heard a woman cry out, "Don't take away my children!" Looking up from her knitting, she recognized the two Brattleboro men who were the cause of the disturbance. One was the village sheriff, the other an old gentleman of means from the town. Later she would learn that the mother was suing for divorce, citing domestic abuse, but without waiting to hear the mother's story Nichols immediately rose and went to her defense.

"My friends," she announced, "the lawmakers of this Christian country have given the custody of their babies to the fathers, drunken or sober." Her words incited the others in the car to turn against the two men.

She reported, "The excitement was intense; except the two child-stealers, every man there (I need not speak of the *women*) was for women's rights to her babes."

The sheriff and grandfather had planned to grab the children off the train while it was in the depot and whisk them to a carriage waiting to return them to Brattleboro. But Nichols barred the door to the mother's compartment and, before the second child could be seized, the train pulled out of the depot. Suddenly the men found themselves in a car full of hostile passengers on a train moving rapidly toward the Vermont-Massachusetts state line.

Ever alert to the laws that affected women, Nichols knew that either a father or a grandfather could take children from their mother in Vermont, but in Massachusetts only a father had that right. She warned the sheriff that he was now out of his jurisdiction, "a fact which either he was ignorant of, or supposed the passengers would not detect, or act upon."

As the train rolled through the countryside, she and her new allies in the car discussed "a plan of operations for the rescue." They were not unduly alarmed when the two men hopped off the train at the next stop with the four-year-old in tow. Nichols enlisted a trustworthy-looking man to escort the mother to local authorities and press charges against the kidnappers, something a woman could not do on her own. The baby attended her first women's rights lecture that evening, after which Nichols deposited her in the safe hands of mutual friends. Meanwhile, a Massachusetts sheriff had tracked down the two "child-stealers" and hauled them into court, where they were ordered to return the older child and pay expenses for the trouble they had caused.

News of the rescue arrived home before Nichols did. The story must have included the detail of her knitting, for people sent her skeins of yarn to show approval for what she had done. She gratefully accepted these gifts as evidence that people saw her as she wanted to be seen. She was someone who had "home interests" at heart; someone knitting society together instead of unraveling it.

———————

When she returned to Vermont from her temperance tour, a great national debate was underway. The cause of it all was the Kansas-Nebraska bill. This bill proposed opening the vast Kansas-Nebraska Territory — then known as Indian Country — to white settlement.

At the time of this great debate in the United States Senate, some twenty Indian nations owned every acre of land in eastern Kansas. They had been uprooted from their homes in the East and Midwest and forced to move west to Kansas where, in the words of President Andrew Jackson, "your white brothers will not trouble you...and you can live upon it, you and all your children, as long as the grass grows or the water runs, in peace and plenty." Not only did the sponsors

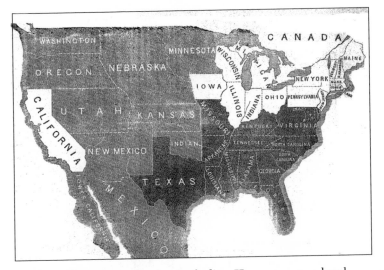

United States territories, including Kansas, were a legal
grey zone between slave and free states, as seen in this
1860 newspaper graphic. *(Library of Congress)*

of the Kansas-Nebraska bill disregard this promise; most of
the senators acted as though it was hardly worth mentioning.
The Kansas-Nebraska Territory was the next big parcel of
land available for white settlement, and many land-hungry
pioneers would not be denied. Some historians believe the
real reason for opening up the territory was to build a railroad
across it, linking East and West, promoting trade, and making its backers rich. Whatever the real scenario involved, it
required removal of the Indians.

The Kansas-Nebraska bill raised another thorny issue.
Would the new states carved out of the territory allow slavery
or ban it? The chief sponsor, Senator Stephen A. Douglas of
Illinois, said this question should be decided by the people
who actually settled on the land, a policy known as "popular
sovereignty." Antislavery forces were horrified by that possibility. They believed passage of the Kansas-Nebraska bill

would be a victory for the South and a major shift in the country's official policy on slavery.

Since 1820, when Congress passed the Missouri Compromise, slavery had been illegal north and west of Missouri in the remainder of the lands of the Louisiana Purchase. Under the new law, however, the citizens of the territory would be allowed to renegotiate the legality of slavery.

No one thought that Nebraska, being farther north and abutting the free state of Iowa, would allow slavery. But Kansas was another matter. With enough settlers entering the territory from neighboring Missouri and other slaveholding states, slavery was sure to be voted in under popular sovereignty. Kansas would be bound to the slave economy of the South, and slavery would have a foothold in the West.

Three thousand New England clergymen sent Congress a protest against the Kansas-Nebraska bill in March 1854. They called it "a great moral wrong" that endangered "the peace and even the existence of our beloved Union." Despite fierce opposition to what became known as "Nebrascality," the bill became law in May 1854. The fate of Kansas would be decided by the people who settled there. The call went up in New England and other Northern states to flood the territory with "free-state" settlers.

That same month, Chapin Howard died. If the passage of Kansas-Nebraska exerted a pull on Nichols, the passing of her father removed one of the tethers keeping her in Vermont. Once again, she began thinking of moving west — this time, far west. Despite her reputation as a genteel voice on behalf of women and children, Nichols had a restless, adventurous spirit that looked outward instead of inward in times of stress or challenge.

———

Since 1847 she and George had been out of step with their less progressive neighbors. They had broken with the Demo-

cratic Party over the slavery issue and allied themselves with
the free-soil coalition that opposed extending slavery into the
Western territories. In New England she was beginning to
despair of what she called its "fossilized conservatism." Now
there was a new territory beckoning settlers like themselves.
Having moved many times in her life, the prospect of a cross-
country move was perhaps less daunting to Clarina Nichols
than it would have been to most women in middle age.

She began meeting with others who were thinking about
moving to Kansas Territory. These meetings led to the formation of an emigrant aid society in Brattleboro, aligned
with the New England Emigrant Aid Society. Its purpose
was twofold: to give people who invested in the company a
good rate of return, and to help "free-state" settlers move to
Kansas. Traveling in a group rather than alone appealed to
many of the would-be emigrants. Those who bought stock in
the company were promised an experienced guide who would
accompany them on their trek and make arrangements. These
pioneers did not head west in white-topped wagons as earlier
pioneers had done. They journeyed by train to St. Louis and
then took a steamboat across the entire width of the state on
the Missouri River. Only when they reached the western
border of Missouri would they step back in time and travel
as their grandparents and great-grandparents had done — by
horse and wagon, by oxcart, or on foot.

With eighteen-year-old Relie and twenty-year-old Howard,
Clarina Nichols went to scout out Kansas Territory. She left
her husband, youngest son, and daughter behind, for she
reasoned that there was no point in dragging the whole family
out to Kansas if it turned out to be an unsuitable destination.
On the other hand, Nichols saw that resistance was growing
to progressive legislation for women in her home state. In her
mind, New England was compromised by its history, while
Kansas — where the laws were yet unwritten — could devise
its future from scratch.

ELEVEN

Mush and Molasses

In October 1854 Nichols and her two older sons boarded the train for the trip west. Over two hundred people were in her particular group, the fourth party of the New England Emigrant Aid Society heading for Kansas that year. There were thirty women and forty-five children in this group, many more than in previous groups. She saw this as a good sign, for where women went, home — and civilization — followed.

These westward-heading emigrants received the kind of patriotic sendoff that soldiers receive in the early weeks of a popular war. At the Boston station crowds of well-wishers joined them in singing the "Hymn of the Kansas Emigrant," written by poet John Greenleaf Whittier.

> We cross the prairies as of old
> The pilgrims crossed the sea.

To make the West, as they the East,
The homestead of the free!

In a week they reached St. Louis, where they boarded a westbound steamboat on the Missouri River. "Picture the writer surrounded by some twenty emigrants...under six years of age, who are laughing, crying, tumbling, and being tumbled over," she wrote in the Boston *Evening Telegraph*. All around them were groups of adults and "snatches of song and cheerful, sometimes hilarious, conversation from surrounding groups. Who can think in such a scene?"

The ship's captain asked Nichols to lecture on women's rights during the ten-day journey up the Missouri, and she obliged him two nights in a row. Another passenger, whom she described as "a pious doctor," sent his young wife to bed, so she wouldn't get any new ideas. Knowing where the wife's cabin was located below deck, Nichols positioned herself so that the woman could hear even if she couldn't see.

"Next morning, poor man! His wife was an outspoken advocate of woman's rights," she later wrote. "The next evening she punched his ribs vigorously at every point made for suffrage, which was the subject of my second lecture."

———

The new pioneers docked on the levee in Kansas City, Missouri, toward evening on a cold, rainy, Saturday. What little they could see of the city did not lift their spirits. Rickety houses were perched atop steep hills that overlooked narrow, muddy streets.

Their welcoming party was a band of rough-talking, pro-slavery Missourians who boarded the boat uninvited and proceeded to scare the daylight out of the weary travelers with wild tales about savage Indians and starving pioneers. As they carried on, the atmosphere grew increasingly tense, with the New Englanders unsure of how to respond, and the

Missourians growing more outrageous in their descriptions of pioneer life in Kansas.

One of their party introduced himself to Nichols as Colonel Scott. "Can you tell me where all these people are from, and where they are going?" he asked, though he knew perfectly well the answer to his question.

"They are from the New England States and are going to Kansas," she replied, playing along.

It was a popular Southern conceit that the Yankees emigrating to Kansas Territory would be unable to plow its tough soil. The colonel declared that she and her compatriots wouldn't be able to farm these prairies without slave labor.

Nonsense, she said, New Englanders were tough and ingenious. "Did you never hear how in New Hampshire and Vermont the sheeps' noses have to be sharpened so that they can pluck the spires of grass from between the rocks?"

The colonel couldn't help laughing at the thought of sharp-nosed sheep plucking grass from the hillside, and with that the tension eased. By the time he and his men departed, Colonel Scott had invited Nichols to bring her lecture on women's rights to St. Joseph.

In 1854 Kansas City, Missouri, was a crossroads of East and West. Pioneers setting out on the westward trails outfitted themselves in Kansas City or nearby Independence or Westport. They bought wagons, ox teams, horses, cattle, saddles, bridles, blankets, camp equipment, flour, coffee, and guns. Indians, of many different tribes wearing a variety of traditional dress, rode in from the Territory to trade wares and buy supplies.

Kansas City is a "homesick" place, Nichols reported to the Eastern press. "We were all in haste to get away." Trappers and tradesmen swigged home-brewed whisky in public, used swear words liberally, and urinated on the ground when they felt like it. They carried pistols on their belts and bowie knives in their boots and seemed ready to use both at the slightest provocation.

When the pioneers crossed the Missouri state line into Kansas Territory, they were overjoyed to find beautiful prairie rolled out as far as the eye could see. To the north stretched a line of forested hills decked out in fall colors familiar to every New Englander. An eagle looking down on the scene would have seen a long, unbroken ribbon of pioneers moving slowly across the prairie on foot, on horseback, and in every kind of rig that could be pulled by horse, mule, or ox.

Emigrants were pouring into "K.T.," as it was called, from every direction. Most of the new arrivals were there for their own piece of cheap land, but some settlers were passionate about seeing that Kansas became either a slave state or a free state.

Nichols and the others in her party were heading for the new town of Lawrence. Missourians had already dubbed it "Yankee Town" because of all the New England abolitionists moving there. At the time, Lawrence looked more like a refugee camp than a town. People lived in widely spaced white cotton tents or crude huts with earth floors. They ate mush and bacon three times a day, often mixed with the ashes scattered by their outdoor fireplaces.

Nichols rode into Lawrence ahead of the others in a covered wagon driven by Colonel Samuel Pomeroy, the guide for her emigrant group. As their coach came to a halt, a burst of loud cheering erupted. She soon learned that some of the young men had been arguing about women's rights. When the announcement came that Mrs. Nichols, the famed lecturer from the East, had just arrived, they let out a whoop and began pestering her to lecture that evening. She begged for a night's rest, was taken to the lodging-house, and given armfuls of prairie hay for a bed.

The next evening, the town dinner bell announced her lec-

Sketch of Lawrence, Kansas Territory, fall 1854, attributed to Clarina Nichols. *(Spencer Museum, University of Kansas)*

ture. The emigrants gathered in their new meeting house, a crude structure made of ridge poles thatched with prairie hay. She stepped up to her podium, two tool boxes piled on top of each other, and surveyed the "novel" scene before her. Men lounged on bundles of hay strewn about the floor, while the women sat on the emigrants' trunks that lined the sides of the meeting house. If anyone got too close to the sloping walls, the hay tickled their noses. Glass lanterns hung from the ceiling cast a hazy light on the upturned faces of her audience.

That cool evening in early November of 1854, Clarina Nichols delivered the first lecture on women's rights in Kansas Territory. She later wrote that she enjoyed it "as I have seldom [enjoyed] a lecture."

In the morning she joined other small groups making breakfast on the levee. "Some twenty families and companies...have kindled as many fires, some with two or three stones to hold up kettles and pans," she wrote in the Boston paper.

She watched one middle-aged man try to boil tea and fry sidepork on the same fire without tipping either over (without success). But at least there were as many men cooking their meals as women, Nichols observed with satisfaction. Nearby, a woman made breakfast, her skirts scorched with burn holes from her outdoor fireplace and fringed by prairie stubble. "Her breakfast is a simple one," Nichols noted, "coffee or tea and mush, which is eaten with molasses." A baby's cries sent the woman scurrying back to her tent. In another corner Nichols saw "a group of men standing round a frying pan, each with a piece of bread in hand, dipping in the gravy and eating with slices of bacon."

In health-conscious Brattleboro she had become a vegetarian. In Kansas, meat was one of the few food items that was plentiful and cheap. She was soon eating it along with everyone else, and passing it off as a necessary price for moving away from settled areas with markets, gardens, and mature orchards. "The climate is the finest," Nichols told her Eastern readers, "and if sickness comes, I shall attribute it to exposure and change of living from a vegetable to a meat diet."

In the days that followed, she borrowed a horse and rode to the top of Mt. Oread, the highest point in Lawrence. From its crest, she could see the countryside spread out like a table before her. She propped herself against a stack of hay, imagined the "embryo city" that would soon come into being, and made a pencil sketch (reproduced on page 104) of the panorama of woodlands and plateaus surrounding her. You have to look hard at this sketch, recently identified as Nichols's work, to locate the handful of widely-spaced huts that comprised the "city" of Lawrence. They are dwarfed by the enormity of the tiered plains, the wooded belts along the river, and the vast unbroken sky.

Before her visit came to an end, she helped her sons prepare for the winter by building a sod house, made from chunks of earth cut from the prairie. She noted that men who came west with womenfolk fared better than those who came alone. "The women are 'strong-minded,'" she told the Springfield *Daily Republican*. "And by the way, 'strong-mindedness' will be no objection to a woman, among the pioneers to Kansas."

———◆———

At the end of November 1854, Kansas Territory's first election was held. Hundreds of Missourians streamed across the border to vote, defiant, rowdy, liquored up, and well armed. From a high bluff Nichols watched in astonishment as they brazenly stole the election. In Douglas — a town named for the Illinois senator who sponsored the Kansas-Nebraska bill — three hundred ballots were cast, nearly all of them for proslavery candidates. At the time, Douglas had only fifty inhabitants. The proslavery ticket swept to an easy victory, but the tug of war over the fate of Kansas had just begun.

By December, Nichols had decided to return to Vermont and prepare the rest of her family for the move west. She told old friends that she thought she knew a few things about pioneer life from the stories her grandparents had told her. "But that was all *head* knowledge," she admitted.

Her son Relie gave this advice to the people out east who were thinking of coming to Kansas: "Do not expect to eat oysters or go to a ball the first thing on landing. You must make your arrangements to live on mush and molasses for a week and sleep on a log for a fortnight."

TWELVE

Life and Death
on the Prairie

When Nichols returned to Vermont, she immediately began preparations to move her family to Kansas Territory. But she couldn't leave home without giving her former neighbors a report on the situation in the territory where she now lived. New Englanders were anxious to hear any word of encouragement from Kansas, because what they read in the newspapers was uniformly discouraging. The "slave power" in that part of the country was described as nearly indomitable. David Rice Atchison, the powerful senator, was riling up his fellow Missourians. If they lived "within one day's journey of the territory," Atchison declared, it was their "duty" to ride across the border and vote to ensure that slavery would become permanently ensconced in Kansas.

"Mrs. Nichols is yet hopeful for liberty in Kansas," said a reporter for the *Vermont Phoenix* who attended one of her lectures, "Kansas and Its Chances for Freedom." The reporter, identified only as "H," said he wished Nichols had given her audience more reasons for hope: "The slave power is united, it is close at hand, no free territory touches the borders of Kansas, the slave interest is fully awake to the importance of the contest, [and] the free States are not so One and determined," he wrote.

On the domestic front, "H" had a somewhat sunnier report. The pioneer life Nichols described was "not without attractions," he admitted, but he drew the line at her glowing account of evening gatherings with men and women lounging on hay or stretched out on buffalo skins. In his opinion, "the fastidious in our cities" would not tolerate such an earthy, unhygienic, and "promiscuous" mixing of the sexes.

———◆———

After a couple months of preparation, Nichols was ready to make a permanent move to Kansas Territory. This time she brought along her husband, who was feeling a little better, and Howard's fianceé, Sarah Jones. Nichols's other children, twenty-three-year-old Birsha and eleven-year-old George, were left behind. They were at the progressive Eaglewood School, run by the Raritan Bay Union, a Utopian community in Perth Amboy, New Jersey.

Raritan Bay was home to three of the country's most revered antislavery activists, Sarah and Angelina Grimké and Angelina's husband, Theodore Dwight Weld. The Grimké sisters had done more than any other women to link women's rights and the antislavery movement, but it had been an uphill battle. Antislavery reformers feared that a close association between two unpopular causes would do more harm than good and urged the sisters to stick with antislavery — which they had not.

The Welds promised to keep a watchful eye on George and Birsha while the two were in Perth Amboy. Birsha, who may have been taking advanced study in art and music as well as teaching, kept them apprised of her mother's adventures. "Mr. and Mrs. Weld express a great deal of love & interest always," she wrote her mother. It was Birsha's responsibility to look after George and to make sure he made the right connections in New York when it was time for him to come to Kansas after school let out. Before leaving Vermont, Clarina packed a trunk with his things. Birsha wrote to her mother, reminding her not to forget George's bow and arrows and sled. The two women would not see each other for a much longer time. "Two long years will pass away without my seeing my more-than mother," she wrote. "God only knows what changes time may have wrought in our little circle."

———————

The spring rains hadn't come yet, and the Missouri River was low on water and hard to navigate. Steamboats kept hitting sandbars and running aground. At one point the boat the Nicholses were on, the *Kate Swinney*, was stuck on a sandbar for eighteen hours. As the men waded around with long poles prying the boat loose, Nichols delivered a lecture on women's rights to the captive audience.

From Kansas City they headed for the Baptist Mission on the Missouri-Kansas border. The mission had become a popular stopping-off place for people leaving the States to enter Kansas Territory. The day before they arrived, a New Hampshire couple came to the mission bearing the body of their young son, who had taken sick on the river and died. Unwilling to leave him behind in a slave state, they were bringing his body with them to bury on the free soil of Kansas Territory.

The West continued to exert its pull as a steady stream of new arrivals poured over the Missouri state line. One night more than fifty people slept at the Baptist Shawnee mission, bedding down on the floors, the attic space, and the bare ground outside. Mice occasionally nibbled on the sleepers' toes, but things like this no longer disturbed Clarina's sleep. After her first trip the previous autumn she had noted, "If any of our company of 230 left their Eastern homes with the starch of aristocracy in their dickies or their stomachs, it was all shaken out before they arrived on the Territory of Kanzas."

What she brought with her to "K. T." is unknown, but we can gather some idea from the belongings of another woman who traveled there at about the same time. The woman, Susan Stone, lost her trunk en route and made a list of its contents. The list — found decades later in the files of her lawyer — shows what one woman considered essential goods to take on her westward migration:

Shawl	$ 8.00	Delaine Dress	9.50
White Basque	3.50	5 Night Dresses	6.50
4 Chemise	6.00	2 Skirts	2.00
3 Pr Drawers	4.50	3 Yds Cotton Cloth	0.38
Thread	.60	1 Brush & 2 Combs	1.50
1 Accordian	2.00	1 Finger Ring	3.00
2 Fine Collars	4.00	1 [Ring]	2.00
1 Pr Mitts	.50	2 Linen Hdkfs	1.00
1 Veil	1.00	1 Rosewood Work Box	3.00
1 Pr Boots	2.50	1 Bible	0.75
1 Pr Ear Rings	2.00	Books	2.00
3 Aprons	.75	3 Daguerrotypes	2.50
Trunk	2.00	4 [items not named]	15.00
1 Wool Plaid Dress	8.00		
2 Calico	3.00		$ 98.73
3 Belt Ribbons	1.25		

In March 1855, a second election was held in Kansas Territory, and it fared no better for the free-state settlers than the previous one had. With the help of five thousand illegal

This illustration satirizes the voting in a Kansas border town that resulted in a heavily pro-slavery vote.

Missouri votes, the proslavery side won.

"The Missourians came boldly up the river, or by teams and horseback several days' journey from the interior of Missouri to vote," Nichols wrote in the *New Hampshire American News*. If they came across suspected abolitionists, "the cry was raised, 'Shoot!' 'Hang!' and 'Lynch him!'" There were reports of free-state men being assaulted and threatened if they tried to cast their votes.

Clarina Nichols was as outraged as any other free-state man or woman, but she had a bride to deliver to her son in Lawrence and was eager to get settled herself. A few days after Howard and Sarah wed, she set off from Lawrence in a wagon pulled by a pair of mules. She was heading for the town of Osawatomie to meet up with her husband, who had gone there from Kansas City by another route.

Her driver and guide struck out across the open prairie, "as if such things as surveyed roads were entirely unnecessary," she wrote in the New Hampshire paper. They followed the old Santa Fe Trail at one point for two miles and crossed two prairies, one twelve miles and one eight miles across. "I would not be willing to live *so far from land* as in one of these, where no tree nor spring greets the eye," she wrote. "I can think of nothing more solitary, more desolate." She kept an eye out for land with timber, for she knew that nearby there would be water, and both were necessary for survival. Across hill and valley, through woods and across rivers and creeks, they rattled and bumped along. Some of the ravines were so steep they almost tipped over. When the exhausted mules could no longer pull the loaded wagon, she hopped out and walked the last thirteen miles on foot.

During this trip, she was struck by the "solitude of the prairies." She was a city girl from the East who had a romantic view of country living, but no experience beyond occasional visits to someone's farm or country home. Now she found herself in the middle of an endless wilderness. In some places, for as far as she could see in every direction, there was no sign of human life, no voice except her own and an occasional grunt from her driver. In another month the prairie would be blooming with pink, yellow, blue, and violet wildflowers, but in early April the hills were as brown and barren as a camel's humps.

In the spring of 1855 George, Clarina, and her sons took possession of four claims on Ottawa Creek. "I liked this region of country better than any I have seen," she told her Eastern readers. "Wood and water are abundant and the prairie high and very rich, besides being beautifully broken in upon by wooded ravines sweeping out from the timber on the streams."

From the nearby timber they built a one-room log cabin that could not have been bigger than their parlor back east. Humble though it was, her family was happy to give up several weeks of camping and gain a roof overhead. Next in importance for the family was growing their own food, so they would have something to eat when the supplies they brought with them ran out. Stores were as yet nonexistent, though they were able to buy some supplies from "Tauy" Jones, a wealthy, Eastern-educated Indian farmer who lived on the nearby Ottawa Reserve. Nichols duly reported the going prices of some common food items:

> Provisions are scarce and high. Potatoes to plant are hardly to be had, and are at from three to four dollars per bushel. Indian meal is from $1.50 to $1.63. Flour $13. Lard 12 1/2, Ham 12 1/2, Pork 11 cts.

Neighbors, she noted, were "fewer and farther apart than were angels' visits."

George had bargained with the Missourians for a few scrawny head of cattle and had turned them loose to fatten up. He was feeling better than he had in a long time, and Clarina was pleased to see how things were shaping up, even though the work was more arduous than anyone had ever imagined. She had promised to report back to some Eastern newspapers on life in the territory, but by the end of each day she felt exhausted.

"Your Kansas correspondent feels very little like writing, though the skies are bright, and birds are singing outside her log cabin," she wrote in an article that appeared in the *Vermont Phoenix* in June.

She, George, and the boys had built their cabin, broken up forty acres of tough prairie sod, and planted corn, wheat, potatoes, beets, tomatoes, and melons. They did all the work by hand in three weeks.

Though she had a much smaller home to care for than her house back in Vermont, she discovered it was nearly impossible to keep the cabin clean and dry. Dust sifted through the chinks in the logs. Raindrops fell on them when they slept, and during the wet spring they tracked in mud so thick it had to be sliced off their boots with a knife. If they left their muddy boots outside, they needed to remember to give the boots a good shaking-out before putting them on. Rattlesnakes were known to curl up inside shoes, boots — or any place warm.

After the school term was finished, Clarina's youngest son, George, joined them in their new home. Birsha had begged her mother to come east to get George, but it seems he came out with another company of pioneers. John Speer, editor of the *Kansas Tribune*, visited Nichols to recruit her for his paper and passed along this glimpse of her family to his readers. "Our dinner was spread upon the lids of three trunks around which we gathered with our benches or stools," Speer wrote. Despite the humble setting, the meal had "all the aristocratic feelings common to the western world." After this pleasant repast, "Mr. Nichols mounted his large bay [horse] with Mrs. N on behind, and in company with them and another friend we crossed the country."

Fate, however, delivered two cruel blows that first summer. In early June George Nichols was injured in a farm accident. Then, in August, a heavy hickory rail struck young George, causing his head to swell to alarming proportions. There was no medical help available for miles, and even if there had been, little could have been done. To the relief of his anxious mother, the boy regained consciousness and began a full recovery.

Then his father caught cold, or perhaps developed pneumonia. The elder Nichols had already been weakened from several weeks spent in bed recovering from his injury. For nine days he teetered between life and death. In late August of 1855, George Washington Nichols died.

During their twelve-year marriage, he had been an exemplary husband and a kind father to all four of her children. Birsha Carpenter remembered her stepfather fondly as the only father she had ever really known. George taught his wife and stepson Relie the newspaper business. He introduced Clarina to politics and encouraged her — as few men of that day would have done — to strike out on her own, to speak up for what she believed in, and to go places without him. Maybe he knew she would need that independent spirit some day. She knew how lucky she had been. "I know what a good husband is," she wrote Susan B. Anthony, "better than one who has never tried a bad one."

As she prepared her husband's body for burial, she snipped a strand of hair from his head, as she had done when her father died the year before. Then they buried George Nichols on the prairie in a grave marked only by a pile of stones.

Even with George's death, there was no letup in nursing duties. Relie fell ill, as did Howard, who lived nearby with Sarah. Half the territory was sick, it seemed, with what people of that time called "ague," or sometimes "chills and fever." Ague was actually malaria, a common malady throughout mid-America in the nineteenth century. The epidemic that year was probably spread by mosquitoes that came out in full force after a week-long rain in August. Ague could be fatal, but more often the symptoms merely made its victims wish they could die. It often recurred and plagued pioneers who thought they were rid of it. In other parts of the territory cholera was ravaging the population. At Fort Riley fifty soldiers died from cholera the same month George Nichols died.

Only after she had nursed her sons back to health did Clarina allow herself to get sick. Her nineteen-year-old son Relie cared for her "with the tenderness of a woman," she wrote in later years.

Political tensions were building throughout Kansas Territory. The proslavery men were in power and their Law and Order Party began passing draconian laws. Writing and

All existing pictures of Clarina Nichols (such as
this one, circa 1854) are solo portraits.
(Grace Hudson Museum, Ukiah, California)

speaking out against slavery were criminal offenses, punishable by fine and imprisonment. Aiding fugitive slaves became
a capital offense.

The free-state men responded by writing the antislavery
Topeka Constitution and forming their own government.
(Charles Robinson, the leader of the free staters, invited Nichols to their organizing convention. Because of her husband's
illness she had to decline.) Reflecting the sentiment of many
free staters, the Topeka Constitution not only banned slavery
in Kansas Territory, but also prohibited free blacks from taking
up residence there (and, presumably, competing with white
men for land and jobs). With the formation of the Topeka
Constitution there were now competing governments, each
claiming to represent the people of Kansas as the legitimate
ruling body of the territory.

Throughout the summer, the two sides eyed each other

warily. Taunts, threats, and fistfights were common when they crossed paths. A minister who bravely (or foolishly) preached abolition in the proslavery town of Atchison was beaten by a mob, tied to a raft, and set adrift in the Missouri River. The clashes grew more violent. A free-state man was murdered over a claim dispute. An abolitionist was killed in Lawrence.

In October 1855 a man arrived in the territory who began keeping score of the wrongs committed against antislavery settlers. John Brown was in Kansas for one purpose: to see that it never became a slave state. He joined his sons, who were sick like everyone else and unprepared for the winter ahead. Brown was heavily armed, unshakable in his beliefs, and determined to wage war against slavery. The territory was a tinderbox waiting for the spark that would ignite it. Both sides bolted their doors at night, stockpiled weapons, and talked anxiously about what they would do if attacked.

Nichols and her boys were no exception. "Sharps rifles are in all our cabins," she wrote in the *New Hampshire Sentinel* the month Brown arrived. Arms, particularly Sharps rifles, were indeed flowing into Kansas, sometimes in boxes marked "Bibles" or "Dry Goods." She once considered herself a pacifist, but a few short months in the territory had changed her mind as it had changed her mind on eating meat.

In December proslavery forces lay siege for a week to Lawrence. Nichols's older sons rode over to assist the free staters. She recalled one anxious night during the siege sitting in her cabin, "the little boy sleeping in his berth," as she worried about Relie and Howard's safety. As she listened for the sounds of approaching "border ruffians," the derogatory free-stater term for Missourians, the "fearful silence" was suddenly broken by the hoot of "the cheerful owl," echoed by the hoot of another, until there was a chorus of owls serenading her cabin. It was so incongruous that she burst out laughing.

The siege ended without bloodshed, although property

was destroyed and many families were robbed at gunpoint. Afterward, Nichols prepared to return to Vermont to wrap up the details of her husband's small estate before the weather made any travel impossible.

The Missouri River was already closed to navigation for the season. The roads through the interior of Missouri were perilous due to rain, mud, snow, or ice, depending on the temperature and weather on any particular day. Nichols convinced the mail carrier to take her along "against the united protests of his agents at every point," she wrote in the *Greenfield Gazette and Courier.* She was advised in Independence to take the Vermont labels off her baggage, lest Missourians discover she was one of those Yankees who had come to make trouble in Kansas Territory.

Missourians had a long list of unflattering things to say about the new Kansans as they moved onto land that the locals had been using for years and considered rightfully theirs. Particular dislike was reserved for the Yankees, who in the Missourians' estimation had peculiar speech, were sloppy, did not know a plow from a harrow, couldn't steer an ox if their life depended on it, and put on airs of moral superiority.

To her surprise, though, Missourians were more gallant than she imagined they would be. Whenever her coach got stuck in the mud or snow, she would jump out and walk to the nearest cabin to warm up while the men worked to free the carriage. Invariably she would be welcomed, no matter what the hour or how humble the dwelling.

In the gray dawn of morning on one of these unannounced visits, she roused a dishevelled family of eight who had been living in a windowless cabin with an open doorway for the past four years. When she asked the man of the house where the door had gone, he said. "I hung it there, but my wife thought it was in the way, and I took it down again!" However chivalrous and hospitable the Missourians were, she concluded from this and other encounters that they were less refined, intelligent, and industrious than the new Kansas emigrants.

Regional prejudices ran deep in antebellum America, and people saw what they wanted to see. Neither side had to look far to see trouble.

THIRTEEN

Bleeding Kansas

On Christmas Day of 1855 it was thirty degrees below zero and snowing in Kansas Territory. The new pioneers gave up trying to stay warm and concentrated on not freezing to death. They strung sheets above their beds to keep the snow that sifted through the cracks from falling on their beds. Water hauled in from the creek froze into solid blocks of ice by midnight and had to be thawed to make coffee in the morning. Icy winds whipped through the uninsulated walls of their cabins as wolves howled in the timberlands.

Nichols, who had gone east, was back in Brattleboro, settling her late husband's affairs. After his debts were paid, his daughters given their inheritance, and the lawyers' fees deducted, she received $200. From her father's estate the previous year she received over $1,400. Over the course of her life she would eventually inherit several thousand dollars

more from her father's and mother's estates. The inheritance
from her father was not enough to make her a wealthy woman, but it did give her a cushion against financial ruin for a
number of years and a sum of money for land or other large
expenditures.

As a lasting memento to the two most important men in
her life, Clarina took the strands of white and brown hair she
had clipped from her father's and her husband's heads and
wove them into a brooch. Many Victorian women remembered loved ones in this way (including, it was said, Queen
Victoria herself, who wore a bracelet woven from Prince
Albert's hair). The brooch's special meaning was not lost on
the descendants of Clarina Nichols, who have preserved the
keepsake to this day.

———————

Exhausted and "broken in spirit," Nichols recovered her
strength in Townshend at the home of her mother, like herself a recent widow. Once she did, she re-entered the public
sphere well before it was customary for widows in mourning
to do so.

"You cannot know how anxious I am to hear from and
all about Kansas," she wrote in the *Herald of Freedom* in early
February of 1856. "I would have written you before, but I
have hardly recovered my strength and health sufficiently to
be 'moved by the spirit' to make any communications." She
said she hadn't seen a copy of the *Herald* since she left Kansas
and begged them to send her all the back issues.

In a message delivered to Congress on January 24, 1856,
President Franklin Pierce denounced the free-state movement as "revolutionary" and a "treasonable insurrection." He
reiterated his support for the tainted election results and commanded all free staters to accept the proslavery legislature, or
as the opposition called it, the "bogus" legislature.

Nichols, in commenting on President Pierce and the pro-

In this 1856 *Harper's Weekly* cartoon, "Liberty, the Fair
Maid of Kansas" begs for mercy from Democratic Party
leaders aligned with pro-slavery Missourians. Liberty and
Freedom were invariably portrayed as women — ironic
given their lack of rights under the law. (*Library of Congress*)

slavery administration, quoted Euripides: "Whom the gods
would destroy, they first make mad." She said that all "free
hearts" were "swelling with ominous indignation" toward the
Missourians and their federal "aiders and abettors."

Northern newspapers were reporting every indignity
toward the free staters that they heard about, often adding
dramatic embellishments to make the story more fantastical but
overlooking the villainy and thievery from the free-soil side.

Nichols encouraged the free staters to stay the course. The
"strong-minded women" of Kansas, she promised, would "run
bullets, tranfer ammunition, and inspire their husbands and
sons with hope, faith, and courage."

Because of her husband's final illness, she had been unable to attend the first meetings of the free staters, and now
she was going to miss the formation of their assembly. "Alas,
that I cannot get back in time to be at the organization of the

Legislature!" she wrote to the Lawrence newspaper.

The free staters who wrote the Topeka Constitution had already served notice that they would be looking out for the interests of white males. "But the black male and the white females," she wrote, "what will she do for them?" Many free staters did not want African Americans as neighbors or co-laborers in the fields or cities of Kansas. At least, she wryly noted, white women would not face that problem: "Happy circumstance—the free 'white males' can't get along comfortably without them!"

She backed the free-soil cause one hundred percent, but she knew that in one way both the free-state and proslavery legislatures were "bogus," since neither would consider rights for females. Moderate, progressive, or radical though they might be in other respects — the free-state men were unenlightened when it came to women's rights.

As a new widow, she had seen first-hand the peculiar disabilities of that subclass of women. The "widow's dower" gave a woman only the use of one-third of the estate, whereas a widower had no such restriction. She could not fathom why the legislature would not grant widows and widowers equal access to their own property. "Is this asking too much?" she fumed.

Despite this less-than-total support for her agenda, Nichols believed the political situation in Kansas Territory was fluid and more open to influence than it would ever be again. Just as Abigail Adams had urged her husband to "remember the ladies" in 1776, when he was helping draft the Declaration of Independence, Nichols began urging the free-state men to do the same in 1856:

> I entreat you to legislate for the mothers, legislate for your wives as you legislate for yourselves. Make them your companions, your equals, in legal rights, that in case you die first, your children may still nestle in a mother's

arms, be restrained by the loving authority of a mother,
and never fail of a protector.

That spring she wrote a series of articles for the *Herald of
Freedom* on women's rights. She reminded the men that their
forefathers had fought a bloody revolution to gain their rights.
Then they had turned around and denied women and blacks
those very same rights. Just that year North Carolina had
become the last state in the Union to drop the property test
for white male suffrage. Now all white men across the country were eligible to vote regardless of class. This was a great
achievement, but Nichols wondered why men — and even most
women — couldn't see the hypocrisy in one newly enfranchised
group of citizens denying that right to another.

By spring the situation in Kansas Territory had grown critical. A proslavery judge had rounded up the free-state leaders
in the territory, including Clarina Nichols's friend and ally,
Charles Robinson, who had been elected president of the free
staters. Robinson was accused of treason, imprisoned, and
threatened with execution.

Back in Washington, D.C., Senator Charles Sumner of
Massachusetts delivered a blistering speech to the Senate
titled, "The Crime Against Kansas." He shocked everyone by
singling out certain proslavery senators, including Andrew
Butler of South Carolina, whom he compared to a deluded
Don Quixote. Senator Butler, he said, was in love with "the
harlot Slavery," who, "though polluted in the sight of the
world, is chaste in his sight." Shortly afterward, one of Butler's
relatives came onto the Senate floor and nearly beat Sumner
to death with a cane. Most Northerners were incensed by the
attack, while most Southerners thought Sumner had gotten
what he deserved.

The following day, May 21, 1856, proslavery forces

launched their largest attack on Lawrence. A massive posse that supported the "bogus" legislature descended on the town and destroyed the Free-State Hotel with cannonfire. They took sledgehammers to the offices of the town's two newspapers, the *Kansas Free State* and *Herald of Freedom*, and dumped the *Herald*'s presses into the Kansas River. Nichols said later that the last article in her series on women's rights — the article that included her plea for women's voting rights — went down with the presses to the bottom of the river.

Outnumbered, the free-state men once again stood back as the Missourians ransacked the town. By the time John Brown and his sons arrived on the scene, much of the city was destroyed or in smoking ruins. Furious at what they saw and unable to comprehend why no one had put up a fight, Brown stormed out of town to plot his own revenge.

Meanwhile, Nichols had received news at a friend's house in New York of both attacks. "The late news from Kansas and the horrible outrage on Senator Sumner in Congress have roused me from the stupor of my grief," she wrote a friend in Wisconsin, "and I feel an intense desire to be up and doing.... Only when an evil becomes intolerable do men or states rouse themselves to eradicate it. Then let the darkness deepen and the great wrong fill the heavens with wailing."

When John Brown and his sons got back to their camp, they received word about the assault on Senator Sumner. For them it was the final straw. They all went "crazy — *crazy*," said one of the sons. "It seemed to be the finishing, decisive touch."

Under cover of darkness, Brown, his sons, and other men attacked proslavery settlers along Pottawatomie Creek. They called five men from their cabins and executed them at close range, attacking the bodies with broad swords, slashing throats, and hacking off fingers and arms. All the murdered men were proslavery settlers, but none owned slaves. Two of the victims were brothers, barely out of their teens.

After the Pottawatomie Massacre, as it came to be called, civil war broke out in Kansas Territory five years before the officially recognized opening of the Civil War. The first pitched battle took place at Black Jack in southeast Douglas County, a few miles east of the Nichols farm.

Howard and Relie Carpenter joined John Brown's small band of men as they fought Federal troops who had been sent in to capture Brown. It was the first regular battle between proslavery and antislavery men anywhere in the United States, and the Federal troops were fighting on the proslavery side. After a brief skirmish, Brown's small band of guerrilla fighters forced the Federals to surrender, a stunning turn of events that gave heart to the beleagured free staters.

Relie, however, had been seriously wounded. The McCowens, a family caught in the crossfire of the region, took him in and nursed him back to health over the next several weeks. They sent the bullet, which had just grazed his heart, to his anxious mother in Vermont. She later used it as a visual aid in her lectures.

"My son lives to fight another day in the hand-to-hand struggle against the most monstrous oppression that the civilized world has ever seen," she wrote in the *New Hampshire Sentinel*. "I thank Heaven that I have sons ready to live or die for the rights for which their great-grandfathers fought."

When the Kansas-Nebraska bill passed in 1854, it motivated Clarina Nichols to change the course of her life and move to Kansas. The sacking of Lawrence, the attack on Senator Sumner, and the epic battles of John Brown's guerrilla fighters drew her into what she called a "semi-political" role at a time when she was expected to be in deep mourning. But writing for the newspapers was no longer enough. Nichols left her mother's house and set out to lecture on behalf of free-state Kansas.

Returning to Kansas Territory at that time would have been

John Brown instigated the Battle of
Black Jack, in which Clarina Nichols's
two sons fought. *(Library of Congress)*

difficult and risky. Proslavery forces had taken control of the
ports along the Missouri River, the liquid highway into the
territory. Reports filtered back that free-soil emigrants were
being stopped on the river, harassed, stripped of their weapons,
robbed of their gold, and turned back. Emigrants determined
to bypass Missouri entirely began taking an alternate route
across Iowa.

Nichols decided she could do more good for the cause by
staying out east. A presidential election was coming up, and
she began stumping for the new Republican candidate. John
C. Frémont, a dashing adventurer, was running for President
on the first Republican ticket. She declared her support for
"Frémont and Freedom." Anyone would be better than the current pro-South Democratic administration, she reasoned, but
the campaign was an uphill battle from the start. New England
and New York were leaning heavily toward the Republican

ticket, but Pennsylvania, home to the Democratic candidate James Buchanan, was disputed territory. So Nichols went to Pennsylvania where she thought she could do the most good. To convince voters to support Frémont, she told them what was going on in Kansas, the hotbed of the growing crisis. People knew she had first-hand knowledge of the situation in Kansas, and she had plenty of lurid stories to share with her audiences about the dastardly Missourians and the noble free-state freedom fighters.

Her calendar quickly filled with speaking engagements. Many times, audiences received a double dip: a lecture on free-state Kansas in support of candidate Frémont, followed by a lecture on women's rights.

It is unknown whether she had any formal commission from the Republicans to canvass Pennsylvania, but on one occasion she said they used her name and notoriety to draw a crowd in a heavily Democratic district. After the people had assembled, they were told that the lady from Kansas had not showed up, but that they had some fine Republican speakers on hand. "I suspicioned then it was jest a republican trick," an old Pennsylvanian farmer told Nichols. She commiserated with him, even if he was a Democrat.

On the circuit she averaged ten dollars a lecture or fifty dollars a week after expenses. She sent back money to her sons who were fighting in the "Free State army of Kansas." One day, she predicted, the country would "wreck itself on the dark rocks of slavery." The South was protecting the "viper" of slavery, and the North "will strangle it in return."

While Nichols was touring Pennsylvania, she received a letter from free-state leader Thaddeus Hyatt, asking if she would work for the cause of Kansas in western New York. She replied that if she took that assignment instead of lecturing on her own, her sons would have to be provided for. "I will never desert them for any post that promises less," she told Hyatt, who agreed to her terms. He also agreed to pay for an assistant, and she had the perfect choice in mind. "Susan B. Anthony of Rochester has the executive ability & the experience admirably adapted to the work....She has a brother in the Free State army in Kansas & if I take the post you propose, I would solicit her as my right hand woman." Anthony, however, was busy organizing an upcoming women's rights convention in New York and could not accept the offer.

"Poor bleeding Kansas — how the soul sickens," Anthony wrote her in September of 1856. "All free State men & women will be crushed out, ere the North will awake."

Near the end of October, Nichols finally made her way to New York City. Leaders of the National Kansas Committee were holding a big rally in lower Manhattan and wanted her on hand to share her perspective and to plead for aid. Rallies like this were being held across the North in 1856 on behalf of "bleeding Kansas," which was now a national rallying call, not only for abolitionists but for growing numbers of Northerners, as the country became more and more polarized.

Women who belonged to various types of ladies' aid societies were meeting and pledging their benevolent energies to Kansas instead of overseas missions. They held clothing drives and quilting bees; sponsored bake sales and ice cream socials; sold flowers and fruits — and donated what they earned and collected to the National Kansas Committee. Nichols's job was to motivate and mobilize this important segment of the population, to identify leaders in each community who would continue to work for Kansas after she left. She was not averse to using a little guilt if she felt it would aid her cause.

> Don't ever tell me 'your eastern friends sympathize with you in your noble struggle for liberty.' Such friends, if one were hanging to a rope for dear life, would look over from the ship's side and cry, 'my sympathies are with you, hang on till you drown!'

She claimed the situation in Kansas was far more dire than

most people realized. Some of the women there were "so poorly clad that they are ashamed to be seen by strangers, and many of them have cut up their undergarments to make pantaloons for the men who were obliged to stand guard."

———————

In November 1856 the Seventh National Woman's Rights Convention, the one Anthony had been organizing, was held in New York City. Nichols did not attend, though she was in striking distance at the time and might have taken a few days off to go back to the city and reconnect with old friends and colleagues. Right before her Wisconsin trip the *New York Tribune* had called her "one of the leading champions of the Emancipation of Woman," but in moving to Kansas she was unable to continue her leadership role in the movement.

There was another factor at work. Clarina Nichols was becoming a Westerner, or at least a hybrid of Easterner and Westerner. She lived in a very different world than the one she had once inhabited, and her experience set her apart from her Eastern sisters. Though she longed at times to live near women "whose whole souls were in the movement instead of unused scraps of heart," it is clear from her writings that she found satisfaction in her new life, despite its hardships, and that she came to prefer it over life in the East. Though she spent all of 1856 outside Kansas Territory, there was never any doubt that she would return.

By 1856 the women's rights movement had come of age. Those involved now had a common history, and they recalled it like old soldiers telling war stories at a reunion. At most conventions someone recounted the advances that had been made in the past year. Lucy Stone, president of that year's convention, enumerated the strides that had been made across the nation. In Ohio, New York, Maine, Vermont, New Hampshire, Rhode Island, Massachusetts, Pennsylvania, Illinois, Indiana, and Michigan, women were working to reform property rights and gain other advances.

"And Wisconsin — God bless these young states! — has granted almost all that has been asked except the right of suffrage," Stone enthused. She assured the delegates that suffrage would not be long in coming.

The Reverend Thomas Wentworth Higginson, the man who would lead a black regiment in the Civil War and later bring Emily Dickinson's poetry to light, gave an impassioned report on his recent fact-finding trip to Kansas. Like many partisans on both sides of the issue, Higginson was prone to exaggeration in his accounts. He told of Missouri "wretches" who "would come at night, discharge their rifles, and howl like demons," striking terror into the embattled free staters, including a child who had "died from sheer fright."

But there was no disputing Higginson's descriptions of the unbelievable hardships faced by settlers in Kansas Territory. He was particularly moved by the example of Kansas women, who lived an arduous and even heroic existence on the frontier. Having seen "what woman had done there," he could not help but feel disgust for the "little men who squeak and shout on the platforms in behalf of Kansas," yet adamantly opposed any political relief for women.

Meanwhile, Nichols was making the rounds of western New York state, meeting with old friends and raising awareness and funds for the free-state settlers in Kansas. One of her speeches, which was published in the New York *Tribune*, contained an impassioned appeal to the women in her audience:

> Are you mothers? Let me speak to you for the mothers of Kansas. I am one of them. My sons are among the sufferers and defenders of that ill-fated territory. Their blood has baptized the soil which they yet live to weep over, to love, and to defend. I ask of you, mothers of New York, but a tithe of the sacrifices and devotion of

the mothers of Kansas....To many of you I may speak as personal friends and former co-workers in the cause of Humanity. I know your zeal. I know your labors. I count upon your utmost efforts in this the crisis hour of the accumulated oppressions of the past — in this the grey dawning of a resurrection day for Humanity such as the world has never seen.

FOURTEEN

Quindaro

Though thousands of determined souls moved to Kansas Territory in the 1850s, many soon moved on. They found the unending hardships too much to bear. The brutally hot summers and bitterly cold winters, the shortages of food, clothing, and decent shelter, and the ever-present threat of violence took their toll.

By the spring of 1857, a new territorial governor had quieted down the region. Howard and Relie Carpenter were no longer in immediate danger, but Relie told his mother that he, too, had had enough. During the weeks he spent recuperating at the McCowen's cabin after the Battle of Black Jack, he got to know the family well — especially their pretty eighteen-year-old daughter Helen. The McCowens, too, had seen their share of trouble. "Border ruffians...invaded the neighborhood with no regard for life or property," Helen wrote in her journal.

"The mother of our little colt was taken and our only cow."

She wasn't very fond of Kansas: "The violent thunderstorms are enough to wreck the nerves of Hercules, and the rattle-snakes are as thick as the leaves of the trees." After all they had been through both physically and mentally, she concluded, "I can bid Kansas goodbye without a regret."

Clarina Nichols was still out east raising funds for the embattled territory when Relie married Helen McCowen on Christmas Day, 1856. Nichols returned the following spring. By then Relie, Helen, and the McCowens had made up their minds — they were going to California. Late that spring five wagons, their white tops gleaming in the sun, began rolling westward, across the green grass prairie. On a bright red seat in the middle wagon, rode Relie and Helen, side by side, just like the pioneer couples Nichols had observed in Wisconsin.

She must have been sad to see them go. Relie was the child most like her — intelligent and thoughtful, but restless and ambitious too. She still had her other three children nearby. Young George lived with her along with Birsha, who had come along on this trip. Howard and wife Sarah had a new baby and were eager to settle down near the rest of the family.

Upon returning from New York, Nichols set out on a whirlwind tour of the territory. She had promised her Eastern donors that she would give them a report on how the supplies they had sent to Kansas Territory were holding up. Everywhere she went she saw people drinking "charity tea" and "charity coffee" sweetened by "charity sugar." Everyone seemed to be making good use of all the other contributions as well.

In many places it looked like people had just reached into the donated barrels of clothing and put on whatever they pulled out. Kansas immigrants weren't particular about what they wore. They desperately needed clothing and proudly

Clarina's three oldest children, in a portrait from 1853
(clockwise from top): Birsha Carpenter, C. Howard
Carpenter, and A. O. "Relie" Carpenter. *(Grace
Hudson Museum, Ukiah, California)*

stretched extra life out of their garments. When their skirts
started to wear out, the women turned them "wrong side
out" or upside down and wore them that way. Some of the
women wore men's pants or a Western version of the bloomers their more-fashionable sisters in the East had abandoned.

Housewives cut the legs off trousers, gave the legs a quarter turn, and sewed them back on again before the knees wore through. They repaired cuffs, replaced collars, and patched holes with whatever scrap of fabric was at hand. Their patchwork sometimes looked comical, but their thriftiness and "good housewifery" warmed Nichols's heart.

"I was always in love with the country," she later told a friend. What she did not love, however, was the isolation of "4 base walls in the desolate prairie." When her inspection tour was complete in early 1857, instead of returning to her claim, Nichols and what remained of her family moved to a new town springing up on the ragged eastern edge of Kansas Territory.

Quindaro was a free-state settlement defiantly perched on the banks of the Missouri River. Because of the proslavery blockade along the Missouri, the free staters needed to establish a port of their own. They sent out a surveying team, and a few miles upstream from the juncture of the Kansas and Missouri rivers, they discovered a natural rock harbor. A group of Wyandotte Indians held claim to the land, but they welcomed the free-state settlers and proposed to name the town after a respected Wyandotte woman, Quindaro Brown Guthrie. When Nichols arrived, Quindaro was only a few months old, but already it was taking shape at a dizzying speed. Bushes, small trees, and undergrowth had been cleared out and burned on several acres of bottomland. In a short time "a hundred buildings — many of them of stone and brick — including hotels, Dry Goods, Hardware, and Grocery stores, a Church and School house, had been built," Nichols reminisced later in the Wyandotte *Gazette*. The town boasted the second largest sawmill in the territory and was growing so rapidly that settlers started to pay it the ultimate compliment of frontier boomtowns, predicting that Quindaro would some day become the greatest city west of Chicago.

But there was more going on in Quindaro than met the eye. While all the racket of building a new town was going on in broad daylight — blasting, banging, hammering, and saw-ing — another project was quietly taking place out of public view. When word came that a fugitive slave needed help, certain people in town were alerted. Staying in the shadows, keeping one eye open for those who couldn't be trusted, these abolitionists hid slaves, supplied them with food and clothing, and transported them to the next safe house.

All three races — Indian, black, and white — cooperated in the work of this secret network sometimes called the under-ground railroad. In later years Nichols called Quindaro "the Canada of the escaped slave."

A slave master would have had a difficult time finding a runaway slave there. From the harbor the terrain rose sharply into rocky bluffs and steep hills with deep ravines and valleys cutting across them. Much of the area was heavily wooded but opened into a high meadow that allowed a keen-eyed lookout to spot slave catchers from afar. "Of the many slaves who took the train of freedom there," Nichols wrote, "only one, and he through lack of caution in his approach for help, was ever taken back to Missouri."

Quindaro lay directly across the river from Parkville, Mis-souri, an area with a large slave population. Freedom lay within sight if that river could just be forded. One night two men ran away from a plantation near Parkville, one still dragging his chains behind him. They "borrowed" a canoe to cross the Missouri River and hid in the brush at the foot of the bluff. There they made contact with some young free-state men, barely out of their teens, who lived in a place insiders called "Uncle Tom's Cabin." After the manacles were filed off the one man's ankles, both fugitives were hidden inside wooden crates marked "Dry Goods" and sent off to Lawrence. On a lecture tour out east the following year, Nichols brought along the shackles, so her audiences could feel the weight of slavery for themselves.

Another time, a neighbor came to her house at dusk with a fugitive named Caroline, whose little daughter had been wrenched from her earlier that day and sold to a slave trader on his way south to Texas. Caroline had broken her arm, either holding onto her daughter or in trying to escape and was in physical and emotional agony.

Fourteen slave hunters were scouring Quindaro, hoping to collect the bounty offered by Caroline's slave master. They came up empty because Nichols had hidden her in a cistern, the brick-lined pit many settlers dug outside their homes to catch rain water. She set washing equipment next to the cistern, so that passersby would assume the pit was full of water. She handed down a chair, pillow, and comforter to Caroline, who would spend the night in the seven-foot-by-twelve-foot hole. As a further deception, she enlisted the aid of her teenage son George, who slept on a cot in the kitchen, pretending to be ill. His mother lined up medicines next to his bedside, so she would have a ready answer for anyone who wandered by and inquired why she was up at such a late hour.

"All night I crept to and fro in slippered feet, whispering words of cheer to Caroline in her cell," Nichols recounted years later. At midnight, "I passed a cup of fresh hot coffee to Caroline, and sitting by the open floor drank my own with apparent cheerfulness, but really in a tremor of indignation and fear." Thoughts of the day her own children had been stolen by their father must have crossed her mind. Caroline, she knew, would not be as lucky as she had been. Caroline's daughter was gone, and it is unlikely that her mother would ever see her again.

The next morning the slave hunters rode out of town empty-handed. By that evening Caroline and another young woman had hidden themselves in the back of a wagon and were on their way north to Leavenworth and the next stop on their journey to Canada and freedom.

Birsha had been hired to teach in the new Quindaro school-house, and Clarina helped her daughter launch the school. Both women insisted that the facility be open to black as well as white children, an unpopular decision even among the progressive white citizens of Quindaro. Nichols wrote to an abolitionist friend at that time that if the school had excluded blacks, they could have had three or four times as many tuition-paying students.

"We have concluded," she added, "though it looks like [we are] starving for our principles, that we will wait till we *have* starved before we abandon them."

Like her father, Chapin Howard, she was civic-minded and as interested in progress and reform on the local level as she was on the state or national levels. She supported Birsha's efforts in organizing a school and helped the local temperance society rid the town of its rummeries (ale and beer were exempt from the cleanup). She took an active role in the town's literary society and provided hospitality to visiting dignitaries and newcomers.

There was no Baptist church in Quindaro, and even if there had been, it might not have been a church that suited Nichols. She was growing increasingly impatient with churches where women were told to be silent, wives were told to submit to their husbands, and suffrage was denounced as an infidel doctrine. Without fail, she found comfort and inspiration in nature and in long rambles through the woods. She complained about the developers who were clearing acres of trees outside Quindaro. In the local paper, the *Chindowan*, she urged others to enjoy the natural surroundings while they could:

> Do our sister citizens know how beautiful are the woods of Quindaro? If they have not penetrated the undis-turbed portions of the town plat and its environs, we beg them to do so at once, before the woodman fells the

Quindaro Chin-do-wan.

PRINTED AND PUBLISHED BY

J. M. WALDEN & CO.

J. M. WALDEN,..................EDITOR,

MRS. C. I. H. NICHOLS,.....ASSOCIATE.

Mrs. Nichols' articles marked..........N.

Saturday, June 6, 1857.

The *Chindowan* published for a year; Nichols
stopped contributing after three months.

> grand old trees and works the ruin of beauty which it
> has taken ages to perfect....Go to the grand old woods,
> sister, go and gather cool shadows, and music of bird
> and bee, the beauty of climbing vine, and clinging ivy,
> and forget the weariness of the toil and the disorder of
> the path of progress.

Nichols had become associate editor of the *Chindowan*, a
four-page weekly that began publication shortly after the
town's founding. She wrote on many subjects: education, gar-
dening, the joys of motherhood and clean laundry, the virtues
of paid labor (as opposed to slave labor), the Wyandotte lands,
and of course, temperance.

This article, about a method she used to keep bugs off cu-
cumber vines, reveals not just keen observatory powers but a
fastidiousness that extended into every corner of her life:

> We will tell our readers a better way with less trouble
> and sure to kill every kind of bug that destroys vines. We
> have practiced it these ten years and with entire success.
> These bugs all lay their eggs in patches on the under
> sides of the vine leaves. It is only necessary to visit the

vines every other day for some ten days, and pinch out, or break off the portion of the leaf to which the eggs are fastened, and the original pair will die without posterity. The labor is very little and the good housewife will find it a benefit to herself to spend so much time among her vines each evening or morning as will suffice to keep out the bugs.

What she did not write about was her favorite subject: women's rights. The editor of the *Chindowan* was passionate on the subjects of abolition and free-state Kansas, but not on women's rights. In particular, he did not believe that women needed — or should have — the right to vote. Before long she realized she could not continue working for an editor who opposed one of her core convictions. After three months, she quietly resigned.

———

Throughout the territory, the tide was starting to turn. By the fall of 1857, the number of free-state immigrants began to exceed the number who favored slavery. They were coming in not only on the Missouri River, but on the overland Lane Trail across Iowa. In October of that year, free-state men went to the polls and won an overwhelming victory. Their party gained control of both houses in the territorial legislature.

As the election returns started rolling in, Nichols wrote to a Vermont newspaper that Kansas was about to see the "dawn of freedom on her glorious prairies." After the election, proslavery settlers began leaving Kansas Territory in droves. There would be more violence in the years ahead. Terrible atrocities would be committed by both sides that would be remembered by people in that region to the present day. There would even be an attempt in 1857 and 1858 to bring Kansas into the Union as a slave state under the farcical Lecompton Constitution — which came perilously close to ratification by the United States Congress. But popular opinion had swung inexorably to the free-state side. Eventually, Kansas soil would be free soil. The march of slavery would be halted at the Missouri-Kansas border.

That victory, however, proved to be Quindaro's undoing. As the ports up and down the Missouri River were opened, residents began moving to less rugged townsites, and the town began to empty out. Nichols kept a residence there until 1868, when she moved to nearby Wyandotte City. She may have been hanging on to her property in the hope she could recoup the money she had invested, but Clarina Nichols had more than a monetary interest in Quindaro. She loved the beauty of the surrounding woods, and she loved the town for what it was and what it stood for. "Many a brave deed was done there," she would recall, "and many a mean one circumvented, of which the world outside knew nought."

FIFTEEN

Woman on
a Mission

A convention was planned for the summer of 1859 to draft yet another constitution for the would-be state of Kansas. With the free-state forces firmly in control of the territory, the delegates who gathered in Wyandotte City in July 1859 knew that they were likely determining the laws that all Kansans would eventually abide by. Various groups of men had created three earlier constitutions that failed to be adopted for one reason or another. These ran the gamut on race and gender. The Topeka Constitution, in 1855, had outlawed slavery, but it also prohibited African Americans from living or working in the state. There was the notorious Lecompton Constitution, which had come close to passing Congress in 1858 and would have admitted Kansas to the Union as a slave state. A third constitution, drafted in Leavenworth in 1858, probably in reaction to Lecompton, outlawed slavery and gave black males the right to vote. Within Kansas Territory there were sentiments for all three points of view.

Nichols's views on race and gender cast her as an "ultra," an extremist on both issues. "My blood boils at the efforts to drive out the col'd freeman & exclude [blacks] from educational advantages," she wrote to a friend.

She had, of course, another reason for coming to Kansas, and this one was shared by even fewer people. Nichols believed she could midwife the birth of woman suffrage there. Her plan was a time-honored one: to circulate a petition throughout Kansas Territory and to deliver as many signatures as she could gather to the men at their convention. This would legitimate her advocacy. If enough respectable citizens of both sexes signed her petition, she would at least be given a hearing. The petition expressed its opposition to "any constitutional monopoly or pre-eminence of rights, based on sex."

She considered adding *race* to her petition but decided against it. "I am forced to the conclusion that it would mar our effort and do no good to them," she wrote to a friend who brought up the subject. She also expressed a belief that if women got the ballot, they would soon legislate slavery out of existence and grant black suffrage as well.

Clarina Nichols was not the only woman in the territory thinking about women's rights. In the southeast, two sisters-in-law, Susan and Esther Wattles, along with Esther's husband John and more than forty others, formed the Moneka Women's Rights Association, the first such organization in Kansas Territory.* The Wattles women were bloomer-wearing, abolitionist Quakers who wanted to see the higher-paying professions, like doctor and lawyer, opened to women. Two of Susan's daughters would later become physicians, and Esther's three daughters all did advanced study at Oberlin College.

When the Moneka group learned of Nichols's plan to attend

---

*Appendix B contains the constitution of the M.W.R.A.

the Wyandotte convention, Susan Wattles contacted her to seek an alliance. "We are none of us competent to speak or write on the subject," Wattles wrote, "and with great pleasure shall we look to you to take the lead in this movement."

Nichols sent a copy of her petition. "I am ready to act at the Convention, speaking before Committees; or the [full] Convention if allowed to do so," she wrote back. "But to feel perfectly in place I want to be authorized by petitioners — by my own sex especially." The Moneka organization elected Nichols as their official representative and agreed to help collect signatures.

She was short on cash and had no money to spare for traveling expenses, but she and Susan Wattles had read an item in *The Lily* that said the abolitionist Wendell Phillips was handing out money from a fund promoting women's rights and other reforms. Both women wrote to Phillips asking for support, which he agreed to provide.

Undertaking a petition drive in Kansas Territory was no simple matter, for there were no trains, and roads were often little more than trails that in bad weather turned to mud. That spring the creeks and rivers were swollen and overflowed their banks. Swift currents and driftwood made fording rivers dangerous. One observer said the mud was as slippery as lard and as sticky as tar. After the flooding subsided, everyone went out into the fields to put in the crops that had been delayed. There were no extra horses or rigs to hire, and no men with the time to haul Nichols around the territory.

"There is no man to go with me & I don't want one," she wrote to Susan B. Anthony in New York. Nichols was confident that she could handle the strain of a difficult petition drive by herself. "I am in perfect trim physically," she declared, "which is what I never was [back] east."

She decided on a plan that would allow her to visit the most people in the shortest time in the sparsely settled territory. She would visit only the largest settlements and ask around at each one until she had identified townfolk sympathetic to her cause. Then she would ask those people to circulate the petition while she moved on to the next town. In this painstakingly slow way she collected almost six hundred signatures. Borrowing a pony from Quindaro Brown Guthrie's family, she rode the five miles to Wyandotte, where the delegates had begun assembling. Just in case the petition was not enough to gain her admittance to the convention, she had also obtained a press pass. "So you see I am doing all I can in every direction," she told Susan Wattles.

The fifty-two delegates gathered in a large, unplastered hall under a second floor saloon in Wyandotte City. Three windows in front and three in back provided the only ventilation as the temperature outside climbed over the one hundred degree mark and stayed there. An early observer of Kansas made up a humorous "forecast" that perfectly described weather conditions in the summer of 1859:

Day 1 — hot.
Day 2 — hotter.
Day 3 — hottest.
Day 4 — hottentot.
Day 5 — *hottentissimo!*

The air inside the convention hall was stifling hot and foul-smelling, for many of the men smoked or chewed tobacco and spit the sickly-sweet juice on the floor as was the custom in all public buildings at the time.

During the proceedings tempers occasionally flared, as delegates boiled over with shouts of "Liar!" and "Coward!" and threats of physical violence. The spectators, separated from the delegates by only a wooden railing, egged them on. But the convention's president, seated on a raised platform at one end of the hall, managed to keep things under control. On the rough wall behind him, a United States flag had been

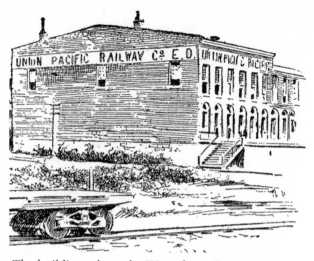

The building where the Wyandotte Constitution was
hammered out in 1859 was later used as railroad offices.

draped, reminding the delegates of their solemn duty to earn
Kansas a star on that flag. These men were determined to get
the job done.

To no one's surprise, Republicans — the antislavery party —
outnumbered Democrats two-to-one. The Republicans agreed
that the institution of slavery should be outlawed in Kansas.
But they argued over whether blacks should be allowed to live
and work there and haggled at length over the exact boundar-
ies of the new state.

Nichols had known from the start that she would not be
allowed to speak or vote at the convention, but she knew she
could be a presence, and she felt confident that she would
find ways to influence the proceedings. "I felt my wings grow,
fearing no disappointment," she told Anthony before the convention began.

Wearing a Sunday dress that made some observers wonder
if she was a Quaker, she took her assigned place beside the

convention's chaplain, writing paper and knitting in hand. At her side most days was her faithful friend, Lucy Armstrong, a missionary's daughter who had become a Wyandotte Indian through marriage. She was a longtime leader in the local community, and together with Nichols they made a formidable twosome. On many of the days other women sat in the convention in a quiet show of support. Nichols was fully aware of the need to make a favorable impression that balanced strength with propriety. In discussing her desire to give a "womanly" presentation of the subject, she told Susan Wattles that "my age, my past history, and actions endorse my suitableness."

The *New York Times* sent a correspondent to cover the historic proceedings. He wrote on the paper's front page, "Mrs. Nichols sits at the reporter's table every day; some of the time plying her needle, some of the time her pen."

During the afternoons and evenings when the convention was not in session, she lobbied the delegates, drew up the resolutions on women's rights, and planned how to steer them through the committees.

Lucy Armstrong, who was also a widow, provided room and board for her during the convention and a base to operate from. "The hospitable tea table of Mrs. Armstrong ...offered abundant womanly opportunity for coffee and discussion with the delegates," Nichols said.

The citizens of Wyandotte City took a lively interest in this addition to the usual cast of characters pontificating on matters of state. They were used to seeing lawyers, doctors, editors, farmers, merchants, and mechanics wrangle over Kansas affairs, but they weren't accustomed to seeing a woman right in the center of things, calmly knitting and taking notes as though she were sitting in the middle of her parlor. The townfolk drew up their own petition, asking the delegates for permission to use Constitution Hall for a lecture from Nichols. "They say I have accomplished a great change in public sentiment," she reported to Anthony during the convention.

Her allies urged their colleagues to let her address the convention, and a lively discussion ensued. The most eloquent among her defenders was John Ritchie, a close ally of John Brown and a radical Republican from Topeka. "In this age of intelligence — in the noon of the 19th century, I hope we will not take the position that we will not hear a woman in her own cause," he said. "Every man has received his first and best impressions from his mother. Therefore, when the mothers speak, don't let us become so full of Democracy and Republicanism as to stop our ears."

Nichols was allowed to speak twice in Constitution Hall —once to the Republican delegates and once to the citizens of Wyandotte. Both meetings took place after hours, for the delegates weren't radical enough to allow a woman to speak during their regular sessions. The Democratic delegates, outvoted as usual, took off in a group to attend a circus in Kansas City. Her talk drew plaudits from some papers and faint praise from others. "Her audience was large, promiscuous, and quite attentive and respectful," the New York *Evening Post* reported. "She is a tolerable speaker and rather a decent person for a reformer; pays some regard to feminine attractions in the way of ribbons and silver-gray curls, which give her a frisky appearance, somewhat inconsistent with her years. Proper culture and direction would undoubtedly have rendered her a worthy and useful member of society."

For the first half of the convention, Clarina Nichols believed that the delegates would delete the word "male" from the constitution and grant women full suffrage. She wrote a resolution for a proposed section of the Bill of Rights that said taxation and representation were inseparable and that "no Constitutional distinction on account of Sect or Sex" should be made."

In a sign of things to come, however, her old friend, Horace Greeley, had warned the Republicans when he met with them in May at Osawatomie that granting woman suffrage might endanger Kansas's chances of being admitted to the Union.

On July 18 her resolution on suffrage was finally voted down. She was disappointed and later blamed the defeat on "too many old lawyers," though most of the delegates were under thirty-five. No one knows whether Greeley's fears were well-founded, but she believed that the threat of not being admitted to the Union played a major role in Kansas's failure to grant women the franchise in 1859. Twenty years later she wrote in the *History of Woman Suffrage*:

> I believed then and believe now that Woman Suffrage would have received a majority vote in Kansas…if it could have been submitted unembarrassed by the possibility of its being used as a pretext for keeping Kansas out of the Union.

She also faulted the men for falling under the sway of a single influential delegate, Judge Samuel Kingman, who, as she put it, "played upon the old harmonicum," arguing that political rights for women would upset the biblical ordering of society.

What Nichols and the others in the antebellum women's rights movement were unwilling to acknowledge was that the country was not ready for woman suffrage and would not be ready for a long time. Various scenarios can be entertained under which suffrage might have been adopted in Kansas —if the country had been less fractured, if Judge Kingman had taken ill — but the truth is that a majority of men were not ready to grant suffrage, and a majority of women were not ready to demand it. Nichols had no way of knowing that full suffrage for women in Kansas would not happen until 1912. And that all women in the United States would not be given the vote until 1920. In the mid-1800s, especially in Kansas, it seemed like suffrage was just around the corner.

Though she failed to achieve her most ambitious goal, she

succeeded in getting other rights for women written into the constitution. From the first, Kansas mothers had equal custody considerations with fathers in cases of divorce. Married women had the right to inherit, control, and bequeath property in their own names. "Equality in all school matters" meant that the University of Kansas was coeducational from its founding and one of the first public universities to admit women.

Perhaps most significantly in terms of political advances, Kansas women could vote in school district elections. Nichols believed that this precedent would someday pave the way to full suffrage.

To her dismay, however, school suffrage was "extensively denied" in the early years by local judges and politicians. This was the common fate of every significant advance made by women, in Kansas or elsewhere. Even if a new law was as clear as a sunbeam at noonday (to quote a popular saying of the period), it could be — and often was — drained of its original intent or simply ignored.

Despite these setbacks, Kansas was regarded as a pioneer in the rights it extended to women. When Nichols wrote Anthony in 1870 to report the work that still needed to be done, Anthony replied, "If it be so in Kansas, the most liberal state in the Union, how is it in the other states?"

———◆———

When the convention was over, Nichols again crisscrossed the territory, this time seeking support for the new state constitution. She traveled any way she could — with the mail coach, by steamboat, with friends and strangers, by pony, and on foot.

In Atchison, she was invited home by a gentleman who had attended her lecture and wanted to share her message with his wife and three daughters. As it turned out, his wife was not interested in women's rights and scolded her husband for bringing Nichols to their home. The wife could not turn out her unwelcome guest into the streets at so late an hour, so Nichols and her female traveling companion were put up in a roomful of the family's hired men. The two women slept in the middle of three beds, with only a chair on either side separating them from their male sleeping companions. Additional hired hands stretched out in bedrolls on the floor. She found the scene highly amusing, at least in retrospect.

In Lecompton, performers rehearsing for an upcoming minstrel show drowned out her lecture, forcing her to cut it short. That left her unable to take up a collection to help defray expenses. Four generous men pitched in fifty cents apiece to help cover her costs. And so it went.

In early September she toured southeastern K.T. and finally met all members of the Wattles family, though she had been corresponding with Susan for some time. Esther Wattles's husband, John, an ardent supporter of every progressive cause, had ridden over to the convention in Wyandotte, ready to help lobby for women's rights if need be. When he saw how well Nichols was doing on her own, however, he turned around and trotted home. One argument against women's rights had always been that if women wanted their rights, they were the ones who needed to speak up. Their silence was taken as assent to the status quo, though women were also silent out of ignorance of the issues or fear of reprisal.

In the fall of 1859, the Moneka group held back-to-back women's rights and temperance conventions and asked Nichols to be their featured speaker. The Wattleses were longtime reformers from Ohio who were eager to bring this mark of civilization to the frontier. John Wattles gave an extensive report to the Lawrence *Republican* on Nichols's presentation in Moneka. He called her lecture "one of the most thrilling and convincing" he had ever heard and said her words "had more real *gospel* in it than often falls to the lot of mortals to hear."

The Monekans clearly understood that women needed rights for exactly the same reason men needed them — because they were citizens. There was no talk at their conventions of women needing rights to fulfill their responsibilities. In their resolutions they declared that women were not inferior to men "physiologically, intellectually, or morally" and asserted that the institution of marriage needed a major overhaul to correct its lopsided balance of power. They did allow that there was one major difference between the sexes: "We use the pen, the press, and the living speaker, they the sword, bayonet, the rifle, cannon, and hosts of murderous men." (It was, after all, Kansas.)

The delegates authorized Nichols to continue as their representative. She was free to schedule lectures and meetings throughout Kansas as she saw fit. John Wattles planned to accompany her on the circuit, and they began laying out their route.

The final day of the convention "was as hot a day as ever I experienced," Esther Wattles recorded in her memoirs. That night, however, while John Wattles was giving the final speech of the evening, the temperature plummeted, and they all had to walk home in the chilled air in their light summer clothing. John already had a bad cold, and the extreme change in temperature apparently triggered a recurrent bout of ague. Nine days later he died, leaving his widow Esther with three little girls and Nichols without the strong ally who had promised to help her campaign for women's rights and passage of the Wyandotte Constitution. Once more she would need to carry on alone. It seemed to be her fate in life.

"You must remember," she told Susan B. Anthony, "that all my life I have been separated from my peers in the work."

———◆———

In October the voters approved the Wyandotte Constitution by a three-to-one majority, forever ridding the territory of slavery and allowing the settlement of free blacks in Kansas. The constitution also set the stage for a segregated school system, which Nichols saw coming. She told Anthony that anything not written in "block characters" in the constitution would be used by the "negro hating people, as in the river counties the majority are," to prevent black children from attending school with white children. It would take ninety-five years and a lawsuit filed against the Topeka school district — *Brown v. Board of Education* — before school segregation was declared unconstitutional by the United States Supreme Court.

Rounds of cannon fire echoed up and down the Missouri River as Kansans celebrated the results of the voting. Only one hurdle remained. The U.S. Congress needed to approve Kansas's application to become the thirty-fourth state admitted to the Union.

But the good news from Kansas was soon eclipsed by dramatic reports from Harpers Ferry, Virginia.

SIXTEEN

'A Vast Army
of Widows
and Orphans'

On the night of October 16, 1859, John Brown led twenty-one men on their ill-fated raid of the Federal armory at Harpers Ferry, Virginia. His plan was to arm and free the slaves of the South, but its execution was a fiasco almost from the start. Brown's tiny legion of black and white abolitionists held the armory for only a few hours before federal troops stormed in and killed or captured most of his party. Brown was tried, convicted, and ordered to hang on December 2.

Throughout the South, he became the symbol of Northern treachery. Among the "ultra" abolitionists, Brown was on his way to sainthood, but among antislavery Republicans, opinion was divided. Abraham Lincoln, who had come to Leavenworth to help free staters organize the Kansas Republican Party, measured his words carefully: "Old John Brown has just been executed for treason against a state. We cannot object, even though he agreed with us in thinking slavery wrong. That cannot excuse violence, bloodshed, and treason."

Nichols had been on a lecture tour in Missouri when news of the Harpers Ferry raid reached her. She was scheduled to give a speech in the proslavery border town of Westport that evening. People in this part of the country had no trouble believing that Brown was capable of such a plot. They remembered the Pottawatomie Massacre and the raids he had made in their own state to carry off slaves and "liberate" cattle.

The streets of Westport quickly filled with citizens anxious to trade news and rumors. Many believed Brown was part of a broader conspiracy against the South and spoke of tracking down his allies and stringing them up. Nichols's lecture that evening was boycotted, then cancelled. The nervous innkeeper at the hotel where she was staying urged her to leave quickly, and she slipped quietly out the back door.

She had been looking forward to an all-out lecture tour in a slave state. Now she would not be able to fulfill the promise she had made to Colonel Scott when he and his cohorts had boarded her boat upon arrival in Kansas City five years earlier. An extended lecture tour in Missouri would no longer be possible for a woman so strongly identified with the abolitionist cause. In some Southern communities, abolitionists were being threatened, rounded up, or driven out of town. At least back in Kansas Territory she was safe.

That wasn't the case for fugitive slaves. In the so-called "free" territory of Kansas, they could still be hunted down and dragged back to Missouri in chains. Not even free blacks were safe, as roving bands of slave hunters from both sides of the border could kidnap them and sell them back into slavery. Only in Canada, Mexico, or some parts of the Caribbean were blacks truly safe, for in those places slavery had been outlawed years earlier. In a letter to Susan Wattles, Nichols relayed the story of "Missouri wretches" who had kidnapped a free black woman she had hired to keep house for the family when she was away on business. The woman's husband was able to get her back, but Nichols knew that such outcomes were rare.

She was outraged that human beings could be stalked like prey, and expressed her sentiments in a poem for the Lawrence *Republican*. The impetus for the poem was a handbill that offered $500 for the return, dead or alive, of a young enslaved Missourian. A gang of bounty-hunters and dogs had chased the fugitive to the Kansas bank of the Missouri River. There the "chattel" had disappeared into the underbrush.

> To the hunt! to the hunt!
> Take bloodhound and gun;
> The quarry is noble —
> a chattel has run.
> O hush, "mad Missouri,"
> your ravings be still —
> There's hope on your bosom,
> and chains on your will.
> "Ter hoot! ter hoo!"
> who'll follow the game?
> "Ter hoot! ter hoo!"
> who'll rivet the chain?
> — the shame!

When it came to the underground railroad, she had to be cautious about what she said in public. One detail let slip to the wrong person could endanger the lives of a whole chain of fugitives or those helping them. Even her letters had to disguise any mention of the underground railroad. In a letter to Susan Wattles, she said that some "blessed events" had recently occurred in Quindaro. She did not say what those events were but wrote, "Humanity can have railroads without grants from Congress." Wattles would have known immediately that Nichols was not talking about the transcontinental railroad that would soon run through Kansas. The underground railroad was "Humanity's railroad." The "blessed events" were the successful escapes of slaves on the "train" to freedom that regularly pulled out of the Quindaro "station."

Legend has it that the underground railroad got its name from a frustrated slave master in Kentucky who watched a runaway swim across the Ohio River and disappear into the underbrush. After a futile search of the riverbank, the man grumbled that the slave must have gone off on an "underground railroad." Whether or not the story is true, the fact that it was set in Ohio makes sense, for Ohio had one of the most active fugitive slave networks in the country. It also had one of the earliest state organizations of women working for equal rights.

In the winter of 1861 Nichols and other women's rights advocates were called to help out in Ohio. Year after year the women of the Buckeye State had been petitioning for a married women's property rights law, and this was a pivotal year. It was not unusual for women's rights workers in one state to put out a call for help to their counterparts in other states. They all knew each other. In the Ohio campaign Frances Gage and Jane Elizabeth Jones welcomed Ernestine Rose from New York, Hannah Tracy Cutler from Illinois, and Clarina Nichols from Kansas. They were all veteran reformers, dedicated to the triumvirate of mid-nineteenth century reforms: temperance, antislavery, and women's rights.

Nichols knew Rose from out east and had stayed with "Aunt Fanny" Gage's family in St. Louis during one of her trips in and out of Kansas Territory. The early advocates were connected with one another in a myriad of ways. They corresponded, stayed at each other's homes while traveling, met one another at conventions, and traveled to each other's states when the call came forth that a special campaign was underway. They strategized, canvassed, and lectured together, and sometimes looked out for each other's children. Women were brought into the movement by their sisters, mothers, aunts, cousins, in-laws, friends, and schoolmates, and as they got older, they passed the torch to the next generation.

In Massilon, Ohio, Nichols reported hearing a tragic story that underscored what happened when women were denied their property rights. An eight-year-old boy had been recently orphaned by the death of his mother. By law her property was controlled by her second husband, the boy's stepfather. After laying his beloved to rest, the second husband skipped town without making any provision for his stepson. A good family had taken the boy in and saved him from the poorhouse, but Nichols reminded the public that this situation could have been prevented if the mother had been able to make legal provisions for her son and to control her own property. "The State...had paupered the helpless boy!" she declared.

She spent nine weeks in Ohio; after she left, a married women's property rights law was passed by the legislature. Of the role played by Nichols in the 1861 campaign, Jane Elizabeth Jones wrote,

> Perhaps no person was ever better qualified than she. Ever ready and ever faithful, in public and in private and ever capable too, whether discussing the condition of woman with the best informed members of the legal profession, or striving at the fireside of some indolent and ignorant sister.

While Nichols made stops in Illinois and Wisconsin to deliver lectures and visit old friends, the country's crisis over secession was deepening. In the weeks since the Republican candidate, Abraham Lincoln, won the 1860 election, South Carolina had led a withdrawal of Southern states and the formation of the Confederacy. Other slave states closer to the North, including Missouri, were being urged to desert the Union.

Kansas was admitted to the Union as a free state on January 29, 1861. Despite clouds on the horizon, the free-soil settlers celebrated their hard-fought victory. The new motto of Kansas perfectly described its odyssey to statehood: *Ad Astra per Aspera* ("to the stars through difficulties").

Nichols returned to Kansas in late March and wasted no time making her way to Topeka, where the new state legislature was in session. She met daily with lawmakers, accompanied by a traveling companion identified only as Miss Grant. They lobbied the assembly successfully to give married women the right to sue and be sued in their own names, an important advance that allowed women to defend their right to property in a court of law.

The ladies' constant presence at the capital had led one irritated observer to write in the Atchison *Union*, "The everlasting Mrs. Nichols and her yoke-mate Miss Grant are prepared to resign their knitting work, and take upon themselves the business of legislation." Nichols clipped the article and sent it to the more sympathetic Lawrence *Republican* with a tongue-in-cheek reply that she would be happy to knit the author of the piece a pair of stockings "if he will furnish yarn."

She kept in good spirits despite the continuing hardships and the occasional attacks on her character by opponents of women's rights, for this, indeed, was the whole reason she had come to Kansas:

> In 1854...an earnest friend of our cause [in Vermont] protested that I was 'going to bury myself in Kansas, just as I had won an influence and awakened a public sentiment that assured the success of our demand for equal rights.' I replied that it was a thousand times more difficult to procure the repeal of unjust laws in an old State, than the adoption of just laws in the organization of a new State. That I could accomplish more for woman, even the women of the old States, and with less effort,

in the new State of Kansas, than I could in conservative
old Vermont.

At the 1859 convention she had been told that woman suffrage would be taken up again by the legislature once Kansas
was firmly ensconced in the Union.

In early 1861 she arrived in Topeka to find the new capital
deluged by days of rain that fell so heavily, the plaster inside
the legislative hall was peeling off the walls. Dank clouds of
tobacco smoke fouled the air, and many of the legislators came
down with hacking coughs. Nichols complained of a sore
throat that bothered her for weeks. "I do so long for home,"
she wrote to a friend. But when she returned to Quindaro, she
found an even more distressing state of affairs: rain was pouring into her front room from a leaky roof. Reluctantly, she got
out the money she had set aside to send Birsha to art school
back east and bought new shingles for her roof. With no money
left over to hire laborers, she shingled the roof herself.

Before the downpours of 1861, the infant state had been
tormented by another severe drought that had made the efforts of the early pioneers to transform the prairie into farms
seem hopeless. When the wheat crop failed, farmers dug it up
and planted corn. When that failed, they dug up the corn and
planted buckwheat, and when that too failed, they planted
turnips, which also failed.

There was a mass exodus from Kansas. "All over Kansas,
were vacant homes, telling of an invader more terrible than
'border ruffians,'" Nichols wrote. The heavy rains brought
welcome relief but came too late to save much of the state
from famine. She traveled to Atchison where, once again,
relief supplies from other states were being handed out to the
suffering Kansans. She described the hollow-cheeked farmers who drove in from the interior with their empty wagons.
"Three out of four are afflicted with the scurvy, some to the
extent that their teeth could be taken out with the fingers," she

wrote in the *Chicago Tribune*. Reports like this and the efforts of many others helped mobilize a massive relief effort that saved the infant state from starvation.

Some must have wondered if Kansas would ever be self-sufficient, or if it would always need to rely on outside help to survive. The early years in Kansas Territory were hard for almost everybody who lived there. Prices fluctuated wildly, and political unrest made investments uncertain. In Quindaro, fortunes were made and lost in a matter of weeks. In Wyandotte City, the price of land swung between four dollars and fifty-eight dollars an acre in a six-year period. Nichols was thrifty to a fault, but she wasn't on the lookout for business opportunities and sometimes failed to recognize them when they came to her. A neighbor who wanted to buy a load of apples in Missouri to sell in Lawrence approached her with a proposal. He offered to share the profits with her, fifty-fifty, if she would loan him the money to buy the apples. "I had become so accustomed — indeed so expectant of loss, that the suddenly presented idea of unearned gain was quite unsettling," she told the Wyandotte *Commercial Gazette*. "So I substituted a trifling business commission" and missed an opportunity to share in the tidy profit her neighbor made.

Most settlers struggled to make even a modest living. In 1859 Nichols told Susan Wattles: "The 'times' are so hard it is almost impossible to get money in any business or collect what is due. Once out of the stocking you can't get it in again."

It is unclear at what point Clarina Nichols herself began to experience financial hardship. She had sacrificed most of her lecture income by moving to Kansas, where she earned only occasional honoraria, and the Moneka Women's Rights Association paid her just enough to cover expenses. At home she took in a gentleman boarder, collected tuition for the schools she and Birsha ran, and sold butter and eggs from her farm. She may also have earned money from her newspaper writing. Like the great majority of pioneers, she was self-sufficient, producing and preserving the food she needed, using the wood on her property for fuel, and bartering with her neighbors for goods and services she did not have. Her expertise at knitting and her skill with the needle helped keep her family's clothing in good repair, and she bought a sewing machine at a substantial discount by agreeing to endorse it in the newspaper.

As a well-traveled, well-read, self-educated individual, Nichols found living comfortably in Kansas a challenge, but she cut back on reading material and writing paper only when it was absolutely needed to make ends meet. These literary deprivations must have been especially painful to someone whose public identity had been formed in the printed and written word. The arrival of new books and periodicals were like "food that went to the hungry spot." They "revived" her connection "to the former life and to the world." She read her most treasured books over and over until the bindings were worn.

The Civil War added yet more burdens to the lives of Kansans. Quindaro was soon drained of its military-age men, including Howard, who joined the Union army. From across the river in Parkville, Nichols began hearing enemy soldiers changing guard in the night. Missouri was one of the border states that stayed with the Union during the "War of the Rebellion," but slavery remained legal there until 1865, and many in western Missouri openly flew the Rebel flag and supported the Confederacy.

Twice Nichols was prepared to flee Quindaro. The town, she was warned, would soon be attacked by hostile forces. She packed her carpetbags so she would be ready to leave at a moment's notice but stayed on as the town moved into a state of high alert. Old men became patrol guards along the river, keeping watch for any sign of a coming attack. Residents deserted homes and businesses to move to safer towns. "We expect trouble if the river freezes," she wrote Wattles.

"If I am burned out or driven away I don't know which way I would go."

In later years she would complain, "My children wander from me." By 1862, however, her family was already strung out across the country. She had sent George, now a teenager, off to school in Baldwin City, two counties away. Birsha went back east to stay with friends. Relie was at the other end of the country, in California. He wanted to come east and join the war but was neither able to finance the trip nor willing to leave his family behind. Howard was who-knows-where, serving with the Union army.

Only Howard's wife Sarah was nearby. For a time she stayed on in Quindaro with their two small children, Charles and Irena. Both women had pioneered in Kansas and knew how to take care of themselves under the most difficult circumstances. "She's no mouse," Nichols said approvingly of her daughter-in-law, but even that relationship was disrupted by the war. Sarah left to become a laundress in the army, so she could earn a living and be near her husband.

Clarina continued to tend her gardens and care for her livestock. She was fond of animals and gave names to some of them. Two cows she named Old Polly and Curly, and her little terrier dog she called Phebe. "I think I feel the death of favorite animals more than many," she confessed.

After Quindaro's only doctor joined the Union army, people turned to her for help when they were sick or injured. "Our people are many, and most of them too poor to send out of town," she wrote to Wattles. Though she had no formal training in medicine, her mixture of common sense and optimism and her knowledge of substances like arnica and belladonna served her well. She treated her patients with diet and bedrest, various herbal remedies, and hot and cold packs of water. "I have had several severe cases, one given up by a Wyandotte physician, a pregnant woman in fever — but all have recovered," she reported with satisfaction to Wattles. Her medical services were available to all, regardless of color. Speaking of the woman she had helped through a difficult pregnancy, she said, "She has a fine boy two months old — a *black* boy — the first *free* child out of 11 now in slavery."

As the war progressed, Nichols signed a petition of the Woman's Loyal League, demanding that President Lincoln, who had issued his Emancipation Proclamation in 1863, free *all* the slaves, not just those in the Confederacy over which he had no control. Slaves in the border states of the Union were not freed, for Lincoln feared that such an order would drive those crucial states into the arms of the Confederacy.

She heartily endorsed the call made by Anthony and Stanton to organize the Woman's Loyal League. "I have been feeling for months that [women's] activities should not be limited to the scraping of lint and concocting of delicacies for our brave and suffering soldiers," she said in her letter to the convention. "Women, equally with men, should address themselves to the removing of the wicked cause of all this terrible sacrifice of life." Through the efforts of Anthony and Stanton and an army of women across the nation, some 400,000 names were collected and delivered to Congress demanding an amendment to the Constitution that would ban slavery everywhere in the United States.

Though the emancipation of slaves was the issue, many in the movement felt women would benefit as well. Once enslaved blacks had their freedom, the reasoning went, men would realize that their wives lacked certain liberties also.

"This war is adding a vast army of widows and orphans to this already large class of unrepresented humanity," Nichols complained. Women were performing the duties of both mother and father; for this reason alone, they should no longer be denied their legal and political rights.

———

In late 1863 Nichols joined her daughter, Birsha, in Washington, D.C. Many government jobs had been vacated by men going off to war, creating a great labor shortage. Women were coming to the Capitol to fill those posts, conflating patriotism with opportunity for good pay. The two women were among the first female clerks in the treasury and army quartermaster's departments.

In Washington she joined the Ladies National Covenant, which was leading a boycott of foreign-made goods in order to strengthen the Union's balance of trade. The proposed abstinence pledge said that the women would not purchase any imported article of apparel that was not "absolutely neces-sary" after the coming Fourth of July. Nichols and a delegate from Massachusetts objected to this wording, since it allowed women to stock up on "absolutely necessary" purchases until the deadline, thus defeating the purpose of the boycott. Others, perhaps wondering how they would manage without imported mourning crepe or French underwear, objected.

Lois Bryan Adams, a correspondent for the *Detroit Advertiser and Tribune*, wrote, "Here Kansas came to the rescue again and delivered a stirring little speech, full of pith and patriotism." Nichols reminded the women of the sacrifices the soldiers were making on the battlefield and asked "if their wives, mothers, and sisters could not, for [the soldiers'] sakes, deny themselves for a time these luxuries of dress that were draining the coun-try of its gold." After some discussion, the ladies agreed to the more stringent wording.

During the War Between the States, women became nurses on the battlefront and turned their homes into miniature fac-tories to produce uniforms, blankets, bandages, bullets, and other supplies. Some became scouts and spies, and hundreds disguised themselves as men and served as soldiers. Both in the North and the South, women worked the farms and carried on trades and businesses emptied out by the war machine's unending need for more men.

As the Civil War came to an end, Clarina Nichols agreed to

"Lady Clerks Leaving the Treasury Department," 1863
illustration. Women filled traditional male positions in
government during the Civil War. *(Library of Congress)*

become the matron at a Georgetown home for black orphans
and widows left destitute by the war. It provided food, shelter,
medicine, and education for seventy orphans and a number
of aged widows. During the year she served as matron, she
succeeded in bringing the "chaotic" affairs of the home "to a
most complete system of social and educational discipline with
orderly, cleanly regulations" according to an accolade in the
Vermont Journal. The following year her mother died, and she
probably returned to Vermont for a time, but by 1867 she was
back in Kansas, picking up the pieces of her life.

SEVENTEEN

With Liberty
and Suffrage
for All

The town of Quindaro had started emptying out as the Civil War got underway, and its mostly deserted downtown was gutted during the war by Union — not Confederate — soldiers. The Second Kansas Cavalry tore up many of the deserted buildings and used them for firewood while quartered in Quindaro with their horses. It must have been a depressing sight to come home to, but Clarina Nichols had bought a small farm in 1862 and was planning to move anyhow.

Those plans were interrupted by a dramatic political development in Topeka. Legislators had been discussing woman suffrage ever since Nichols first petitioned for its passage in 1859. But the war had also created irresistible pressure for enfranchising black males. These two suffrage movements would collide in Kansas in early 1867 when, after a surprising turn of events, the Kansas legislature struck both *white* and *male* from the state constitution.

Many in the black male suffrage movement balked at combining the two issues, arguing that woman suffrage would weaken their cause. That led to a compromise in the legislature: two separate amendments were drafted, one for black male suffrage, one for woman suffrage. Both would be put on the fall ballot, and the white male electorate would vote to adopt or reject each amendment. (Black females needed *both* amendments to pass to gain voting rights.) It was the first time that female suffrage was put to a vote by any state, and women's rights leaders across the country saw this as the opportunity they had been waiting for.

Nichols was confident that woman suffrage would win in Kansas this time. "The hour of universal freedom is coming to us without violence," she wrote in the *Vermont Phoenix* in February of 1867. "Those who have fought the oppressor, and freed the slave and demand suffrage for him, will not forget the women who prayed and wept and wrought for them in the battlefield, in hospital and rebel prison. We have been on a political equality with the negro too long not to be lifted with him now."

In early April the Kansas Impartial Suffrage Association was formed to support the two amendments. Nichols was at the inaugural meeting in Topeka, as was an old friend from New Jersey, Lucy Stone, and her husband, Henry Blackwell. The couple had caused a hubbub in 1855 by announcing that their marriage vows would not include the word *obey*, and that Lucy would not take her new husband's name, unthinkable blasphemy in many people's minds. The meeting was orderly until a lawyer "with a hole in his coat and only one shoe" crashed the proceedings with his minister friend. "He made a mean speech," Stone said. After the lawyer spewed a few choice pronouncements ("If I was a negro, I would not want the woman hitched to my skirts" was one), "Mrs. Nichols and I came down on him, and the whole convention, except the Methodist minister, was against him."

The ill-clad lawyer and his minister friend, however, were harbingers of things to come, though no one had any inkling of what trouble lay ahead. Indeed, as Stone and Blackwell set off on a vigorous lecturing tour, they were delighted by the lovely spring weather and emboldened by the same optimism that had kept Nichols going out west all those years. "Everything has conspired to help us in this state," Blackwell wrote to Elizabeth Cady Stanton. "This is a glorious country, Mrs. S, and a glorious people. If we succeed here, it will be the State of the Future." They urged their friends out east to join them.

So did Sam Wood, a colorful local politician who saw the campaign as a way to put Kansas and himself on the map. The referendums became national news and drew Eastern women's rights leaders and journalists to Kansas. The Reverend Olympia Brown (inspired by but not related to the Reverend Antoinette Brown) heeded the call and came west.

The famed Hutchinson Family Singers, songbirds of the reform movement, also made the trek. Their close harmonies and topical themes had made them one of the most popular singing groups in the nation. For the 1867 campaign they composed "The Kansas Suffrage Song," with lyrics set to the tune of the folk song "Old Dan Tucker." It challenged the "Brave defenders of the nation" — the men of Kansas — to "crown their deeds of daring" by being the first state to give women the vote. The song assured the supporters of temperance that newly enfranchised women would "rid the nation of its intoxication." It even tried to assuage the fears of men who worried that suffrage would mean late suppers and neglected children. "Fear not," the Hutchinsons trilled; nothing on the homefront will change.

> O, say what thrilling songs of fairies,
> Wafted o'er the Kansas prairies,
> Charm the ear while zephyrs speed 'em!
> Woman's pleading for her freedom.

(Chorus)
Clear the way,
the songs are floating;
Clear the way,
the world is noting;
Prepare the way,
the right promoting
And ballots, too,
for woman's voting!

We frankly say to fathers, brothers,
Husbands, too, and several others,
We're bound to win our right of voting,
Don't you hear the music floating?

We come to take with you our station,
Brave defenders of the nation,
And aim by noble, just endeavor
To elevate our sex forever.

By this vote we'll rid our nation
Of its vile intoxication.
Can't get rum? Oh, what a pity!
Dram shops closed in every city.

Fear not, we'll darn each worthy stocking,
Duly keep the cradle rocking,
And beg you heed the words we utter,
The ballot wins our bread and butter.

All hail, brave Kansas! first in duty.
Yours, the meed of praise and beauty.
You'll nobly crown your deeds of daring
Freedom to our sex declaring.

The Hutchinson Family Singers combined
popular harmonies with progressive politics.
(Library of Congress)

Had the election been held in the spring, perhaps both
amendments would have passed handily. Crowds at the pro-
amendment rallies were large, enthusiastic, and supportive.
Many state Republicans, however, decided to support black
male suffrage but reject female suffrage. Articles soon began
to appear in the local press that attacked the women's amendment and the character of those who supported it, particularly
outsiders like Lucy Stone. More distressing was the lack of
consensus and support among the old guard from the antislavery movement and the silence of male abolitionist friends
in the East.

The women's rights leaders expected that after all their
years of supporting abolition and the Republican Party, they
would be rewarded with support for suffrage. Instead, Horace Greeley, Wendell Phillips, Frederick Douglass, T. W.

Higginson, and other longtime supporters of women's rights withheld their support. It was the "Negro's hour," they said, a time to enfranchise black males and bring them into the Republican Party. Others went further, saying the women's amendment was *hurting* support for black male suffrage. By fall there was an Anti-Female Suffrage Association — with bipartisan support.

Ministers were among the most strident opponents of woman suffrage, claiming that it would emasculate men, defeminize women, contribute to gender confusion, and lead to a breakdown of the family. They based their sweeping conclusions on a handful of Bible verses, while Nichols and others pointed to an equal number of passages in Scripture that stressed themes of liberty and charity.

For a decade she had been working on a long essay she eventually titled, "The Bible Position of Woman, or Woman's Rights From a Bible Stand-Point." Impelled by her personal faith and informed by her lifelong membership in the Baptist Church, her extensive knowledge of Scripture, and a stack of Bible commentaries, she was prepared to take on the challenge. She had been debating ministers from the very beginning of her political career, and she knew exactly what Bible passages these men used to make their case. Invariably, they would emphasize Eve's role in bringing sin into the world and St. Paul's injunction to wives to submit to their husbands. The clergymen believed that a hierarchical structuring of families (with men in charge) was not only in everyone's best interest but part of the Almighty's plan for order and harmony in both families and society.

Religion exerted a powerful influence on people's thinking, and the majority of churchgoers were, as they are today, female. They could be strong opponents to expanded rights for women if they thought the Bible taught otherwise. A wife's duty to submit to her husband was as universally accepted as the idea that children should be seen and not heard. That idea of wifely submission was broadened to mean that no woman should be in authority over any man, so it is not difficult to see why suffrage was a threat. If women gained suffrage, what might they want next? It was not inconceivable to think they might seek elective office and influence in power structures now dominated exclusively by men.

Opposition ministers used their pulpits effectively, as can be seen in this diary entry of a twelve-year-old Lawrence girl: "I think it is against the Bible and the will of God for a woman to take a man's place," she wrote. "I think the men will not respect the women, and that they will neglect their duties."

Nichols resolutely believed that if she could help both men and women return to the central message of the Bible and see these isolated passages in a different light, she could break down the strongest set of objections to female suffrage and women's rights. Often she used humor when it served her purpose, as when she observed in later years,

> There is not one word in the Bible about woman suffrage. Neither is there one word about apple dumplings. I don't believe they had any in Paul's day, nor man suffrage either, for there is not a word in the Good Book about suffrage for anybody.

In articles for the Wyandotte *Commercial Gazette* she reminded her readers that if their forefathers had adhered to a strict interpretation of the Bible (to honor those in authority) there would have been no American Revolution. Nor would the slaves have been set free, for they too were counseled by St. Paul to obey their masters. It was time, she said, "to abolish the last relic of barbarous government" by granting political rights to women.

At the First National Woman's Rights Convention in 1850

she had been introduced to a concept that the early women's rights advocates called "co-sovereignty." This was the belief that men and women could exist in the world as equals, sharing power while working as partners. Co-sovereignty was arguably the most radical idea to come out of the antebellum women's movement, though it was never fully explored, much less practiced. In the Kansas campaign the role of religion was overshadowed by the singular focus on woman suffrage, and the events that would tear the women's rights movement in two.°

———————

The summer of 1867 was another difficult season in Kansas. Grasshoppers devoured Nichols's crop, and she was forced to replant late in the season. She and other family members were sick for a long stretch; the rest of the time she and Birsha were busy running a tuition-paying summer school. She was also having her house moved ("by my carpenter son") to her new location outside Wyandotte City. With all of that going on, she still managed to bring her message on horseback to every house in Quindaro and Wyandotte, to lecture within the county during the spring and summer, and to spend four weeks in late summer canvassing several counties for both amendments. She received fifty dollars from the Moneka Women's Rights Association for her services.

In the *Western Home Journal*, published in Ottawa, Kansas, she defended Lucy Stone, who was being accused by an influential Kansas politician of promoting free love. "She don't believe in marriage for life, but wishes all to do like her and that seed-wart she carries around with her—called Blackwell," he said. "The women of Kansas must feel themselves

———————

°For more on "co-sovereignty," see Appendix D, "Mrs. Nichols v. Rev. Blachly: An Imagined Debate."

insulted ...that such stock as Lucy Stone was *imported* to tell them what to do."

Nichols called the attack "a gross slander" and said tartly, "To my thinking, men horrified at the idea of women's ears being assailed with rude and obscene language at the polls, should abstain from writing such communications for women and children to read in their homes."

She also took to task a columnist who had warned readers of the dangers of black female suffrage. "The colored women are proposed to be made equal with you and I," predicted the reporter who wrote under the pen name of "Philo" for the Wyandotte *Commercial Gazette*. "Imagine three or four hundred colored women next November, marching to the polls...each one carrying in her arms a squalling brat."

That "brat," Nichols replied, "is an armful of reasons why its mother should exercise the high prerogative." She also argued that "Philo" was condemning the mother to a perennial fate: "So long as they [black females] have no right to the elective franchise, they have no motive to [educate and improve] themselves, and politicians have no motive to enlighten them in the uses of the ballot."

As the campaign wore on, female suffrage and black male suffrage were increasingly pitted against each other, with supporters of each saying that the other was dragging down their cause. The hostility between the two camps helped stir up people's natural resistance to change of any kind, and both causes suffered. The campaign began to wear on everyone's nerves, and support for both causes began to fade as special interest groups became more vocal.

German Kansans organized to defeat woman suffrage out of fear that a fresh influx of female voters would dry up the state and leave them without beer. Rural Kansans feared that giving black men suffrage would encourage poor, illiterate blacks to flood the state and compete with white labor. Editors in many

Lucy Stone, who came to Kansas to rally for suffrage, was branded an interloper by local newspapers. *(Library of Congress)*

papers claimed that both amendments were too radical — or at least premature — for such a young state to experiment with. They asserted that impartial suffrage should be tried in an older, more established state. If it succeeded there, without destroying the social fabric of society, then perhaps Kansas would reconsider.

In a letter to Sam Wood, the Kansas organizer of the campaign, Nichols complained about mixups and miscommunications in scheduling and finances. She bristled at an apparent suggestion from Wood that she was upset because she wasn't the center of the show and wasn't getting enough attention. "Now don't talk of my fearing others will work, or I not get 'all the honor,'" she wrote on June 19th. "Having labored years when it was a reproach to be a Woman's Rights advocate, I may covet my share of the honor of success without a blush."

By the time Susan B. Anthony and Elizabeth Cady Stanton

arrived in early fall, black male suffrage was in jeopardy, and woman suffrage was in disarray. With campaign funds dried up and support eroding for their amendment, Anthony and Stanton made a decision that would taint their reputations and split the movement. They accepted help from George Francis Train, a flashy, rich entrepreneur who was both an ardent women's rights supporter and an unapologetic racist. The two women rationalized this misalliance by claiming they were unconcerned with Train's other views, so long as he supported woman suffrage. They pointed out that the supporters of black male suffrage took money from people who held unenlightened, or even misogynistic, views on women. Anthony and Stanton appeared unfazed by the furor they created. They resented being criticized by their former allies in abolitionist-Republican circles who refused to support female suffrage. They believed they could win Kansas with an all-out, last-ditch, no-holds-barred campaign financed by Train's money and oiled by his supposed charm.

Anthony and Stanton had been seriously contemplating moving to Kansas if woman suffrage passed. Stanton wrote:

> I thought of the novelty of a six-months' journey through the bright spring and summer days in a house on wheels, meals under shady trees and beside babbling brooks, sleeping in the open air, and finding a home, at last, where land was cheap, the soil rich and deep, and where the grains, vegetables, fruit, and flowers grew bountifully with but little toil.

In Kansas, however, Stanton — who lived comfortably out East — found that "a few months of pioneer life permanently darkened my rosy ideal." During their travels and lectures throughout the state in the fall of 1867, the Eastern women found themselves roughing it to a degree they had not anticipated. "The dirt, the food!!" Stanton exclaimed in a letter to a cousin. Seemingly unaware that these were everyday facts of life to Nichols and other Kansas women, Stanton declared that her brief exposure to pioneer life "gave me added self-respect to know that I could endure such hardships and fatigue with a great deal of cheerfulness."

The "rosy ideal" of the Impartial Suffrage campaign, however, had withered by autumn. In the election, the coalition of ministers and turncoat Republicans prevailed. The black male suffrage amendment was defeated by a vote of 10,483 for and 19,421 against. The women's amendment lost by an even wider margin: 9,070 for and 19,857 against.

The vote turned out to be a temporary setback for black male suffrage, which was granted with the passage in 1870 of the Fifteenth Amendment to the Constitution. But women would have to wait another fifty years for the franchise. Anthony and Stanton opposed the Fifteenth Amendment because it failed to include women. Feeling betrayed and unwilling to wait for political deliverance, they broke with the Republican Party and formed an independent organization, the National Woman Suffrage Association. From that point on they were not beholden to any man or any political organization. Lucy Stone and Henry Blackwell remained with the old Republican guard and organized the American Woman Suffrage Association. Each wing of the movement had its own publication. *The Revolution* (financed by Train) was run by Anthony and Stanton, while Stone edited *The Woman's Journal*. Ironically, neither group attracted many black females. The two most prominent African American women in the movement were Sojourner Truth, who remained with Anthony and Stanton's organization, and Frances Watkins Harper, who aligned with Stone's wing.

In a letter to Susan B. Anthony in January of 1870, Nichols called the Fifteenth Amendment "mean," but added, "inasmuch as it is in advance somewhat of former positions, I won't quarrel with it." She retained membership with the National organization but signed the call to organize the American. "I felt assured we were strong enough to swarm," she told Anthony, "and would increase our strength and numbers by spreading ourselves and taking up other and more ground." Her instincts were proven correct. Before woman suffrage could be passed, it would have to become an idea palatable to millions of people across a broad spectrum who embraced suffrage for a variety of reasons.

Over the years, Nichols contributed articles to the publications of both the American and National organizations. She told Susan B. Anthony she would write for *The Revolution* "whenever my breadwinning occupation will allow."

EIGHTEEN

'Grant! Grant! Grant!'

After 1867 Nichols curtailed her public appearances. Her complaints about the intransigence of Kansas legislators since 1859 reflected her growing realization that the conservatism she had seen in Vermont was now taking hold here. The decisive defeat of woman suffrage merely confirmed this fact for Nichols and probably contributed to her withdrawal from active participation in Kansas politics.

In the years ahead, her family situation would grow more complicated, health problems would mount, and the physical demands of speaking and politicking would become too great to bear. Nichols began shifting her energies into journalism, writing for newspapers from Vermont to California, and making an effort to sum up her career for posterity. Many circumstances were beyond her control in the third act of her life, but the years ahead would be no less demanding than those that had preceded them.

By February of 1868 she had settled into her transplanted house on a thirty-four-acre farm on the outskirts of Wyandotte City in present-day Kansas City, Kansas. The editor of the Wyandotte *Gazette* wrote, "She has got one of the most beautiful and romantic situations in the state." Lovely though her location may have been, its proximity to Wyandotte City caused Nichols grief. A small portion of her land lay within city limits, which made her subject to city taxes, though she was too far out to receive services and was irked at the prospect of helping support a city that condoned "rum holes." The following year she led a contingent of her neighbors in an unsuccessful attempt to secede from Wyandotte City.

With her move from Quindaro over and the previous year's unpleasant campaign behind her, she could unwind, putter around the house and yard, and look forward to spring. It had been a rough campaign, especially near the end, and the final tally destroyed any hope that woman suffrage was just around the corner. Each of those "no" votes represented a man who at some level felt his sovereignty threatened by woman suffrage. A change in consciousness was going to take longer than anyone ever dreamed it would take, though the women's rights advocates still couldn't concede the truth.

That spring she planted potatoes, melons, tomatoes, onions, sweet corn, field corn, oats, and wheat. She liked physical work, and she enjoyed being outdoors in the brilliant Kansas sunshine — sowing, weeding, watching things grow, comparing one field with another. "Oats are harvested and heavy," she wrote in the Wyandotte *Commercial Gazette*. "Wheat is splendid. No poor bread this year, sisters."

———

It had looked for a while as though Birsha would be her mother's lifelong companion. The two had spent most of the last decade together. Both were committed abolitionists; they had organized an integrated school in Quindaro and worked together in Washington during the war. Birsha had taken over the household when her mother was on the road. When Clarina's back ached, Birsha lugged the heavy tubs of water for the weekly washing, and in the long evenings they kept each other company, sewing or knitting by the fire while Clarina read aloud to them both.

But in June of 1868 Birsha, now in her late thirties, married a former Civil War general, George Franklin Davis. A widower with three children, Davis was also a native Vermonter. After the wedding he brought his new bride back home with him.

It must have been hard for Nichols to see her daughter go, not knowing if she would ever see her again. She called Birsha her "dearer, sweeter, better self," and her departure filled Clarina with despair. "I seem to have lost power to make sunshine," she wrote a year later.

But Birsha had left her mother in a terrible fix. Shortly after the war the young woman had informally adopted a little African American girl named Lucy Lincoln, probably from the Georgetown orphanage where both women had worked. In a letter to her daughter-in-law Helen in California, Nichols said that she had opposed the adoption, but when Birsha "wept and begged," saying she wanted a child "to love and care for" and promising she would take sole responsibility, her mother relented. When Birsha married, however, her interest in Lucy waned. She wound up leaving the girl behind, and Nichols quickly developed a dislike for the troubled child.

"She is a natural born thief and liar," Nichols said of Lucy in a letter to Helen Carpenter. "I shall get rid of her as soon as I can." She was frustrated and angry at the situation she found herself in, but her wrath was misdirected at Lucy instead of at Birsha, who had broken a promise to her mother and abandoned Lucy like an unwanted pet. It would be natural, especially at Nichols's age, to feel put upon by the responsibil-

Birsha Carpenter Davis. *(courtesy Grace Hudson Museum, Ukiah, California)*

ity of caring for a child she did not want in the first place. Yet given her own trials, she displayed a curious lack of empathy for Lucy, whose young life had been filled with upheaval and loss. There are racist innuendos in Nichols's assessment of Lucy's "natural" propensity for deceit, as well as in her comment that Lucy had been "so white and pretty" when she was younger. Still, her forebearance with Lucy Lincoln probably was a step up from the average white person of that day, and despite her threat to "get rid of her," Lucy remained in the household for at least three years and was at one point nursed by Nichols through a long convalescence.

———————

The summer after Birsha left, Nichols went on a memorable field trip with an old friend from the early days of the women's movement who was visiting from Pennsylvania. The two arrived in Manhattan, Kansas, in time to see the most famous man in America.

On the morning of July 18, 1868, a train carrying General Ulysses S. Grant pulled into town. Three years removed from his triumphs as the commander of the Union Army, Grant had declared himself a Republican and was running for President. Along with other Civil War heroes, he was making an inspection tour of the new Union Pacific Railroad that now ran through Kansas to Denver. Since Abraham Lincoln made a brief campaign tour of eastern Kansas in 1859, development in the state had proceeded apace, and the coming of the railroad was its most visible sign.

As Grant's train came to a halt in Manhattan, he stepped out of his private railroad car and bowed to an enthusiastic crowd that was chanting "Grant! Grant! Grant!" Though people were close enough to reach out and touch him, no one moved, and Grant was not the kind of back-slapping, hand-shaking politician who makes the first move.

Holding her long skirts in one hand and parting the crowd with the other, Nichols began making her way toward the general. Halfway across she caught his eye, and he gave her a cordial nod.

When she reached him, she thrust out her hand. "General," she announced, "as one of the mothers of Kansas, I bid you welcome!" Before the celebrated war hero and presidential hopeful could reply, she had another message for him, also from the mothers of Kansas: "If we could vote, we would vote for Grant!"

"You can electioneer for us," he said, pumping her hand.

"Aye, aye," she said. "That we can."

The ice was broken, and the men in the crowd surged forward. A few minutes later the train started up again, and Grant disappeared inside the railroad car, leaving behind a sea of outstretched arms.

The professor who had accompanied Nichols and her friend

Ulysses S. Grant, as depicted in an 1868 *Harper's Weekly* cartoon, cast a large shadow. *(Library of Congress)*

on this outing said, "You were acquainted with him at Washington? No? I thought from the cordialty of his manner and the way his face lighted up, that you had met before."

Nichols shook her head. She had merely sensed Grant's discomfort at being stared at "like an elephant" and decided to use her "motherly intervention" to put him at ease. The occasion had also given her the chance to deliver a message to the man who would soon occupy the highest post in the land, and opportunities like this didn't come along every day, especially in Kansas.

Following the morning's excitement, she toured another sign of progress — Kansas State College. Professor Benjamin Mudge, an old neighbor and co-worker on the underground railroad in Quindaro, proudly showed her around the campus.

Now the state geologist, Mudge was cataloging a fine collection of fossils that he had gathered from his expeditions. She gave a glowing account in the newspaper of the new land-grant college and assured her readers that none of the professors she had met were of the "gassing type."

———

If the railroad and the new college were signs of the future, the Indians of eastern Kansas were evidence of what that future had cost. Delawares, Kanzas, Kickapoos, Miamis, Osages, Ottawas, Sacs and Foxes, Shawnees, Wyandottes and other smaller tribes were all being removed to the *new* Indian Country — Oklahoma.

Clarina Nichols had more than a passing interest in the fate of one of these tribes. Her son George had married Mary Warpole, a fifteen-year-old Wyandotte, shortly before the war ended. Her friend Lucy Armstrong was a Wyandotte by marriage, and another Wyandotte family, the Brown-Guthries, had been good neighbors to Nichols during her years in Quindaro.

Wyandottes were respected farmers, merchants, and public officials in Kansas. They practiced Christianity and adopted the dress of their white neighbors. Many had intermarried. None of this saved them from the fate of all the other Indians in eastern Kansas. Those Indians unwilling to give up their tribal identities for United States citizenship were forced to leave Kansas for Oklahoma. Whether they stayed in Kansas as citizens or moved to Indian Country, they did not receive fair compensation for lands that had been allotted to them after they had been removed from their former homes in the East and Midwest.

Mary Warpole was paid between two hundred dollars and three hundred dollars for property that was probably worth five times that amount. Nichols was away from home when Warpole accepted partial payment on her land. "They were so needy!" Nichols said, explaining to family members why Mary had sold out so cheaply.

Though a hard worker and a temperate man, George Bainbridge Nichols was never able to get ahead in Kansas. His young wife had borne three children before the age of twenty-one and was in such poor health that both he and his mother had to help out with household chores and minding the children. "I am sewing, tending baby, and [doing] my own work," Clarina wrote to Helen in California.

She investigated the probate books herself and confronted the Indian agents with proof that they had siphoned money from Mary's account. Despite incontrovertible evidence of mishandled transactions and chicanery, every sale of Wyandotte land was upheld as legal. Nichols said that it was common knowledge that Indian agents had cheated Wyandottes out of $30,000. She decried the transaction as "rascality revealed too late."

The ongoing removal of Indians from eastern Kansas made the last Green Corn Festival of the Wyandottes in 1868 a poignant occasion. Wyandottes held the festival every year to celebrate the corn harvest, commemorate the day when they had accepted Christianity, and give new names to children and any tribal member who wanted to assume a new identity. Writing for the *Gazette*, Nichols reported that the gathering was large, respectable, orderly and without the wholesale smoking of tobacco that made the Fourth of July celebration an "endurance" for people like her who were bothered by smoking. Indians from other tribes attended, and Wyandotte leaders recited the long saga of their people from Canada, where they were part of the Hurons, to Ohio and Michigan and finally to Kansas.

After the speeches, "Big iron kettles of succotash were free to all," along with baskets of bread and meat, fried cakes, and melons, Nichols reported. She pronounced the celebration superior to the showy, pretentious affairs that white members of the community seemed to favor.

Native dances wrapped up the day. Nichols could not take her eyes off the older women taking part. "They moved in a circle outside the men, erect, calm, dignified and self-possessed with slightly undulating forward steps, bowed heads, and grave, pensive faces that I will not soon forget."

———

As Clarina Nichols neared sixty, Relie and Helen began urging her to move to California, where the winters were less harsh and she could garden all year round. She was reluctant to make another move halfway across the continent. She had been transplanted so many times she wasn't sure if she had the ability to grow roots one more time. "I never can make another home," she wrote to Relie.

The years of campaigning and homesteading had worn her down. She also seems to have felt that, as in Vermont fifteen years earlier, her moment had passed. She had pushed hard, and now Kansas was pushing back. Although voting in school elections had been guaranteed by the Wyandotte Constitution and reinforced by a later law, Nichols discovered that school suffrage was widely denied across the state and ridiculed where it was not.

Writing in October 1869 in the *Daily Commonwealth* of Topeka, where she had become a regular correspondent, she recounted a recent visit — on horseback — to a district school meeting in which women were taking part in a vote on whether to hire a male or a female teacher. When the vote went in the male teacher's favor, one of the men at the meeting leaped to his feet and exclaimed, "We can wear our breeches yet!"

Nichols found this sentiment throughout Kansas, not just in the legislature. There was widespread fear that women were looking to take over men's roles to the detriment of their homes and families. Alarmist voices warned that women's rights would lead to an outbreak of free love, or even worse, communism, which was at that point some twenty years old.

It didn't help that in 1872 Victoria Woodhull, the first woman to run for President, would espouse both free love *and* communism. Woodhull was the first woman to hold a seat on the New York Stock Exchange and an outspoken advocate of women's rights. She had seemed like a natural leader for the movement, a godsend even — until she started spouting ideas that sent horrified women's rights leaders running for cover.

"Yes, I am a free lover," Woodhull declared in a public meeting in New York during the campaign. "I have an inalienable, constitutional and natural right to love whom I may, to love as long or as short a period as I can, to change that love every day if I please." Despite quickly distancing themselves from Woodhull, all women's rights leaders were tarred with the same brush by those who were looking for a reason to bring out the tar.

For many women in the East, a shortage of lovers, rather than an abundance, was the issue. Nichols responded in the *Daily Commonwealth* to a Boston minister who had asserted that wedlock was the only natural state for women. Marriage wasn't always possible, Nichols argued, even when women desired it. In Massachusetts following the Civil War, for example, there were 75,000 more women than men. What were these single women, many of them widows with children, supposed to do? Apparently they were to "fold their hands and starve, or be restricted to starvation wages," she said.

The minister had argued that if women were given good jobs, men's wages would be cut in half. "Poor fellow," she responded with mock pity. Like many women, she had supported herself and a family for most of her life on "women's wages." If men's wages were halved, "both will have bread," she said. "If they marry ... the halves make a whole loaf, just as sweet as if the man had brought it all."

Despite earlier objections to another move, Nichols's resistance began to weaken as the health problems in her family

worsened. Both Mary's and her baby's health were so poor
that Clarina feared for their survival and thought a move to
a more temperate climate might save them. She herself was
not well, despite more or less constant self-doctoring. Her
back problem had gotten worse after she fell from the loft in
the barn while putting up clover, and her bronchial condition
flared up during the long Kansas winters and led to fits of
coughing that wore her out.

In addition to health problems, her financial situation was
making her anxious. In a letter to Anthony in 1870, she said
that she had to withhold a subscription to the *Revolution* because she lacked the funds. She explained:

> With a snug little farm and good crops, the improve-
> ments, farming tools ... and taxes have taken all I could
> rake together with a fine tooth-comb economy, and
> then I am often so uncomfortable at being in debt; $250
> yet to pay, I can't get to any of our conventions, even
> in Kansas — *expenses*! It costs $10 to go to Topeka and
> back, and I am behind that much on my taxes yet, and
> must get it from butter and eggs, one new milch cow and
> thirty hens! Ah, Susan, you are a favored individual, to
> be allowed to fight a big fight. These petty struggles are
> hateful, belittleing.

NINETEEN

Third Class
to California

Clarina, George, and Mary Warpole Nichols dreamed of California and worried about how to get there. The overland trip took three or four months, which meant they could take more of their household goods, and George wouldn't have to leave behind his beloved team of horses, Kit and Fanny. However, for the sake of Mary and the baby, who were both in delicate health, they decided to take the train. The transcontinental railroad, completed just two years earlier, ran at twenty-five miles per hour, cutting the trip to a fraction of the time it had taken Relie and Helen to travel by oxcart from Kansas to California fourteen years earlier.

Throughout 1871 Clarina Nichols worked on settling her affairs in Kansas and preparing for the move west. "I feel so unsettled — homeless," she wrote to Helen in March. "Of course I can't feel at home where I am, only staying till I can

sell." She sold her pigs, an old stove, and wood off her property as fast as George could haul it away. Her chickens and
milch cows she held onto to supply her with eggs, milk, and
ready cash. In the end she decided to rent her farm instead of
selling it. She held an auction sale in early December to get
rid of everything nonessential.

She had seen Kansas through its troubled labor and delivery
and now that it was a strapping ten-year-old, she left it behind
forever, along with her oldest son Howard and his family,
many friends, a house she could not transplant a second time,
her wisteria-draped elms, gooseberry and raspberry bushes,
and a mature orchard that supplied her and her family with
enough peaches for "an eat" every day through the winter.

The trip from Kansas City to California took twelve days,
including four extra for minor mishaps and delays. Heavy
snow on the track blocked their path several times; the engine
on the train ahead of them broke down at one point; and the
steamboat that was supposed to take the passengers across a
submerged patch of track ran aground.

Before she settled in Kansas, Nichols had traveled first class,
but on this trip she and her family traveled third class, the
compartment preferred by poor immigrants new to America.
A California friend had assured her that third class would
be more roomy at that time of year than first or second class
accommodations, and far cheaper. For the first few days
their railroad car was dirty, crowded, and untended, and she
wondered if they had made a big mistake. Soon, however, she
began to realize the advantages of immigrant class:

> You may be sure it was a privilege we will never forget,
> to lay aside our wraps, spread a mattress for the little ones
> and their invalid mother, and make our tea as a family at
> home. The weather was not very cold, and the car always
> warm enough. Fare from Kansas City to California $62.
> Freight 6 cents per pound and no extra charges.

In addition, though they sacrificed the magnificent views afforded to customers in first and second class, they enjoyed a camaraderie with the other occupants in third. In fact, what Nichols enjoyed most about the trip were the people traveling in her car, several of whom "could discuss any topic of general interest with sense and feeling." There was a Danish scholar, fluent in several ancient languages, who was traveling with his sister and trying to learn English ("with excellent success," Nichols said), merchants accompanying their freight, French immigrants, and American pioneers heading for California to make new homes wherever their prospects were brightest. "All together we were a sort of family party," she said. She had always been an enthusiastic traveler who enjoyed going places and seeing new things. She was soon looking forward to California almost as much as she had once looked forward to seeing Kansas Territory.

They crossed the continental divide and began their new life in California on January 1, 1872. Relie had settled in the city of Ukiah, northeast of San Francisco, where he and Helen had become leading citizens, involved in a great variety of entrepreneurial and civic activities. Opting for the rural life, Clarina, George, and Mary settled on land owned by Relie in Pomo, a rural settlement twenty miles northeast of Ukiah in the geographically isolated Potter Valley.

With characteristic optimism, Nichols shared her first impressions of the Golden State with readers of the Wyandotte *Gazette*:

> I was prepared to like California, yet feared that seeing would 'let me down,' other people's spectacles magnify so differently from our own. But there is a great deal more of California, and all unlike my imaginings. The whole country is made up after patterns I am not familiar with. I was born among the Green Mountains of Vermont, explored its gorges and climbed its granite rocks. But

these mountains, though green with evergreen trees and shrubs, are all unlike any mountains I have ever seen. The rocks, heavy with the moss of ages, might be taken for remote ancestors of New England boulders. Hurled by the warring elements into the deep gorges, they are eminently suggestive of 'an awful power behind the throne.' Mountains, rivers, valleys, gorges (canyons) are put together in unique and ever varying relations. The effect is always grandly beautiful; nothing suggestive of pettiness anywhere meets the eye or oppresses the thought.

She was quick to note that California had good-paying work for females; what's more, the men there were not constitutionally incapable of housework. "Some of the nicest housekeepers and cooks here are the men and boys," Nichols wrote. She had feared that she was too old to be transplanted one more time. But the old habits of industry, orderliness, and ingenuity took over, and she was soon hard at work making a home for the family, meeting older pioneers in the valley, and acquainting herself with the lay of the land and its history. Although Mary had been able to rest comfortably during their journey west, the trip had been hard on her, and she was too exhausted and frail to join in the work of setting up a new household.

Four months after their arrival, Nichols provided an armchair tour of sunny California for curious Kansans: "To the eye of an insider, the valley is oval in form and framed by mountains, rising tier above tier," she wrote in the *Gazette*. "The pine, cedar, fir, medone, manzanita, live oak, pepper are very fine trees — the three latter blossoming in January." Even though Potter Valley had been settled by Anglos for only a dozen years or so, the land had already been divvied up into forty- and eighty-acre lots, each enclosed by redwood fences which she pronounced both "durable and beautiful."

George B. Nichols and his children by Mary
Warpole (clockwise from top right): Birney
Nichols, Katherine Howard Nichols, Helen Clarina
Nichols. *(Wyandotte Nation of Kansas Tribal Archives)*

"And the flowers!" she exclaimed. There was no need to
plant any as they were everywhere underfoot. She rued the
fact that she had no botany book at hand to help her make
proper identifications, but she had counted more than fifty
varieties right around her cabin. She and her grandchildren
were delighted by the profusion of beauty that greeted them
every morning. "'Fower! Fower! Gramma,'" cries the little

two year old, his chubby little hands full of yellow, blue, red, pink, and purple beauties."

In California she found the climate was, for once, as mild as advertised. It agreed with her, and her health and stamina improved. She marveled at the warm days and chilly evenings and enjoyed keeping windows open day and night to let the fresh breezes flow through. Winter as she had known it in Vermont and Kansas was nonexistent in California. "The ground has never frozen excepting two or three nights in February, just to stiffen a half inch of the bare surface," she said, adding, "Grass and flowers took no note of the fact."

She soon learned that the much drier climate created essential differences between Kansas and California that she hadn't counted on. The growing season for hay and small grains was longer in this Western land; nothing molded indoors or out; the thunder-and-lightning storms so characteristic of life in the middle of the country were all but unknown in the valleys of northern California. Wildlife lived in the wooded areas and scampered across the fields and upland meadows. George brought down thirteen squirrels with his shotgun one rainy afternoon. He furnished their table with a steady supply of venison, hare "the size of jack rabbits in Kansas," and quail. Between what George could hunt and trap and his mother could pick, grow, and preserve, they knew they would never go hungry.

For a continuous source of cash, Clarina turned to something she was familiar with from her Kansas days. "Poultry raising is one of the most, and excepting sheep at present prices, the most profitable investment of farm labor," she observed. In a few months she had her own business up and running and was selling both chickens and eggs to buyers who came directly to her door. Six months later she was enlarging the business, getting dry sheds and shelters built for setting and hatching eggs in the coming winter months. "The grand old Oak just outside the yard, with its gnarled, horizontal branches, is the most healthy roost for the grown poultry, and a splendid orchestra for the crowing choir," she told the *Gazette*.

She liked hearing the chickens in the morning, for her new home in California, far from any city of size, was almost preternaturally quiet in the evenings. The climate was too dry for the insect sounds that she had grown accustomed to hearing in the Kansas evenings. "I miss the cheerful hum of the mosquito [sic], the brusque good evening of countless moths and bugs around my evening lamp, and the song of the Katydid, in gay concert with myriads of evening vocalists," she wrote, making herself one of the few early pioneers to express affection for mosquitoes and other biting insects. "Frog concerts ceased when the creek went dry; pasture fences dispense with cowbells and the railroad has not arrived at the crossing when you 'look out for the engine when the bell rings.' Primitive silence reigns supreme."

That silence was intensified by grief when Mary Warpole Nichols, age twenty-four, died a year after the family arrived in California. The change in climate had not been enough to save her. Mary left three small children for George and Clarina to raise: Birney, a two-year-old boy prone to bouts of ill health, and his two older sisters, Helen and Katie, ages four and six.

At this point there is a three-year gap in references to Clarina Nichols's personal life. The hard work of making a living, caring for home and garden, and looking after three little ones undoubtedly consumed her time and energy. Words were unnecessary to convey to George how well she understood their situation. She had gone through a similar bereavement shortly after emigrating to a new and foreign land, but her children had been older at the time. There was no way that she would have abandoned her son in his hour of need. She confided to Susan B. Anthony later that she had received an offer of marriage during these years (the suitor was a "tender love from life-long acquaintance"), but had turned it down because of her responsibilities to George's children and her fear that marriage would interfere with any small amount of time left over that she might devote to the women's rights cause.

TWENTY

'The Heart of a Loving Woman'

Throughout 1876 the United States held a joyous celebration of its centennial. Parties, parades, and a World's Fair in Philadelphia commemorated one hundred years since the signing of the Declaration of Independence, proclaiming the country free from outside oppressors. The new republic had survived a revolutionary war and a civil war. Independence — its once-impudent act of defiance — was now an established fact.

Many in the women's movement, however, saw little reason to celebrate. In 1776 Abigail Adams had declared, "We will not hold ourselves bound to obey laws in which we have no voice or representation." Brave words indeed; but a century later one half of the United States's citizens still had no political rights.

A gala celebration was planned in Philadelphia to commemorate the nation's first Fourth of July. The women who had been working for thirty years to secure rights for their gender decided to seize the moment. At their May meeting, the National Woman Suffrage Association drafted a "declaration of rights of the women of the United States, and articles of impeachment against the government." Susan B. Anthony wrote to the head of the centennial commission, asking to be seated at the ceremony and to be allowed to present their declaration.

She was told that "only officials were invited" to the event, and furthermore that this was not the time and place for a protest, even one that took less than a minute's time. Besides, the program had already been printed. Undeterred, Anthony secured a press pass through her brother Daniel, editor of *The Leavenworth Times* in Kansas. Four other women managed to gain entry as well. When the day came, they took their places in the meeting hall. As one speaker finished an eloquent rendering of the Declaration of Independence, the women rose from their seats on cue and began making their way toward the stage.

Unsure how to respond, the military guards, civil officials, and foreign guests who were flanking the speaker's stand gallantly let the women pass. Anthony approached the flabbergasted speaker and presented him with their declaration, which was "signed by the oldest and most prominent advocates of women's enfranchisement," thirty-one signatures in all, among them Anthony, Lucretia Mott, Elizabeth Cady Stanton, Paulina Wright Davis, Ernestine Rose — and Mrs. C. I. H. Nichols. Although she was in California, 3,000 miles away, she had somehow managed to sign the declaration.

As the officer in charge pounded on his podium and futilely called for order, Anthony and her cohorts fanned out across the room, handing out copies of the declaration to the invited guests. "On every side eager hands were stretched," the *History of Woman Suffrage* recorded. Some men even "stood on seats and called for copies." It was a Pyrrhic victory for the women, but offered a moment of juicy satisfaction during a long dry spell in the march toward suffrage.

Back in California, Clarina Nichols was undertaking new domestic responsibilities more suited to someone half her age while struggling to stay connected to the larger cause that had given her life its central defining purpose.

Each year, she composed a long, carefully crafted letter to the annual meeting of the National Woman Suffrage Association. For the *Pacific Rural Press*, published in San Francisco, she wrote about women's rights, prison reform, immigration, and national politics. "I believe my interest in the progress of affairs all over the world keeps me alive," she wrote to a friend in Kansas.

One of her favorite targets was the clergy, the group she had identified as having the most obstructionist stance against women's rights. In response to the question posed in the *Woman's Journal* in 1877, "Shall Women Preach?" she wrote the following:

> Yes, they must preach, and preach they will....From the beginning our pulpits, more especially those of the Orthodox sects, have taught and fostered a despotic relation of the sexes. Man to rule; Woman to be ruled. In the marriage relation, he with the powers of a despot, she with no rights and the obligations of a slave. Her person, her conscience, her children, his to control; the very bread she earns to keep starvation at bay, his to convert into liquid fire! – in all but the name and power to sell – a relation the counterpart of negro slavery, and defended from the same theological platform. During my thirty years of earnest labor, at home and abroad, by lecture and pen, and in social converse, I have found the clergy, with noble and multiplying exceptions I am

glad to admit, opposing our demand both for legal and political equality, as being antiscriptural and infidel.

She continued:

> Do I charge them falsely? Their Bible commentaries, their periodicals, their theological schools bear witness. The clergy themselves bear willing testimony in the pulpit, in conference, and on the lecture platform; with notable exceptions, they stigmatize us as 'unsexed women,' 'Amazons,' 'the self-willed women of the period,' etc. Yet two-thirds, at least, of the women prominent in the movement for legal and political equality are or have been, members of Christian churches, in the Church or out of it, holding fast to the teachings of the Saviour as the Magna Charta of their freedom and of human rights.

"An Old Friend Returns," read the headline of the *Pacific Rural Press* on May 8, 1880. Nichols had not appeared in its pages in more than a year, and the editors welcomed her back with pleasure. To the readers of the *Press*, she attributed her extended absence to illness. She wrote that "a brief exposure to the cold wind" on New Year's Eve 1878 had triggered a painful bout of rheumatism, and that she spent much of her time in "utter prostration." What she did not mention was that her household had been shaken by the loss of another family member, her seven-year-old grandson Birney, who died after a long illness.

Her ailments continued to mount during the last years of her life: bronchitis, a kidney disorder that she treated by applying hot rags; "nervous rheumatism"; and a pain in her spine that was so sharp it made any travel an ordeal.

"I am still confined to bed and lounge-chair," she wrote,

"with little hope — my 70 years being against me — of regaining power to return to the pleasant occupations of the garden, the orchard and the noisy farmyard." Yet she had no intention of remaining idle "while head and heart respond intelligently to the demands of practical life." The census that year did not report Nichols as an invalid, a housekeeper, or retired, as might be expected, but rather as a "teacher and correspondent." Since she could no longer go out into the world, her students came to her, and with the aid of the laptop desk her parents had given her as a child, she continued to write from bed.

> The compensations — for I would rather have you rejoice than grieve with me — are nights of sweet, unbroken sleep; an unvarying appetite for plain, wholesome food; books and papers to read; worn garments to repair; sewing and housework to suggest and direct; and sandwiched between, the manifold duties of teacher of 'mother tongue,' homely arts and sciences and general literature to students on foot.

She also home-schooled her two granddaughters, who had taken over performing the daily household chores now that she was no longer able to do them. She enjoyed the stimulation of teaching, free from the confinements of a schoolroom and a set curriculum:

> I know too well the doubt and anxiety that harass the educator who, under the pressure of necessity must grade, survey, and run the enginery of a side track in education. But the world furnishes too many examples of self-educated men and women for vague doubts to shake the faith or damp the courage of mother or child when pledged to the pursuit, even though the instruction must be fragmentary, and given and received over the steam of the wash-tub, the bread-kneading, or the click click of the sewing machine.

In 1880 the women who had organized the first National Woman's Rights Convention in Worcester, Massachusetts, celebrated their thirtieth anniversary. Even if her health had been excellent, Nichols could not have spared the funds or the time to make such a long, expensive trip across the country. She had finally sold her farm in Kansas, but at only half of its value.

Writing from home, probably in the bed that had been set up for her in the big room with the fireplace, she sent a message which was read aloud at the convention. In her mind's eye she returned to that life-changing women's gathering. From Brattleboro she had journeyed to Worcester not knowing what to expect. She had left with a head full of new ideas and a note-pad covered with the addresses of new friends. Together they had hammered out a set of resolutions and aligned their cause with the fight against slavery. It was at Worcester in 1851 that she had discovered her voice and had begun to use it.

In thirty years the movement had grown into a truly national organization, with chapters and local affiliates in most states. The movement was still divided into the National and American factions that formed after the 1867 Kansas debacle — and would not reunite until 1890 — but Nichols took the long view. Differences in philosophy and strategy were inevitable in any great movement. What mattered was the common goal, the attainment of suffrage. It had assumed the place of the Holy Grail in the women's rights movement and become the focus of all their efforts. Nichols knew that she would never see the day of universal suffrage, and she was at peace with that. In her letter to the 1880 Worcester Convention she made a prophecy that would be fulfilled in a way she could not have anticipated:

> The leaders in the Suffrage Movement may all die — two to one will spring from the ranks to bear aloft the glorious banner of a free womanhood. Differences as

to ways and means will now and then, as in all human associations, agitate the surface of affairs, but the deep underlying love of humanity for humanity's sake, which is the life and sinew of our cause, will restore the disturbed equilibrium.

By this point Anthony, Stanton, and Matilda Joslyn Gage were writing their epic account of the women's movement. The first volume of the *History of Woman Suffrage* was published in 1881. Nichols happily submitted her reminiscences and felt honored that she was to be featured in a chapter devoted to her life's work. She did fuss, however, over the picture that accompanied her chapter. She felt it showed a "wooden" face instead of the "motherly" image that she wanted people to remember. Unfortunately, the photograph of herself that she liked best — one that showed her with knitting in hand — has disappeared, as has much of the documentation for her life. In her final years she began to regret that she had never kept a diary or written the story of her life. She wanted to be remembered, and she was acutely aware that those who do not write history are likely to be forgotten by it. She also realized, too late, the legacy she could have endowed to those who knew and loved her: "What a book I might have given to my dear children, relatives and personal friends," she wrote in 1880.

In the sunset years of her life Nichols began thinking of her legacy, of what she had done and what had been left undone. She was trying to tie up loose ends. In 1881 she wrote to Abby Hemenway, a Vermont historian who had written to her twenty-seven years earlier, asking her to contribute to a volume on Vermont authors. In a lengthy reply that is amusing for its sincerity, Nichols wrote, "Your request found me anxious and overburdened in preparations for the removal of myself and family to Kansas." After apologizing and explaining why she had never replied to the request — a busy life and "the old haunting fear of seeming to seek publicity" — she asked

The undated photograph (top) that served as the
model for the steel engraving (inset) accompanying
Clarina Nichols's chapter in the *History of Woman
Suffrage*, published in 1881. *(Photo courtesy Grace
Hudson Museum, Ukiah, California)*

if it was too late to contribute something. Enclosed with her
letter were materials on her early work in Vermont that she
thought Hemenway might find interesting. She responded to
another request from the Wyandotte *Gazette* with three lengthy
articles of recollections from her pioneer years in Kansas.

To Anthony she expressed a desire to "map out my plan of
work for humanity," but that ambition was never fully realized. In the fall of 1881 the *Woman's Herald of Industry* in San
Francisco published her article, "Christian Civil Government,"
in two installments. Abstract doctrines like predestination

and vicarious atonement were "beyond my comprehension,"
she wrote. Christianity could be boiled down to one central
and essential tenet: the Golden Rule. Thus, when Nichols put
together the words *Christian* and *Government*, she was not en-
dorsing theocracy but a codifying of fairness and benevolence that
she saw as religion's most important contribution to society:

> A Christian government simply makes this regard for
> individual rights a matter of individual obligation, in
> order that any not disposed to act justly may be coerced
> into good citizenship and restrained from abusing their
> power to do wrong. The two great reforms that had
> begun in antebellum America — freedom for slaves and
> equal rights for women — started with individual acts
> of Golden Rule conscience.

In this way, she argued,

> through revolution and reconstruction, the grand
> ultimate of Christian civilization is coming to us in a
> Christian government…a government which recognizes
> Christ's teachings of love and duty as practical rules and
> not abstract principles to be admired in theory….Again,
> the germs of progress are with the individual, and while
> a nation seems to stand still under the shadow of some
> great wrong, in the soul of a Garrison, or the heart of a
> loving woman, the fires are lighted.

For Nichols that understanding explained why progress was
so maddeningly slow — why it had taken decades to convince
the public of the evils of slavery and why it was taking even
longer to change opinion on woman suffrage. Truth needed
to stir one soul, and then another, until it began to "permeate
the masses," challenging conventional wisdom, overcoming

prejudices, and winning popular support before it could be written into law.

"With only the right of petition, free speech, and pen," she observed, women had made great strides. "Who can doubt what would have been the influence of women in the past, or what it will be in the future as a political element in the government of State?"

Women needed to have their legal and political rights acknowledged because they were citizens, taxpayers, and above all, human beings. Nichols believed that women were destined to play a saving role in the world. A woman who had given birth or raised a child felt a special connection to the future, a link to the world, and an obligation to protect and nurture life. In "The first Baby," which appeared in the *Windham County Democrat* and was later reprinted in the Quindaro *Chindowan*, she wrote as follows:

> To a mother's heart, every mother's baby is the representation of inestimable treasure; is an estate held 'in fee simple'; a little subsoiler that leaves no affections fallow, no sympathies isolated from the claims of a common humanity....That baby is the medium through which the helplessness, the wants and the promise of humanity have appealed to the *woman*. In behalf of the race it has whispered *mother*, and looking into its trusting, worshiping eyes, she accepts the consecration, answers the appeal with a deep, an eternity-echo'd — my *child*!

Once again, Nichols used a conventional ideal — motherhood — as a bridge to a broader plane. Those who wanted to maintain the status quo used motherhood as the supreme justification for keeping women out of the public sphere. Her response — which could only be effective coming from a woman with an untarnished record for protecting motherhood — was that because mother-love was so pure, self-sacrificing, forgiving, creative, beautiful, powerful, noble, and wise, it must be transfused *into the public realm*. Motherhood made women's participation in public affairs not only desirable but imperative.

What she did not anticipate was that suffrage itself would be merely another beginning, that the way the world conducted its business would be relatively unaffected by women gaining the vote — at least in the short run.

———

As she was nearing the end of her life, Nichols put together a final puzzle. Over the years she had suffered from bronchial ailments and a "depression of vitality," in certain situations. "I put this and that together, or rather, this and that came together with a rush of recognition," when she realized what the common denominator had been: second-hand smoke. She recalled that in all-female assemblies she was unaffected, for no well-bred female smoked in public. But men puffed on tobacco everywhere — in public buildings, in their homes, in closed carriages, even inside churches.

In an article for the *Pacific Rural Press*, titled "The Tobacco fiend," she wrote, "I was often faint in a crowded assembly, and to my great mortification, had to leave church, even in cool weather if windows and doors were closed." Then, this lifelong temperance supporter made a bold claim: "I am satisfied from observation and experience that tobacco is more destructive to health than alcohol." She warned "all who value God's breath of life" to stay away from both smoking and second-hand smoke. The article appeared, appropriately, as Nichols took to bed with her final bout of bronchitis.

Her friends and the California half of her family gathered at her side. She had supported her family and maintained bonds of connection, in good times and bad, while continuing her life work. Relie later reported that his mother's mind was clear to her final hour. Four days before she died, she wrote one last letter to an old friend and comrade-in-arms. Later that month it was read at the annual convention of the National Woman Suffrage Association in Washington, D.C.

"Dear Susan," it began, and continued:

> I am very sick of acute bronchitis. I am not utterly hope-less of rallying for a few weeks or months longer, but my friends think I have little expectation of many days. My last words in your (our) good work for humanity through its author is, 'God is with us – there can be no failure and no defeat outside ourselves that will not roll up the floodwood and rush away every obstruction. 'Farewell! Farewell!' if forever (but I have hope yet). Remember my granddaughters when I am gone and don't forget my loved ones.

Clarina I. H. Nichols died peacefully on January 11, 1885. She was buried alongside her daughter-in-law Mary and grandson Birney in Potter Valley, California, surrounded by fields, vineyards, upland meadows, and a ring of gently slop-ing mountains.

Epilogue

*"The leaders in the Suffrage Movement
may all die – two to one will spring from
the ranks...."*

Clarina Nichols's declaration to the 1880 Worcester Convention proved, in her own case, to be remarkably prescient. On the very day that she died — January 11, 1885 — Alice Paul was born into a Quaker family in New Jersey. Beginning in 1913, a radical wing of the suffrage movement emerged under Paul's leadership. The women staged parades, protests, and hunger strikes that propelled suffrage to the front page of newspapers across the country and ultimately forced Woodrow Wilson to support suffrage. The Nineteenth Amendment to the United States Constitution was passed in 1920, giving women at long last the right to vote.

Susan B. Anthony did not forget her old friend or the family.

She wrote to George Bainbridge Nichols, visited Relie Carpenter's family in Ukiah, California, and was a witness at Clarina's granddaughter's wedding in San Rafael, California.

Birsha Carpenter Davis spent the rest of her life in Vermont. Howard Carpenter stayed in Kansas, and Relie Carpenter and George Nichols remained in California. Clarina Nichols's best-known descendant was Grace Carpenter Hudson, Relie and Helen's daughter. Her home and the adjacent Grace Hudson Museum in Ukiah, California, have become a cultural

Hudson

center for art and artifacts related to the West and the Pomo Indians, of whom Grace Hudson became a well-regarded painter. The museum also houses the only permanent exhibit devoted to Nichols. Her laptop writing desk is on display, as is the brooch woven from her fathers's and second husband's locks of hair, and other effects: family china brought from England, a beaded purse, textiles, her still-life painting, and an ivory carved jewelry box that, according to family legend, was given to her by Mary Todd Lincoln in appreciation of Nichols's service to the Georgetown home after the Civil War.

After her death, the Wyandotte County Women's Club commissioned the Kansas artist George Stone to paint a portrait of Clarina Nichols. It was displayed in the Kansas Pavilion at the 1893 Columbian Exposition in Chicago. The painting was later presented to the Carnegie Library in Kansas City, Kansas, but after a fire it was taken down and has never been recovered.

Today, Nichols's home town and state are beginning to pay tribute to her life and achievements. Roadside markers were commissioned by the Vermont Division for Historic Preservation for Nichols and her cousin Alphonso Taft, the father of William Howard Taft. Originally, the placards were to be placed on the grounds of the church that Nichols and Taft attended, a classic white building with the date *1817* clearly visible at the base of its steeple. Church officials agreed to place Taft's placard on their property — but declined to accept Nichols's. Both historical markers are now permanently positioned just off church property, side by side, facing Route 30.

Perhaps the most fitting tribute, however, is a living one: the Clarina Howard Nichols Center in Morrisville, Vermont. This is a shelter for victims of domestic abuse and rape. She would have been honored to have her name associated with such a sanctuary, though also saddened to know that domestic abuse and violence against women are still enormous problems in this country and almost everywhere in the world. She would have been surprised at how far we have come — and how far we have yet to go.

Taft

The stories of the early women's rights movement have faded from memory. Today few people know more than the name of Susan B. Anthony. History textbooks often overlook the Worcester conventions and all the women of the antebellum women's movement except Anthony and Elizabeth Cady Stanton — but they almost always include a cartoon of a woman wearing bloomers in the 1850s.

Others, including the pioneers mentioned in this book, remain largely unknown outside the circle of women's studies scholars. Frances Wright. Angelina and Sarah Grimké. Lucretia Mott. Jane Swisshelm. Lucy Stone. Ernestine Rose.

Sojourner Truth. Antoinette Brown Blackwell. Paulina Wright Davis. Abby Kelley Foster. Frances Dana Gage and Matilda Joslyn Gage. These women were as important to the future of this country and to liberty as the Founding Fathers of the eighteenth century or the Civil War generals of the nineteenth. They did not fight their revolution on battlefields but in the hearts and minds of citizens of both sexes. They challenged ancient laws and customs that seemed as impenetrable as Vermont granite.

When the movement started in the years before the Civil War, few thought that women were men's intellectual equals. Even fewer believed females needed the same rights and opportunities as males. The concept of co-sovereignty seemed ludicrous — as it still does in some circles today. Despite backlash and retrenchment, dramatic and subtle shifts have occurred in every institution in American society from the law, education, and medicine to religion, the family, and male-female relationships.

The movement to win equal rights for women began long before the twentieth century, and those who were there at its founding deserve to be remembered today. Clarina I. H. Nichols was one of them. As she followed the western expansion of the United States, she helped spread the idea that all people are created equal. That no one has the right to bully another. That all citizens have the right to vote and be treated fairly. That everyone has the right to go as far in life as her dreams, talent, and hard work will take her. And that together, men and women can make the world better, if they will.

Acknowledgments

I will always be grateful to three people, all since deceased, who began gathering Clarina Nichols's scattered writings in the 1960s and 1970s: Patricia Rabinovitz, a great-great-granddaughter of Nichols; Vermont historian T. D. Seymour Bassett; and, most of all, Joseph G. Gambone, who collected, footnoted, and published the eight-part series, "The Forgotten Feminist of Kansas: The Papers of Clarina I. H. Nichols, 1854–1885," in the *Kansas Historical Quarterly*. This collection remains the starting point for anyone seriously interested in her life work. Mona Gambone told me her husband was so preoccupied with Nichols that she began calling her "the other woman." I am only sorry that none of these individuals will be able to read the biography they helped make possible.

A chance conversation introduced me to Clarina Nichols in the summer of 1999. At the Wyandotte County Museum in Bonner Springs, Kansas, archivist John Nichols (no rela-tion) shared enough stories about one of the state's leading female pioneers to pique my interest. As it happened, a local professor named Steve Collins was in the museum that same day looking through issues of the Quindaro *Chindowan* — the newspaper Nichols briefly edited in 1857. Steve took me to the ruins of Quindaro in Kansas City, Kansas. That trip through the tangled woods to see what remained of stone foundations from the 1850s helped me appreciate what it took to carve a town out of such a hilly, rocky, inhospitable site. Nichols's story interested me from the start, but the trip into the Quin-daro ruins touched something deeper.

My initial plan was to spend a year or two researching and writing a young adult biography of Nichols, thereby making my modest contribution to this underserved genre. The result was an audiobook, *Frontier Freedom Fighter*, which is being released concurrently with this book. But then the Clarina Nichols story took on a life of its own.

In early 2002, the Kansas Humanities Council announced it would observe the 150th anniversary of the opening of Kansas Territory with a chautauqua — a traveling history festival fea-turing first-person characterizations of historical figures. One of the six subjects selected was Clarina Nichols. I auditioned for the role and in 2004 began touring Kansas with a newly scripted monologue, comprised mostly from Nichols's own words. While on the chautauqua circuit, I was continually approached by people who wondered why they'd never heard about Nichols before and wanted to learn more.

Early in my research I had met Marilyn Schultz Blackwell, a Vermont historian who had been studying Nichols's politics and her life in the East. Our approach to the material is quite different, as Lyn is writing for an academic audience and I am writing for a general one. Nonetheless, sharing research, questions, and insights has been invaluable.

"It's nice to know that someone outside the family feels that Clarina was slighted when it came to recognition for a life of work for important issues of the time," wrote Juanita Johnson, another of Nichols's great-great-granddaughters, after I located her in Florida. She has been very helpful in sharing the Union army records of Howard Carpenter, as well as memorabilia that was passed down from Nichols to her descendants. Juanita's daughter, Janice Parker, generously allowed me to reproduce an original image of Nichols and to wear the 170-year-old brooch (seen on the cover of this book) for my final performance of the 2004 Kansas Chautauqua.

In California, the extraordinary Karen Holmes at the Grace Hudson Museum in Ukiah has helped us at every turn. It was she who encouraged me to come and see Nichols's grave in Potter Valley and to look over the rich store of artifacts that have found their way into the museum. During my trips to California in 1999 and 2005, Karen went beyond the call of duty to help me. On the other end of the country, Tiz Garfield and Tom and Joan Lyman provided hospitality and supported my research efforts in Windham County, Vermont, when I visited in 2000 and 2004, and I have cheered their efforts to gain recognition for Townshend's most distinguished daughter.

I am grateful to the Kansas State Historical Society in Topeka for their extraordinary collection on territorial Kansas, including a vast collection of early newspapers, an extensive collection of Nichols's writings, and a fine online resource; the Vermont Historical Society in Montpelier; Mary Jo Gigliotti and the Drake Memorial Library at SUNY-Brockport, for additional information on the elusive Justin Carpenter and for copies of the *Brockport Free Press*; the American Antiquarian Society for copies of the *Windham County Democrat*; Karen Board Moran and the Worcester Women's History Project;

KanColl, an online resource for materials on territorial Kansas; the Missouri Room of the Kansas City, Missouri, Public Library, and the University of Kansas libraries; David Boutros of the Western Historical Manuscript Collection at the University of Missouri-Kansas City, for help in locating images of early Kansas; the Newberry Library in Chicago; the New York Historical Society; and the San Francisco Public Library, where I was delighted to find bound copies of the *Pacific Rural Press* (print is preferable to micro-anything).

Thanks also to people who dug through their files when I needed it. Tim Rues of the Kansas State Historical Society not only took time to explain territorial politics, he introduced me to Howard Duncan and the Lecompton Reenactors and issued the earliest invitations for me to speak about Clarina Nichols. Ola May Earnest of the Linn County Historical Museum provided information on the Wattles family and the Moneka Women's Rights Association. Patrick Sumner lent me his expertise on the Wyandotte Constitutional Convention. Thomas St. John uncovered some useful nuggets about Nichols's early career in Vermont. Barbara Brackman not only supplied information on Lois Bryan Adams but also graciously loaned me her beautiful Civil War-era dress for my performances. John McClymer of Assumption College provided insights on the Worcester conventions. Adrienne E. Christiansen of Macalester College had great thoughts on Nichols's rhetoric. Bob and Bette Fairbairn took me to the Potter Valley cemetery. A friend, Ric Hudgens, finally put an end to the ongoing game of Name That Book by suggesting *Revolutionary Heart*.

One summer day, early on in this project, we were in Lane, Kansas, looking for Pottawatomie Creek, when we found five boys swimming and fishing in the creek. It seemed so incongruous — this bucolic scene of carefree boys near a place that had once been the scene of grotesque nighttime mayhem by

John Brown and company. The boys asked me to put their names in my book, and I told them I would, so here they are: Josh Needham, Fred Gleason, Billy Bowers, Tyler Mohr, and Erik White, all from Osawatomie.

The following individuals also read drafts and provided valuable feedback: Marilyn Schultz Blackwell, Craig Miner, Kendall Taylor, Sheri Steinberg, Julia Pferdehirt, Lauren Gleason, Jason Mangal, Diane Bourgeois, Marion Cott, Richard Johnson, Barbara Watkins, and Muriel T. Stackley. Special thanks to Linda Williams, who provided great encouragement for the project and many helpful editorial queries and suggestions. I am grateful to them all for finding oversights and errors that I missed. Responsibility for the text in its final form is, however, solely mine.

Thanks to my family — Edward and Anne, Myrna and Carol — for reading my book, telling me it was wonderful, and refraining from asking the dreaded question: "Is it done yet?"

Most of all, thanks to Aaron Barnhart, my husband and life partner. Deciding to write a historical biography after being diagnosed as legally blind was an outrageous move on my part, but he has supported me every step of the way. I was fortunate to regain some reading vision in one eye, but Aaron has spent who-knows-how many hours driving me from one end of the country to the other to visit the places Nichols lived; reading microfilm that would have given me migraines; and helping me decipher page upon page of faded handwriting. Without him, I couldn't have begun — much less finished — this project. He has urged me on when my own courage flagged, and has put up with this project for more time than either one of us imagined it would take.

In this 1792 engraving, Lady Liberty is presented with a copy of Mary Wollstonecraft's book *Vindication of the Rights of Woman*. (*Library of Congress, Rare Book and Special Collections Division*)

Appendix A
The Antebellum Women's Rights Movement

The roots of the antebellum women's rights movement can be traced to the Revolutionary War (1775–81). The founding fathers claimed that certain "truths" were "self-evident" and that "all men" were political equals. "All men" originally included only a small class of property-owning white men, but other men — and women — soon began trying to expand the definition to include all men, all races, and both sexes. ABIGAIL ADAMS (1744–1818) had instructed her husband to "remember the ladies" as he and other delegates were writing the Declaration of Independence (1776). They had not.

Adams

In England MARY WOLLSTONECRAFT (1759–97) published *A Vindication on the Rights of Woman* (1792) in response to Thomas Paine's bestseller, *The Rights of Man* (1791), at the height of the French Revolution. Wollstonecraft's book, which assessed women's current status and the changes she envisioned, influenced all of the pioneers in the movement that followed. LUCRETIA MOTT (1793–1880), a Quaker minister born the year

Wright

after *Rights of Woman* was published, read the slim volume until its pages were as worn as those in her Bible. Mott criticized members of the clergy who taught female submission as God's will. FRANCES WRIGHT (1795–1852), an emigré from Scotland who had no time for organized religion, spoke out publicly on controversial subjects such as race, sex, religion, and birth control. She shocked her U.S. audiences but won admiration from the early women's rights leaders. Ten years later, the GRIMKÉ sisters, SARAH (1792–1873) and ANGELINA (1805–79), renounced their Southern, slaveowning roots and took to the Northern abolitionist lecture circuit. Sarah Grimké had the audacity to compare the legal and political status of married women to that of slaves. In 1845 MARGARET FULLER (1810-50) published *Woman in the Nineteenth Century*, an instant classic that laid out many of the intellectual arguments for woman's

emancipation. By this time individuals in several states had begun working to change laws that automatically divested women of their property upon marriage. ERNESTINE ROSE (1810–92) traversed New York state for a dozen years, collecting petitions for a married women's property rights bill which was finally passed in 1848.

Rose

A year earlier, CLARINA NICHOLS (1810–85) helped secure a modest married women's property rights law in Vermont. Nichols maintained a more moderate tone than some of the early advocates of women's rights but became more radical in later years. Nichols's first forays into the public arena were for temperance. In 1826 the first American temperance society was founded. It was dedicated to reform through cutting alcohol consumption. The movement drew massive support from both conservative clergy and radical reformers. Though agreed on the harmful effects of alcohol, the temperance allies did not agree

on other social reforms such as abolition and women's rights (the conservative ministers opposed both). Ultimately, the movement split over the issue of women's equal participation.

In the early 1830s large numbers of people also began joining forces to confront the evil of slavery. WILLIAM LLOYD GARRISON (1805–79), founder of the American Anti-Slavery Society in Boston in 1833, began allowing women full

Garrison

participation in his organization; ABBY KELLEY FOSTER (1810–87) and others began speaking for the organization. Garrison's egalitarian gesture met with disapproval from members who failed to vote him out of his own organization and later broke away to form the American and Foreign Anti-Slavery Society in 1840.

Another great leveling force was journalism. In the mid-19th century newspapers were abundant, cheap, and Americans' main

Bloomer

source of national and world news and opinion. Nichols began editing the *Windham County Democrat* around 1843. In another decade, the number of women editing reform newspapers included AMELIA BLOOMER (1818–94) of *The Lily*, JANE SWISSHELM (1815–84) of *The Visiter*, and PAULINA WRIGHT DAVIS (1813–76) of *The Una*. Alliances were formed between the movement and progressive newspapermen like Garrison of *The Liberator* and HORACE GREELEY

(1811–72) of the *New York Tribune*. Combined with their work in the temperance and antislavery movements, public speaking, petition drives, and the publication of sympathetic books and tracts, women found numerous ways to educate themselves and others regarding the issues that animated them.

By the late 1840s there was widespread curiosity and interest in the subject of women's rights in various enclaves of New England, New York, Ohio, and other Northern states. In 1848 Mott, ELIZABETH CADY STANTON (1815–1902), and three other women convened a two-day meeting in Seneca Falls, New York, on women's rights. Though the meeting was called hastily — the organizers had two weeks to publicize it — about 300 were present when Stanton read her "Declaration of Sentiments," a watershed manifesto that listed women's grievances and demands. FREDERICK DOUGLASS (1817–95), the ex-slave turned editor and abolitionist, helped

Stanton

pass the most controversial measure at the convention — woman suffrage. By contrast, a resolution declaring "that woman is man's equal — was intended to be so by the Creator" passed easily.

In 1850 Davis and others called for the First National Woman's Rights Convention in Worcester, Massachusetts. This meeting proved that the new movement was not a re-gional oddity or a passing concern. Letters of encouragement were received from as far away as England and France. The only pall cast over the convention was the absence of Fuller, who was expected to play a leading role at the convention but had drowned at sea on her way back to New York from Europe. SOJOURNER TRUTH (c. 1797–1883), an abolitionist and former slave, spoke at the convention, as did

Truth

Douglass. Their early support for women's rights helped link the women's and antislavery causes. That same year, the Fugitive Slave Law passed Congress, which made it a crime not only to help runaways but also to refuse to aid their capturers. Women were quick to see a parallel: sheltering or helping a woman fleeing from a drunken or abusive husband was also a crime punishable by fine or imprisonment. During the 1850s and until the outbreak of the Civil War (1861–65), large women's rights conventions were held across the North. Men as well as women were involved. Women's rights study groups formed in small towns and prairie outposts.

Anthony

In 1851 SUSAN B. ANTHONY (1820–1906) entered and quickly became a leader in the emerging women's rights movement. She had been actively involved in both the temperance and antislavery causes. Women addressed constitutional conventions in several states. Legislatures began passing married women's property rights laws. In 1859, due largely to Nichols's influence, the assembly that would produce the Kansas state constitution voted to include property, custody, and educational rights for women. Kansas also permitted women to vote in school district elections.

The following year, Anthony and Stanton were successful in pressuring New York to pass a comprehensive Married Women's Property Bill.

In the face of enormous social disapproval and resistance, women in the antebellum women's movement relied on ties of kinship and friendship to support and sustain them. Besides the Grimké sisters, a remarkable trio of sisters-in-law were ELIZABETH BLACKWELL (1821–1910), the first female doctor in the U.S.; ANTOI-NETTE BROWN BLACKWELL (1825–1921), the first woman ordained by a mainline Protestant Church; and LUCY STONE (1818–93), a powerful speaker in several reform movements. Lucretia Mott's sister, MARTHA COFFIN WRIGHT (1806–75), was active in the movement. Anthony had a sisterly relationship with Stanton that was extraordinarily strong and productive. And many daughters and nieces, including Stanton's, Anthony's, and Stone's, carried on the work when their mothers or aunts died.

A. Blackwell

Stone

During the Civil War, women willingly set aside their campaign for rights in order to help the Union. Stanton and Anthony collected 400,000 signatures for the Woman's Loyal League, which called for the immediate emancipation of slaves. Many, like Nichols, worked in war-related jobs and helped settle and educate former slaves. At war's end the women took up their cause once more. However, their former male allies had abandoned them, as Garrison, Douglass, Greeley and others focused on obtaining suffrage for black men. A universal suffrage campaign in Kansas in 1867 failed to bring the vote to either blacks or women. The Fifteenth Amendment to the Constitution, ratified in 1870, gave suffrage to black men but not women. Divided and disillusioned over the amendment, the

women's rights leaders — who had seen two
reform movements divide over gender — saw
their own movement divide over race. Women
who supported the Fifteenth Amendment and
the Republican Party formed the American
Woman Suffrage Association, while those
opposed joined Anthony and Stanton in their
new National Woman Suffrage Association.
These two organizations remained separate
for the next twenty years. With the defeat in

Willard

Kansas, the antebellum women's movement effectively came to an
end. As the nineteenth century slipped away, suffrage emerged as
the overarching goal of the women's rights movement. FRANCES
WILLARD (1839–98) organized the Woman's Christian Temperance
Union in 1874, which called for total prohibition of alcohol and
supported woman suffrage. Thousands of less radical women joined
the suffrage cause because they saw it as the best way to achieve
prohibition. In 1890 the National and American groups reunited.
ALICE PAUL (1885–1977) and LUCY BURNS (1879-1966) organized

Paul

the Congressional Union in 1913. Later known
as the National Women's Party, its members
took part in parades, pickets, hunger strikes
and other attention-getting tactics to publicize
"Votes for Women." Their campaign culmi-
nated in the passage of the Nineteenth Amendment to the Constitution in 1920, ending the
longest-running civil rights campaign in U.S.
history. Victory, however, came at a price:
the antebellum movement's larger agenda of
complete co-sovereignty between men and women was forgotten.
It would not be seriously taken up again until the 1960s.

Appendix B
Preamble and Constitution of the
Moneka Women's Rights Association
(Approved February 13, 1858, Moneka, Kansas)

Because Woman is constituted of body and mind and has all the common wants of the one and the natural powers of the other —

Because she is a social being and has all the relations of life to sustain which belong to an Associated condition of existence — and

Because she is a progressive being ever out-growing the past and demanding a higher and greater Future — or in other words,

Because she is a Human Being and as such is endowed by her Creator with the full measure of human rights whether educational, social or political, and

Because by the present arrangement of the world, she is shut out of colleges and the higher order of educational institutions, thereby deprived of great opportunities for intellectual improvements, shut out from most of the lucrative professions and the mechanic arts, thereby deprived of the facilities for the accumulation of wealth and enjoyment of social life, — made subject to laws which she has no voice in making and which deprive her of the ownership of property and of herself, and give even her daily earnings to the control of others; dragged before courts to answer for crimes, against laws to which she has never given her assent, to be tried as a criminal in Halls where she can neither sit as judge or juror or officiate as counsel; and

Because from the Pulpit and the Rostrum woman is called upon to give character to the rising generation and charged with the responsibility of shaping the destiny of the race,

Because she is demanded to make statesmen to wield the fate of Nations, and divines to wake the world to glory,

We therefore, form ourselves into an Association to be governed by the following Constitution.

Article First —

This association shall be called The Moneka Women's Rights Society.

Article Second —

It shall be the object of the Society to secure to woman her natural rights and to advance her educational interests. In furtherance of these objects the Soc. shall consider what woman's natural rights are, and the means best calculated to secure them. It shall also encourage lectures on this subject in the Society and elsewhere; and give its support to some paper devoted to the elevation of Woman.

Article Third —

The officers of the Society shall be a President, Vice Pres., Secretary, Corresponding Sec. and Treasurer who shall perform the duties usually ascribed to such offices. Officers shall be elected quarterly by ballot, a majority of votes constituting a choice.

Article Fourth —

The regular meetings of the Society shall be held monthly. And other meetings may be held as often as the wishes of the Society require it. At the regular meetings an address shall be given by some member of the society appointed at a previous regular meeting. After which some question previously agreed upon shall be discussed by the members.

Article Fifth —

The first Anniversary shall be on the last Wednesday in Sept. At which time addresses, lectures and discussions on the various subjects connected with the rights of women and of progression in general shall be given.

Article Sixth —

Terms of membership shall be a mutual agreement in the objects of the Society, the signing of the Constitution and paying twenty-five cents into the Treasury.

Article Seventh —

The Constitution may be altered or amended by a vote of two-thirds of the membership present at any regular meeting, notice having been given at a previous regular meeting.

(Signatures)

Elvira Andrews

Esther Wattles

Elizabeth S. Denison

Mollie A. McGrath

Emma Wattles

Pamela Doy

Sarah G. Wattles

Susan E. Wattles

Lima S. H. Ober

Angeline P. Crystal

Rebecca E. Hulbert

Mary P. T. Snyder

Ann Schooley

Hulda A. Goodwin

Matilda L. Gibbons

R. W. Gibbons

Joseph Addis

Permelia C. Knox

Charlotte Smith

Rhoda W. Ransom

George E. Denison

John O. Wattles

Hannah Strong

H. P. Danforth

O. H. Stearns

O. E. Morse

C. E. Shearer

Emma L. Burritt

John C. Anderson

R. A. Frazell

John Morrison

E. L. Taylor

Thomas J. Addis, Jr.

Lyman Strong

Hamilton Schooley

J. S. Craig

Thomas J. Addis, Sr.

Timothy Hulbert

P. Frazell

Charlotte S. Anderson

Aggie Lefker

Hetty Addis

Appendix C
'The Birds'

(This satire appeared in June 1852 in *The Lily*, a temperance and women's rights newspaper edited by Amelia Bloomer. Nichols uses the animal world to ridicule the idea of separate "spheres" for men and women.)

Hark! the robins are singing and building in the maple that shades our windows. And what is it ye are singing? Those sweet, responsive notes — are they domestic ditties? Say now, my pretty robin-pair, is not thine a well assorted marriage, a 'match made in heaven'? Shall we humans look and learn of ye our duty?

Ye build together your tiny home! That's not the way, Mrs. Robin. You should smooth your feathers and sit upon the leafy branch and sing and smile, while Mr. Robin builds; then lay your eggs and hatch the little birdies. O fie, for shame, to think of your compelling Mr. Robin to sit in your place and speed the hatching, while you (how could you so unsex yourself?) are away, flitting in the sunshine and singing in the public.

But worse and worse! Mr. Robin — poor bird-pecked husband! — is actually put to nursing and feeding the young ones! Why don't Mrs. Robin attend to matters in her own sphere, and leave Mr. Robin to hunt worms and watch intruders? She should sit in the nest beside her young ones and open her mouth, like them, for Mr. Robin to drop in the bugs and berries and tender insects — indeed she should!

Fie on you, Mrs. Robin, that you should let your husband stay at home and take care of the little birdies, when you ought to know the peculiarities of sex indicate that it is your business, and the masculine pursuit of flying belongs to the Mr. Birds. To be sure,

God has given you wings, and an appetite and a bill for picking up your living in the fields; but then you are a mother bird and should not use these gifts — it is a shame and a scandal to your sex!

'Mr. Robin thinks it is right,' and you are 'perfectly agreed in your domestic arrangements,' eh? Well, we shall see. The State of Vermont is turning its attention to bird-dog pursuit of happiness. The terms of the conjugal relation are very carefully established by human legislators.

So Mrs. Robin, you may as well stick to your nest, for the bugs and worms and small bits and the straws and mud belong, legally, to Mr. Robin, and he is bound in duty to feed you till he dies or flies away. Now sing and dress your feathers and let him hunt worms. It's dirty, masculine business. And sitting in the trees is so nice and lady like — and you will be an honor to your sex!

Appendix D
Mrs. Nichols v. Rev. Blachly:
An Imagined Debate

After years of work on her "Bible Position of Woman," Clarina Nichols finally published the treatise in 1870 as a six-part series in the *Vermont Phoenix*. It appeared as Lucy Stone was canvassing the state for woman suffrage. As in Kansas three years earlier, Nichols believed that the root of Vermont's resistance to women's rights was a faulty interpretation of Scripture that relegated the female sex to second-class status. If people could see that the heart of the Bible was the Golden Rule, not man's rule, she felt attitudes toward women's rights, roles, and suffrage would change.

One of the most intriguing omissions from Nichols's papers is any first-hand account of her many debates with ministers over the role of women in Christian society. So let us imagine one. On August 17, 1867, the Reverend Eben Blachly, a Presbyterian minister in Quindaro, wrote an editorial in the Wyandotte *Commercial Gazette* denouncing the woman suffrage campaign. Nichols responded with her own editorial, published in two parts on September 28 and October 19, 1867. Using their words, and excerpts from her "Bible Position of Woman" treatise, here is how an exchange between these two might have sounded.

———

"If we stand on the *will* of the Creator, we stand on firm ground, Mrs. Nichols," the Reverend Eben Blachly said, turning to face his hearers seated in the pews of the simple frontier church. "Remember that it was *Eve* who brought sin into the world and she who caused Adam to sin. Therefore, God in his infinite wisdom has given man authority and headship over woman. The Bible does not err."

Standing a few feet off to his right, Clarina Nichols smiled.

"You place great stress, Rev. Blachly, on the fact that Eve was first to transgress — as though to have been last were less a sin! Is it not true that Eve was beguiled by her ignorance of evil and by the promise of good? And that Adam acted against his own conscience?

"Any man of common sense" — she paused for comic effect — "would decide it a very bad precedent indeed to give a *willful* criminal authority over his deceived accomplice!"

The reverend straightened his shoulders and mumbled something under his breath.

"It matters not what *man* may think, nor what sort of human logic you may twist out of the text, Mrs. Nichols. The Bible says, 'Thy desire shall be to thy husband, and he shall rule over thee.'"

"That statement was a *prediction*, not a command," Mrs. Nichols said primly. "If it were a command, it would have been addressed to Adam, not to Eve. God could look down the corridors of the ages and see that men would increasingly use brute strength to subdue women. God's *original* intent, however, was quite different — to create humans who were co-equals in sovereignty and dominion."

Rev. Blachly looked at her in disbelief. "On what do you base this bizarre conclusion, Mrs. Nichols?" he asked.

"On the Bible," she responded. "On the Book of Genesis and other texts therein. Genesis 1:26-28 reads, 'God said, let us make Man in our image, after our likeness, and let *them* have dominion over the fish of the sea, and over the fowl of the air. So God created Man in his own image, in the image of God created he him, — male *and female* created he *them*. And God blessed *them*. And God said to *them*, be fruitful and multiply, and replenish the earth.'

"God's perfect will, Rev. Blachly, is co-sovereignty."

Appendix E
The Family of Clarina I.H. Nichols

Chapin Howard
b. 1785 —— m. 3/13/1809 ——
d. 5/6/1854

Birsha Smith
b. 1784
d. 9/14/1866

Clarina	Mary
Aurelius	Laurinda
Catherine	Ellen
Ormando	Bainbridge

Clarina Irene Howard   first marriage   Justin Carpenter
b. 1/25/1810   ——   4/21/1830   ——   b. 8/15/1800?
d. 1/11/1885   (div. 2/16/1843)   d. 9/1/1844?

1. Birsha Clarina Carpenter
b. 3/8/1831   d. 12/11/1907
m. 6/21/1868
Gen. George Franklin Davis
b. 1816 d. 2/27/1901

2. Chapin Howard Carpenter
b. 8/11/1834 d. 7/17/1914
m. 4/1855
Sarah E. Jones
b. 1832   d. 1882

3. Aurelius Ormando Carpenter (Relie)
b. 11/28/1836 d. 2/8/1919
m. 12/25/1856
Helen M. McCowen
b. 4/22/1838 d. 2/13/1917

Clarina I.H.   second marriage   George
Carpenter ——   3/6/1843   ——   Washington
Nichols
b. 1785
d. 8/31/1855

4. George Bainbridge Nichols
b. 2/17/1844 d. 1/27/1935
m. 12/6/1864
Mary C. Warpole
b. 1849 d. 1873

Personal effects of Clarina Nichols on permanent display at the Grace Hudson Museum in Ukiah, California.
(courtesy Grace Hudson Museum)

Birsha's stepchildren
1. Addie Davis
   b. 2/10/1857   d. 3/31/1930
2. Fannie Davis
   b. 1/28/1860   d. 8/31/1928
3. George Davis
   b. (n/a)   d. (n/a)

C. Howard's children
1. Charles H. Carpenter
   b. 12/19/1856   d. 5/28/1943
2. Irena Birsha Carpenter
   b. 5/30/1858   d. 11/9/1923

A. O.'s children
1. May Carpenter
   b. 3/15/1858   d. 9/22/1939
2. Grace Carpenter Hudson
   b. 2/21/1865   d. 3/23/1937
3. Grant Carpenter
   b. 2/21/1865   d. 4/20/1936
4. Frank Carpenter
   b. 11/8/1870   d. 12/6/1951

George's children
1. Katherine Howard Nichols
   b. 2/24/1867   d. 3/20/1944
2. Helen Clarina Nichols
   b. 1/24/1869   d. 2/13/1952
3. Birney A. Nichols
   b. 1871   d. 1878

Unlike many 19th–century families, premature death did not visit the household of Chapin and Birsha Howard, where Clarina and her seven siblings reached maturity. Clarina's four children lived to the ages of 76, 80, 83, and 91, respectively. She did, however, outlive two of her daughters-in-law and one grandson.

Notes

Abbreviations used:

CIHN	Clarina Irene Howard Nichols
HWS	*History of Woman Suffrage*
KHQ	*Kansas Historical Quarterly*
KSHS	Clarina I. H. Nichols Papers at the Kansas State Historical Society, Topeka
MWRA	Moneka Women's Rights Association Papers at the Kansas State Historical Society
PJ	Nichols's poetry journal (begun 1827), in the collection of the Kansas State Historical Society
PRP	*Pacific Rural Press*
SBA	Susan B. Anthony

Note: Originals for KSHS and PJ are in the collection of the Schlesinger Library, Radcliffe Institute, Harvard University, Cambridge, Mass.

Chapter 1: Frontier Justice

Three accounts of the Peck case have survived: Nichols reported for the Lawrence *Republican* in the spring of 1860 as the criminal case against her was proceeding. She wrote a three-parter for the PRP in 1878, and in a letter to SBA she provided a detailed account for inclusion in HWS, although it was left out of the final version. References to the legal aspects of the case can be found in the notes to the undated Anthony letter, quoted in KHQ, v. 39, pp. 422–429.

3 "In 1860 I was arrested": PRP, September 7, 1878, v. 16, p. 150.

5 "The gentlemen advised that": undated letter to SBA quoted in KHQ, v. 39, p. 423.

6 "a hovel": Ibid.

6 "knitting work and reputation": PRP, December 7, 1878, v. 16, p. 358.

7 "intensely political": undated letter to SBA, quoted in KHQ v. 39, p. 426.

7 "conspiring Kansas officials": Ibid., p. 427.

7 "screaming, biting, and scratching": Ibid., p. 429.

8 "wilfully, maliciously, forcibly and fraudulently": "Quindaro" to Lawrence *Republican*, March 29, 1860.

8 "The curtain is about to rise": Ibid.

8 "flourish of trumpets": Ibid., June 28, 1860.

8 "wonderful legal acumen": Ibid., March 29, 1860.

8 "it is not known certainly": Ibid., June 28, 1860.

8 "a little sunny head on each arm": undated letter to SBA, quoted in KHQ, v. 39, p. 429.

Chapter 2: A Vermont Childhood

Nichols's speeches and newspaper writings include many anecdotal references to her childhood in West Townshend. Sources for the chapter include James H. Phelps's *Collections Relating to the History and Inhabitants of the Town of Townshend, Vermont* (Brattleboro: Selleck & Davis, 1877); *Townshend, Vermont Vital Records*; the *Gazetteer and Business Directory of Windham County, Vermont, 1724–1884*, compiled and published by Hamilton Child (Syracuse: Journal Office, 1884); the *Vermont Historical Gazetteer*, v. 5, collated by Abby Maria Hemenway (Brandon: Mrs. Carrie E. H. Page, 1891); and *A Stitch in Time: Townshend, Vermont 1753–2003* (Townshend: Townshend Historical Society, Inc., 2003). Howard family history and genealogical records may be found at the Grace Hudson Museum and the Held-Poage Memorial Home and Research Library in Ukiah, California. The two best biographical sketches of Nichols's life are T. D. Seymour Bassett's "Nichols, Clarina Irene Howard," in James, Edward T., Janet Wilson James, and Paul S. Boyer, eds., *Notable American Women, 1607–1950: A Biographical Dictionary*, v. 2, pp. 625–627 (Cambridge: Belknap Press, 1971) and Joseph G. Gambone's introduction to "The Forgotten Feminist of Kansas: The Papers of Clarina I. H. Nichols, 1854-1885" in KHQ (v. 39, pp. 12-28).

The program from her high school exhibition was no doubt preserved because her cousin Alphonso Taft, father of the 27th President, delivered the valedictory speech. As for the pronunciation of her first name, Juanita Johnson (author interview, 1999) said that her mother, who was Nichols's great-granddaughter, told her to say "Cla-*rih*-nah" with the "i" sound as in *dinner*.

11 William Hayward married his shipmate Marjery Harding. At some point the family name was changed from Hayward to Howard, according to Grant Carpenter's genealogy in the Grace Hudson Museum, Ukiah, California.

11 "packed their brides on horseback": *Kansas Daily Commonwealth*, April 24, 1870, quoted in KHQ, v. 40, p. 257.

12 "That is Clarina all over — so ingenious!": Birsha Carpenter to CIHN, October 17, 1848, KSHS.

13 "We always knit while we read": CIHN, *The Lily*, March 1850.

13 "a handsome suit for summer": *Kansas Daily Commonwealth*, April 24, 1870, quoted in KHQ, v. 40, pp. 257–258.

13 "There is nothing like economy": Ibid., December 9, 1869, quoted in KHQ, v. 40, p. 134.

14 "I took to learning": Autograph essay from the "Nichols Diary,"

quoted in KHQ, v. 40, p. 458.

16 "Only the devil": *Kansas Daily Commonwealth*, November 28, 1870, quoted in KHQ, v. 40, p. 272. For more on religion in nineteenth-century Vermont, the various Baptist sects and their beliefs and practices, see T. D. S. Bassett's *The Gods of the Hills: Piety and Society in Nineteenth-Century Vermont* (Montpelier: Vermont Historical Society, 2000).

16 "rush screaming from the room": *Kansas Daily Commonwealth*, October 6, 1869, quoted in KHQ, v. 40, p. 127.

16 "exploded ghosts": Ibid.

16 "animated discussions that filled": Ibid.

16 central heating: In the above-cited article CIHN also asserts that the "charms of the hearth light has held many a one from the streets and saloons."

17 "O my children": *Kansas Daily Commonwealth*, April 24, 1870, quoted in KHQ, v. 40, p. 258.

18 "Be a little woman": "Early Reminiscences," quoted in KHQ, v. 40, p. 457.

19 equal inheritance: Chapin Howard owned real estate in Vermont, Michigan, and Pennsylvania and was one of the wealthiest men in Townshend. Probate records of his estate are complex, but Marilyn Blackwell, a Vermont historian who has examined them, says it is fair to conclude that Chapin's intent was to divide the inheritance evenly among his children.

19 The wooden laptop desk that Nichols received from her parents on her 12th birthday is on display at the Grace Hudson Museum in Ukiah, California.

19 "frequent opportunities": *Herald of Freedom*, May 17, 1856, quoted in KHQ, v. 39, p. 247.

19 "While I sat in the quiet corner": Ibid. Elizabeth Cady Stanton, Nichols's junior by five years, also records listening to women in distress bring their petitions to her father, who was a prominent judge in New York. Seeing the most powerful men in their lives hamstrung by laws that discriminated against women was a formative experience for both women.

20 "I would shrink from myself": Ibid.

20 "as conversant with the laws": Stanton, quoted in Parton, James, Horace Greeley, T.W. Higginson et al., eds., *Eminent Women of the Age* (Hartford: S. M. Betts & Company, 1869), p. 396.

20 dowry or an education: In her 1851 speech at the Second National Woman's Rights Convention in Worcester, Nichols said: "When a young girl of fourteen, I said to my father: Give me education instead of a 'setting out in the world' if you can give me but one."

21 "Mental improvement a Source of Happiness": For the 1828 pro-

gram, see Phelps's *Collections Relating to the History and Inhabitants of the Town of Townshend, Vermont,* pp. 183–184.

21 "Comparative of a Scientific": Ibid.

22 Girls' brains: Chapin and Aurelius Howard attended a lyceum in West Townshend that debated whether girls had the same capacity for intelligence as boys. The "nays" carried the day. Lyceum records at Vermont Historical Society, Montpelier.

23 "very sensitive to the sensation": CIHN to SBA, December 17, 1880, quoted in KHQ, v. 40, p. 453.

23 "I never desired beauty": Ibid.

23 "I had a longing": *Proceedings of the Second National Woman's Rights Convention,* 1851, Worcester, Mass., p. 31.

Chapter 3: New York Trials

References to Justin Carpenter are taken from the *Brockport Free Press,* available in microform and bound copies from the Drake Library at SUNY-Brockport. Additional information came from Jonathan Mark Smith's "Brockport, New York: A Narrative of That Place" (Ph.D. Thesis: Syracuse University, 1991) and records at Amherst and Union Colleges. Brockport's Erie Canal heyday is recounted in *The Story of Brockport for One-Hundred Years, 1829–1929,* as told by Charlotte Elizabeth Martin and *We Remember Brockport: Reminiscences of 19th Century Village History,* edited by Mary E. Smith and Shirley Cox Husted (Monroe County Historian's Office, 1981).

24 "I go, I go to regions of song": PJ.

25 "three great objects": Constitution and By-Laws of the Adelphic Society of Union College, revised 1877. Justin Carpenter was misidentified by Bassett in *Notable American Women* as a Baptist minister, and that error has been replicated many times. The likely source of the confusion is Justin's brother Mark Carpenter. Both brothers attended Amherst College in Massachusetts from 1826–1828 and then transferred to Union College in Schenectady, N.Y, from which both graduated in 1830. Justin studied law. Mark went on to theological school, became a well-regarded Baptist minister, and married Clarina's younger sister, Catherine. He is probably the brother-in-law who testified against Justin in the divorce suit described in Chapter 4.

29 "coffee, tea, and pure, cold water": *Brockport Free Press,* July 6, 1831.

29 "the most pleasing and heart-cheering": Ibid.

29–30 "by mutual consent": *Brockport Free Press,* March 16, 1831.

30 *Western Star*: Mary Jo Gigliotti at the Drake Library in SUNY-Brockport found this reference to Justin Carpenter's short-lived newspaper in a query addressed to the Brockport *Republic* and dated January

15, 1863.

30 "flourishing female boarding school": "Annie" to the editor, Atchison (Kansas) *Freedom's Champion*, February 25, 1860. Marilyn Blackwell discovered this impassioned account of Nichols's first marriage written seventeen years after its dissolution under the pen name "Annie." Under the cloak of anonymity, Nichols revealed details about her first marriage and her attempts to support the family, that are found nowhere else. She was responding to the newspaper's editor, who complained about "mothers trotting after politicians and conventions and dabbling in State affairs," which he blamed on the invention of the sewing machine.

30 "intelligent mistress": Ibid.

30 "this scene of past sorrows": CIHN to "Dear Parents," Brockport (New York), July 14, 1833, KSHS.

30 New York City: In Longworth's 1834–35 *New York Register and City Directory*, Justin Carpenter is listed as living at 115 Fulton Street.

30 "burned out and lost all": Typewritten note added to the Union College (Schenectady, New York) Record for Justin Carpenter, Class of 1830.

32 "lovely babe" and "treasure sent": PJ.

32 "When her recreant husband failed": "Annie" to the editor of Atchison (Kansas) *Freedom's Champion*, February 25, 1860.

32 "a malevolent desire to wound her": Ibid.

33 "sit and weep": handwritten note added to Clarina Carpenter's poem, "Cheer up my daughter," PJ.

33 "Aurelius, my son": Ibid.

34 "I cannot love another" and "Why do I weep?" and "Days of Sorrow!": Ibid.

34 "I had not a drunken husband": CIHN to SBA, March 24, 1852, KSHS.

34 "I saw a middle-aged, stalwart Methodist": *The Woman's Journal*, August 4, 1877, quoted in KHQ, v. 40, p. 424.

34 "I have less nourishment": Ibid.

34 "The poor mother's eyes": Ibid.

Chapter 4: In Print and In Love

General information on Brattleboro, as well as references to George and Clarina Nichols and the *Windham County Democrat*, are found in the *Annals of Brattleboro*, volumes 1–3, compiled and edited by Mary R. Cabot (Brattleboro: E. L. Hildreth & Co., 1921, 1922, and 1938 [typed manuscript]); *Gazetteer and Business Directory of Windham County, Vt., 1724-1884*, compiled and published by Hamilton Child (Syracuse, 1884); and *Brattleboro, Windham County, Vermont: Early History* by Henry Burnham (Brattleboro: D. Leonard, 1880). One letter from George Nichols to his future wife, dated February 18, 1843, and held by KSHS, is especially telling. CIHN's account of her political career in Vermont is in HWS, v. 1, pp. 171–178.

36 "like a wounded dove": Atchison (Kan.) *Freedom's Champion*, February 25, 1860.

37 "It is when disappointment": *Vermont Phoenix*, March 13, 1840.

37 "heroic sacrifices": Ibid.

37 "The calm monotony of domestic peace": Ibid.

38 "What but lacerated sympathies": Ibid.

39 "plain person": George Nichols to Clarina Carpenter, February 18, 1843, KSHS.

39 "Personal beauty, if I can judge": Ibid.

39 "You must bear with me if your articles": Ibid.

39 formally dissolve her previous union: CIHN shared details of her divorce three times: in a letter to SBA on March 24, 1852; as the anonymous correspondent "Annie" to *Freedom's Champion* on February 25, 1860; and in a letter to Franklin Adams, an officer in the Kansas State Historical Society. "I had never given him [Justin Carpenter] an unkind word and had supported my family from the first," she told Adams. She further claimed that her testimony helped "other poor women escape also." At the time of her divorce, Vermont law "gave no divorces for causes occurring out of the state." She claimed her testimony helped amend Vermont law in 1844 so that women returning to Vermont after unsuccessful marriages outside the state could obtain Vermont divorces (CIHN to Franklin Adams, March 25, 1884, cited in KHQ, v. 40, pp. 557-8).

39 "cruelty, unkindness, and intolerable severity": Supreme Court of Judicature, State of Vermont, February 16, 1843.

39–40 "without exception sustained me": CIHN to SBA, March 24, 1852.

41 "water cure": Much has been written about water cures, vegetarianism, and health reform in the 1840s and '50s. For more information on Brattleboro's water cure, see chapter 6 in Cabot's *Annals of Brattleboro*, "The Wesselhoeft Water Cure," pp. 557-586. Harriet Beecher Stowe visited the Brattleboro water cure in 1846. In her book, *Harriet Beecher Stowe: A Life* (New York: Oxford University Press, 1994), Joan D. Hedrick notes that in the U.S., "the water cure was also an institutional response to what had become a popular expectation: that married women's health would rapidly decline….By taking them away from their husbands and children, the water cure gave them respite from both." Stowe, who had been suffering from chronic mercury poisoning, cholera and miscarriages, stayed nearly a year at Brattleboro and was revived.

42 Longfellow: The Houghton Library at Harvard has a letter that CIHN wrote to H. W. Longfellow dated November 25, 1845, after his

summer stay at the Nicholses' home. In it she expresses her pleasure at having gotten acquainted with him and his family, sends her wishes that his eyesight will improve, thanks him for sending her a copy of *Hyperion*, and offers to advertise it in the *Windham County Democrat*.

42 "I most cheerfully certify": *Semi-Weekly Eagle* (Brattleboro), June 29, 1848.

42 "chronic lung disease": See "Death Notices from Kansas Newspapers," KHQ, v. 18, p. 411.

43 *Windham County Democrat's* political shift: The agitation stirred by the Nicholses' "raising the Free Soil banner" can be seen in a letter George Nichols wrote the Brattleboro *Semi-Weekly Eagle*, August 17, 1848, in which he disputed charges that he was trying to "throw the election of President into Congress" where Cass, the free-soil candidate, would have a greater chance of winning. For an excellent study of the political climate and partisan politics that led to the opening of Kansas Territory in 1854, see *Jacksonian Antislavery and the Politics of Free Soil, 1824-1854*, by Jonathan H. Earle (University of North Carolina Press, 2004).

44 "The bounds of slavery": Harley Smith to CIHN, August 15, 1847, KSHS.

44 "It will cheer them to know": Ibid.

44–45 "I am a walking storehouse": CIHN to SBA, March 24, 1852, KSHS.

46 *coverture*: Unwritten English common law, traced back to medieval King Alfred, was codified by William Blackstone in the mid-18th century and widely used as the basis of law in the American colonies and early republic. The antebellum feminists were united in disputing his description of the marriage relationship, which included the following passage: "By marriage, the husband and wife are one person in law: that is, the very being or legal existence of the woman is suspended during the marriage, or at least is incorporated and consolidated into that of the husband; under whose wing, protection, and cover, she performs every thing...and her condition during her marriage is called her *coverture*." Blackstone also said the husband had the right to use "moderate correction" for his wife's misbehavior (William Blackstone's *Commentary on the Laws of England*, Book 1, Chapter 15).

46 married women's property rights: Opponents of married women's property rights often cited the Bible as their authority. CIHN countered with her own verses from Scripture. One of her favorite Scriptures in this regard was Proverbs 31 (from which the opening quotation to this book was taken), which describes the qualities and activities of a "virtuous" woman: "She considereth a field and buyeth it; with the fruit of her hands she planteth a vineyard" (Prov. 31:16). The woman's husband in King Solomon's day, Nichols said, was not "hen-pecked." The husband's

honorable place in the community was seen as "connected with the virtues of this model wife, who bought and sold and held property" (*The Lily*, September 1850).

47 "the first breath": HWS, vol. 1, p. 172.

Chapter 5: The Road to Worcester

Accounts of the 1840 World Anti-Slavery Convention and the 1848 Seneca Falls Convention may be found in HWS, v. 1, pp. 50-62 and 67-74. The First National Woman's Rights Convention in Worcester is also described in HWS, v. 1, pp. 215-226. The Worcester Women's History Project (WWHP) has made many documents from the two Worcester conventions available online. Two booklets published by WWHP members were helpful: *Window on the Past: Revisiting the first National Woman's Rights Convention*, a script for school use by Karen Board Moran; and *Worcester Women's History Heritage Trail*, which led me to Lucy Stone's home place in West Brookfield, Mass., another evocative glimpse into the past. John McClymer's valuable book, *This High and Holy Moment: The first National Woman's Rights Convention, Worcester 1850* (Fort Worth: Harcourt Brace & Company, 1999), contains many documents and contemporaneous news accounts of that gathering.

For a description of the characteristics essential to an upper middle-class female of that age, see Barbara Welter's "The Cult of True Womanhood, 1820–1860," in *American Quarterly* 18 (Summer 1966), pp. 151–75. Nichols possessed three of Welter's four essential characteristics of "true woman" — purity, piety, and domesticity — but not the fourth, which was submissiveness. As I argue throughout the book, Nichols came by her womanly ways honestly, but her use of them in public life was pragmatic, calculated, and (to her allies, at least) ironic. For another view on CIHN's femininity and a close examination of her political evolution, see Marilyn Schultz Blackwell's "Meddling in Politics: Clarina Howard Nichols and Antebellum Political Culture," *Journal of the Early Republic* 24 (Spring 2004), pp. 27–63.

48–49 On a snowy morning: Details of this account were taken from Cabot's "The Coming of the Railroad — Formal Opening," *Annals of Brattleboro*, v. 1, pp. 611–613.

49 "My husband wanted me": CIHN to SBA, March 24, 1852, KSHS.

50 "They tell about wimin": *Windham County Democrat*, December 10, 1847.

50 "I know some folks argue": Ibid., June 2, 1849.

51 Women in church were supposed to be silent: Nichols asked a "clerical friend" to submit her questions on gender equality to a local meeting of ministers. The friend reported that her questions "were found

to unsettle established tenets." Nichols concluded that "the theological harmonicon" was "too delicate for the touch of truth." (*The Woman's Journal*, August 7, 1880, cited in KHQ, v. 40, p. 444).

52 both sides of the Atlantic: For more information on the international aspects of early feminism and, specifically, the connections between European and American feminists such as Paulina Wright Davis, Lucretia Mott, Ernestine Rose, Elizabeth Cady Stanton, Susan B. Anthony, and others, see *Joyous Greetings: The First International Women's Movement, 1830-1860* by Bonnie S. Anderson (New York: Oxford University Press, 2000).

53 "submerged continent": Inez Haynes Irwin in *Angels and Amazons* (Garden City: Doubleday, Doran & Company, 1933), p. 22.

54 dispelled all doubt: Interview with John McClymer, Worcester, Mass., October 17, 2003. For more on the antecedents to the women's movement, see Kathryn Kish Sklar's *Women's Rights Emerges within the Antislavery Movement, 1830-1870* (Boston: Bedford/St. Martin's Press, 2000) and Nancy Isenberg's *Sex and Citizenship in Antebellum America* (Chapel Hill: The University of North Carolina Press, 1998). Isenberg's discussion of the role of religion and factors other than the Seneca Falls Convention which led to the founding of the first women's rights movement were illuminating. For more on Nichols's ideology and influence, see *Free Hearts & Free Homes: Gender and American Antislavery Politics* by Michael D. Pierson (Chapel Hill: The University of North Carolina Press, 2003).

54 "The room was crowded to excess": *New York Tribune*, October 25, 1850.

55 "In many countries we see women": *Proceedings of the National Women's Rights Convention*, Worcester, Mass., 1850.

56 "The natural rights ... They were both made": Ibid.

56 "the million and a half of slave women": Ibid.

56 "Women are beginning to have": Frederick Douglass, quoted in Michael D. Pierson, *Free Hearts and Free Homes*, p. 57.

57 "There are few papers exerting": Ibid.

57 "You must speak now": CIHN to the National Woman Suffrage Association Convention, February 25, 1884, quoted in KHQ, v. 40, p. 556.

Chapter 6: 'On the Responsibilities of Woman'
Nearly all quotations in this chapter are taken from "On the Responsibilities of Woman," delivered by Nichols at the Second National Woman's Rights Convention, Worcester, Mass., October 15, 1851, and issued thereafter as a tract. For an analysis of Nichols's rhetoric, see Adrienne E. Christiansen's "Clarina Howard Nichols: A Rhetorical Criticism of Selected Speeches" (M. A. thesis, University of Kansas, 1987) and *Man*

Cannot Speak for Her, v. 1: *A Critical Study of Early Feminist Rhetoric* and v. 2: *Key Texts of the Early Feminists* by Karlyn Kohrs Campbell (Westport: Praeger, 1989).

63 "many eyes, all unused to tears": HWS, v. 1, p. 218.

63 "a touching tender pathos": Ibid.

66 "I have found my best success": CIHN to SBA, August 21, 1881, quoted in KHQ, v. 40, p. 514.

Chapter 7: Bloomers and Trousers

No copy exists of the speech Nichols gave to the Vermont Assembly in 1852, but she recorded her memory of the experience in HWS, v. 1, pp. 172-74. The *New York Tribune* provided a synopsis of the speech (December 3, 1852) but curiously did not mention Nichols's demand for school suffrage. For a discussion of the influence of the penny presses on the expansion of the women's rights movement and the political significance of bloomers, see *When Hens Crow: The Woman's Rights Movement in Antebellum America* by Sylvia D. Hoffert (Bloomington: Indiana University Press, 1995). Hoffert identifies fourteen women, including Nichols, and nine men as the "vanguard" whose personal commitment launched the antebellum women's movement.

67 Susan B. Anthony: Most sources say that CIHN met SBA at the Syracuse Convention in the fall of 1852, but the two advocates were corresponding by at least the previous spring. Nichols's March 24, 1852, letter to Anthony expresses her hope to "finish the threads we have commenced winding." The confidential tone and substance of this letter indicates that Nichols trusted Anthony from the start. They began a correspondence that continued for the rest of Nichols's life. "I love Mrs. Stanton & all the faithful workers, but it seems to me that we two more than any I know, live in this woman movement because we see in it the divine development of humanity as a whole" (CIHN to SBA, August 21, 1881, quoted in KHQ, v. 40, p. 513).

67–68 "It is most invigorating": CIHN to SBA, April 1852, quoted in *The Life and Work of Susan B. Anthony,* v. 1, by Ida Husted Harper (Indianapolis: The Hollenbeck Press, 1898), p. 66.

68 penny presses: Hoffert in *When Hens Crow* claims the attitude of the press toward the women's movement was not entirely negative ("anything but uniform") and that "they lifted a movement with little money, no permanent organization, and no official newspaper of its own out of obscurity by bringing it to the attention of a national audience" (p. 94).

69 "The dress — short skirts": Salem (Ohio) *Anti-Slavery Bugle,* June 21, 1851.

69 "inches cut from the tops": Ibid.

69–70 "We can't understand": *Windham County Democrat*, 1853.

70 "being molested by rowdy": Ibid.

70 "Mrs. Nichols and her daughter, in bloomers": *Annals of Brattleboro*, v. 1, p. 380. Many details about Nichols, her family, and her career are erroneous in the *Annals* account. In both the *Windham County Democrat* and the *Anti-Slavery Bugle*, Nichols argued in favor of bloomers yet never said that she had taken up the new fashion herself, nor has any other report asserted that fact.

70 "stumbling block": Salem (Ohio) *Anti-Slavery Bugle*, June 21, 1851.

71 school suffrage: Opponents of woman suffrage (even school suffrage) warned that voting would lead women to neglect their duties in the home. In a fictional story, "Going to School Meeting," published in a Vermont newspaper, a man demanded to know why his supper was late. His son replied, "Mother's got the paper, and it says women's goin' to vote in school meetin' and so she's goin' tonight." This development threw the family into confusion. "Visions of a neglected household, of the late supper, of the children at home in disorder, Lucy Jane's sore foot, and the possibility of the house being set on fire, passed through her [the wife's] mind," while she was away voting, and after a disappointing experience at the schoolhouse, the chastened wife returned home (*Middlebury Register*, December 29, 1852).

71 "entering wedge": CIHN to SBA, April 14, 1858, quoted in KHQ, v. 39, p. 547. Marilyn Blackwell sees CIHN's decision to seek school suffrage as arising out of "her understanding of a mother's role in children's education," rather than as a shrewd decision based on her perception of what was politically expedient (*Journal of the Early Republic* 24, p. 46).

71–72 "Some, it is true": *Windham County Democrat*, October 27, 1852.

72 "Come to Montpelier": HWS, v. 1, p. 173.

72 "Shall I go? ... Have you the nerve?": PRP, January 29, 1881.

72 "If the lady wants to make herself": HWS, v. 1, p. 173.

73 "law adopted by bachelors": HWS, v. 1, p. 173

73 "muffled thunder of stamping feet": Ibid., p. 174.

73 "We did not know" and "unsex herself": Ibid.

73 "Only those who have suffered": *Burlington Courier*, November 25, 1852.

Chapter 8: The World Is on the Move

Numerous newspapers reported on the raucous conventions in New York in the fall of 1853. Reporters from three of New York's daily newspapers (*Tribune*, *Times*, and *Herald*) provided a spectrum of viewpoints in their coverage: liberal, moderate, and conservative. *The Liberator* published a number of first-hand accounts of the conventions, including Nichols's. The first volume of HWS is replete with accounts of the World's and Whole World's temperance conventions as well as the women's "mob convention."

75 "The Crystal Palace is a symbol": *New York Times*, July 14, 1853.

75 James McCune Smith: HWS, v. 1, p. 512.

76 "the scarcity of white neck-ties": Ibid.

76–77 "It was not speeches, nor the singing": *New York Times*, September 3, 1853.

77–78 "I say that woman is the greatest sufferer": Ibid.

78 "You may think me ultra": Ibid.

78 "with a good coat": CIHN speech at Rochester Convention, June 2, 1853.

79 "The most spirited": HWS, v. 1, p. 511. Antoinette Brown was the first woman ordained by a mainline Protestant church (Congregationalist).

79 "We saw, in broad daylight": *New York Herald*, September 7, 1853, quoted in HWS, v. 1, p. 556.

80–81 "The mayor promised": Ibid., v. 1, p. 573.

81 "In the Green Mountain State": Ibid., p. 563.

81 "My husband wishes me to vote": Ibid., p. 561.

81 "Where did your Christ come from?": Sojourner Truth at Woman's Rights Convention (Akron, Ohio), 1851, quoted in Karlyn Kohrs Campbell's *Man Cannot Speak for Her: A Critical Study of Early Feminist Rhetoric*, v. 1, p. 21.

81 "You may hiss as much as you like": HWS, v. 1, p. 568.

82 "several gentlemen" apologized: *The Liberator*, September 30, 1853.

82 "was from God and bound to succeed": Ibid.

82 "His whole appearance and language": Ibid.

Chapter 9: Winning Wisconsin

The *Milwaukee Daily Free Democrat*, edited by Sherman Booth, gave extensive coverage to the 1853 campaign, including routes, speakers, the opposing actions of the Wisconsin Temperance League, and the proceedings of the Wisconsin Women's State Temperance Association which supported Nichols and Fowler after the Temperance League abandoned them. Nichols's reports on her Wisconsin trip appear in some of the few extant copies of the *Windham County Democrat* (Oct. 5 and 12, 1853). She also gave a full account in HWS, v. 1, pp. 178–185.

83 "I wish Mr. Nichols could be relieved": H. M. Darlington to CIHN, August 2, 1853, KSHS.

83 "Go" and "You will be doing just the work": HWS, v. 1, p. 178.

85 "moaning and wretching of passengers": *Windham County Democrat*, October 5, 1853.

86 "stooping to the most disgusting depths": HWS, v. 1, p. 179.

86 "joyfully welcome": *Milwaukee Daily Free Democrat*, September 27, 1853.

86 "We believe that no men": Ibid.

86 "There is no time to be lost": Ibid.

87 "indignant that these funds": Ibid. October 1, 1853.

87 a rousing sendoff: The *Chicago Daily Tribune* shared the *Milwaukee Free Democrat's* enthusiasm for the campaign. "Mrs. Fowler and Mrs. Nichols were present at the organization [of the Wisconsin Women's Temperance Association] and helped to set the ball in motion. If they are only in earnest, the Anti-Maine [anti-liquor] men might as well haul down their colors -- they are bound to be vanquished" (September 30, 1853). Six days later, the *Tribune* issued an even bolder pronouncement of what Nichols and Fowler were accomplishing in Wisconsin: "While in other States they content themselves with TALKING about what their rights are, here we find them practically asserting them by taking the stump." By 1856, the report predicted, "we shall expect to find them so far ahead in this movement that they will be prepared to take to the political field. A mass meeting of the ladies is not an uninteresting idea. We hope yet to see a 'Grand Rally of the Female Democracy, 20,000 petticoats in council. Great excitement, but no fighting'" (October 5, 1853).

87 "We hereby give notice": *Milwaukee Daily Free Democrat*, September 30, 1853.

88 "I am sick of hearing": Ibid.

88 "Broad prairies, gallant lakes": *Windham County Democrat*, October 12, 1853.

90 At a Congregational Church: CIHN records this incident in her "Reminiscences" for HWS, v. 1, pp. 180–182.

90 "My friend had only stood"; Ibid., p. 181.

Chapter 10: A Country Divided

For a study of the fate of the Indians of eastern Kansas before and after passage of the Kansas-Nebraska Bill, see *The End of Indian Kansas: A Study of Cultural Revolution, 1854-1871* by Craig Miner and William F. Unrau (reissued by the University of Kansas Press, 1990). Newspaper articles and letters from Joseph G. Gambone's collection of CIHN's writings, "The Forgotten Feminist of Kansas: The Papers of C. I. H. Nichols, 1854-1885," (KHQ, v. 39 and v. 40) provided many sources for the next several chapters. Past issues of the KHQ include many articles about conditions and politics in territorial Kansas. Two which contain references to CIHN's arrival and early experiences in the territory are

"The Emigrant Aid Company Parties of 1854" (v. 12, pp. 115-155) by Louise Barry and "Emergency Housing In Lawrence, 1854 (KHQ, v. 24, pp. 34-49) by James C. Malin. "Letters of the Rev. Samuel Young Lum, Pioneer Missionary, 1854-58" (KHQ, v. 25, pp. 39-67), edited by Emory Lindquist, gives a vivid description of early life in Lawrence.

93 "Mrs. Nichols has suspended the publication": *The Liberator*, February 3, 1854.

93 four-part series with Lucy Stone: In 2005 a new, authenticated letter by CIHN was purchased by the Vermont Historical Society. In this letter, sent from Brattleboro on December 19, 1853, CIHN describes her upcoming commitments, including the series with Lucy Stone, Antoinette Brown, and Ernestine Rose.

93 "too tame" or "no debate at all": HWS, v. 1, p. 175.

94 "I told you, ladies and gentlemen": Ibid.

94 "clear and convincing" and "masculine brawler": Ibid.

94 "the first tone of her voice": *The Liberator*, January 13, 1854.

95 "Don't take away my children!": *Brattleboro Eagle*, February 24, 1854.

95 "My friends, the lawmakers": HWS, v. 1, p. 176.

95 "The excitement": *Brattleboro Eagle*, February 24, 1854.

95 "a fact which either he was ignorant of": Ibid.

96 "a plan of operations for the rescue": Ibid.

96 "your white brothers will not trouble": This memorable phrase is cited in full in *Fort Benning: The Land and the People* by Sharyn Kane and Richard Keeton (Tallahassee: Southeast Archeological Center, National Park Service, 1998).

98 "a great moral wrong": *The Liberator*, March 10, 1854.

99 the free-soil coalition: The antecedents and consequences of the Kansas-Nebraska Bill have been widely discussed in both the scholarly and popular press for the past 100 years. For a revisionist history of that era, see *Bleeding Kansas: Contested Liberty in the Civil War Era* by Nicole Etcheson (University Press of Kansas, 2004).

99 "fossilized conservatism": CIHN to SBA, August 21, 1881, quoted in KHQ, v. 40, p. 512.

Chapter 11: *Mush And Molasses*

101 "Picture the writer" and "snatches of song": Boston *Evening Telegraph*, October 31, 1854, quoted in KHQ, v. 39, p. 29. CIHN paints a sunny picture of her journey west and the trip up the Missouri River, in part, it seems, to encourage potential free-state settlers to follow. Many emigrants in the New England Emigrant Aid Company, however, complained that the company failed to fulfill its promises. "Coming up the Missouri, we were stowed into a miserable old boat, already half full and

about 75 of us slept on the floor, and many of us found our own blankets....
[In Kansas City] some 75 or 100 slept on the floor, and 20 of us went to
the stable and turned in on the hay. For these accommodations we were
obliged to pay in advance." (George O. Willard, January 7, 1855, to the
[Boston?] *Journal*, quoted in KHQ, v. 12, p. 146).

101 "a pious doctor": HWS, v. 1, p. 185.

101 "Next morning, poor man!": Ibid.

102 "Can you tell me where all these people": Ibid. p. 195.

102 "They are from the New England States": Ibid.

102 "Did you never hear how in New Hampshire": Ibid.

102 "homesick" and "We were all in haste": *Daily Republican*, November 14, 1854, quoted in KHQ, v. 39, p. 32.

103 pestering her to lecture that very evening: Ibid., pp. 185–186.

105 "novel" and "as I have seldom": *Milwaukee Daily Free Democrat*, November 14, 1854, quoted in KHQ, v. 39. p. 37.

105 "Some twenty families and companies": Boston *Evening Telegraph*, quoted in KHQ, v. 39, p. 39.

105 "Her breakfast is a simple one": Ibid.

105 "a group of men standing around": Ibid., p. 40.

105–106 "The climate is the finest": Ibid., p. 41.

106 "embryo city": Springfield *Daily Republican*, November 15, 1854, quoted in KHQ, v. 39, p. 34.

106 a pencil sketch: Nichols's early sketch of Lawrence is now in the
collection of the Spencer Museum of Art at the University of Kansas in
Lawrence. In the *Kansas Home Journal* (September 29, 1870), Joseph
Savage writes, "Mrs. Nichols had from Mount Oread taken a pencil
sketch of Lawrence in 1854." The article referred to her as "Mrs. J. H.
Nichols," raising doubt whether it was the same Mrs. Nichols who had
arrived with the fourth party of the New England Emigrant Aid Society
in the fall of 1854. It is safe to conclude that the sketch was CIHN's
handiwork, for several reasons. Like many well-bred women of her class,
Nichols was an amateur artist; a still-life painting of hers can be found at
the Grace Hudson Museum in California. In one of her first articles sent
to an Eastern newspaper upon arriving in Lawrence (*Daily Republican*,
November 15, 1854, quoted in KHQ, v. 39, p. 33), Nichols describes the
scene that appears in the sketch. She is the only female Nichols listed in
any of the first four emigrant parties, according to Louise Barry's roll
call (KHQ, v. 12, pp. 115–149). Finally, it is not uncommon to see her
name misspelled, even today; she has been variously cited as C. J. H.
Nichols, Mrs. O. H. Nichols, Clarina H. I. Nichols, Clarinda Nichols
and even Clementine Nichols.

106 "The women are 'strong-minded'": Springfield *Daily Republican*,
November 15, 1854, quoted in KHQ, v. 39, p. 33.

107 "But that was all *head* knowledge": Boston *Evening Telegraph*, January 9, 1855, quoted in KHQ, v. 39, p. 38.

107 "Do not expect to eat oysters": Aurelius Carpenter to the *Vermont Phoenix*, May 5, 1855.

Chapter 12: Life and Death on the Prairie

Besides CIHN's writings themselves, two works of fiction were helpful in understanding the turbulent, convoluted history of early Kansas Territory: *The All-True Travels and Adventures of Lidie Newton* by Jane Smiley (New York: Ballantine, 1998) and *Cloudsplitter* by Russell Banks (New York: HarperCollins, 1998), a fictionalized biography of John Brown. See also the early chapters of *Kansas: The History of the Sunflower State, 1854–2000* by Craig Miner (Lawrence: University of Kansas Press, 2002). In Eleanor Flexner's classic *Century of Struggle: The Women's Rights Movement in the United States* (Cambridge: reissued by Belknap Press, 1975), Flexner cites CIHN as the example of "how the new ideas were carried westward with the tide of migration" (p. 93).

108 "within one day's journey" and "duty": *Vermont Phoenix*, February 3, 1855.

108 "Mrs. Nichols is yet hopeful for liberty in Kansas": Ibid.

109 "Kansas and Its Chances for Freedom": Ibid.

109 "The slave power is united": Ibid.

109 "not without attractions": Ibid.

109 "the fastidious in our cities" and "promiscuous": Ibid.

110 "Mr. and Mrs. Weld express a great deal": Birsha Carpenter to CIHN, n.d., KSHS.

110 "Two long years" and "God only knows": Ibid.

111 "If any of our company of 230": Springfield *Daily Republican*, November 15, 1854, quoted in KHQ, v. 39, p. 32.

111 Susan Stone's trunk: KHQ, v. 25, p. 107.

112 "The Missourians came boldly" and "the cry was raised": *New Hampshire American News*, cited in the *Vermont Phoenix*, May 5, 1855, quoted in KHQ, v. 39, p. 52.

113 "as if such things as surveyed roads": *Vermont Phoenix*, June 2, 1855, quoted in KHQ, v. 39, p. 220.

113 "I would not be willing" and "I can think of nothing": Ibid., p. 221.

113 "solitude of the prairie" : Ibid.

113 "I liked this region of country": Ibid.

114 "Tauy" Jones: Ibid., p. 224. John Tecumseh Jones (1800–1872), the son of an English father and a Chippewa mother, joined the Ottawa tribe after emigrating to Kansas. In 1860 he made possible the acquisition of land for the future site of Ottawa University in Ottawa, Kansas, near

Lawrence, which remains in operation today.

114 "Provisions are scarce and high": Ibid., p. 223.

114 "fewer and farther apart than were angels' visits": Boston *Evening Telegraph*, January 9, 1855, quoted in KHQ, v. 39, p. 38.

114 "Your Kansas correspondent": *Vermont Phoenix*, June 2, 1855, quoted in KHQ, v. 39, p. 220.

115 "Our dinner was spread": *Kansas Tribune*, cited in *The Lily*, June 15, 1855, quoted in KHQ, v.39, p. 228, f.n. 17.

115 "all the aristocratic feelings": Ibid.

115 "Mr. Nichols mounted his large bay [horse]": Ibid.

116 "I know what a good husband is": CIHN to SBA, March 24, 1852, KSHS.

116 "with the tenderness of a woman": CIHN handwritten note on letter dated November 28, 1870, to A. O. Carpenter, KSHS.

118 "Sharps rifles are in all our cabins": *New Hampshire American News*, cited in the *Vermont Phoenix*, November 10, 1855, quoted in KHQ, v. 39, p. 232.

118 "the little boy sleeping": *Kansas Daily Commonwealth*, October 6, 1869, quoted in KHQ, v. 40, p. 128.

118 "fearful silence" and "The cheerful owl!": Ibid.

119 "against the united protests": Greenfield *Gazette and Courier*, February 4, 1856, quoted in KHQ, v. 39, p. 233.

119 "I hung it there, but my wife": Ibid., p. 234.

Chapter 13: Bleeding Kansas

Two bestsellers from 1856 give vivid, partisan accounts of life in Kansas. *Six Months in Kansas* by Hannah Ropes and *Kansas: Its Interior and Exterior Life* by Sara T. D. Robinson (wife of one of the two major free-state leaders in Kansas and a friend of Nichols) are both reproduced online (and linked from www.clarinanichols.com). A third source is Julia Lovejoy, whose letters to her mother were printed in the Eastern press; they were republished in KHQ (v. 15, p. 127–142, 277–319, 368–403; v. 16, p. 40–75, 175–211). Though Lovejoy did not approve of "strong-minded women" seeking political rights, she was herself a strong woman: missionary's wife, self-appointed social worker, and writer with a keen eye for detail. The brooch with the intertwined hairs from Nichols's father's and husband's heads is part of the CIHN exhibit at the Grace Hudson Museum in Ukiah, California.

122 "broken in spirit": HWS, v. 1, p. 186.

122 "You cannot know how anxious I am": Lawrence *Herald of Freedom*, March 8, 1856, quoted in KHQ, v. 39, p. 237.

122 "revolutionary" and "treasonable insurrection": Journal of the Senate, pp. 74–79, "Message to the Senate by Franklin Pierce," Janu-

ary 24, 1856.

123 "free hearts" and "swelling with ominous indignation" and "aiders and abettors": Lawrence *Herald of Freedom*, March 8, 1856, quoted in KHQ, v. 39, p. 237.

123 "strong-minded women" and "run bullets, transfer ammunition": Ibid., p. 238.

124 "Alas, that I cannot get back in time": Ibid., p. 239.

124 "But the black male and the white female": Ibid., p. 240.

124 "Happy circumstance — the free white males": Ibid.

124 "Is this asking too much?": Ibid., p. 241.

124–125 "I entreat you": Ibid., pp. 241–242.

125 "the harlot Slavery" and "polluted in the sight of the world": Charles Sumner, *Records of the U.S. Senate*, May 19-20, 1856.

126 dumped the *Herald*'s presses: HWS, v. 2, p. 189.

126 "The late news from Kansas": CIHN to Emma, May 24, 1856, quoted in KHQ, v. 39, p. 253.

126 "crazy — *crazy*": quoted in "John Brown's Body," by Adam Gopnik, *The New Yorker*, April 25, 2005, p. 90.

127 grazed his heart: CIHN to *New Hampshire Sentinel*, undated clipping in "Webb Scrapbooks," quoted in KHQ, v. 39, p. 254.

127 "My son lives to fight another day": Ibid.

127 "semi-political": HWS, v. 1, p. 187.

129 formal commission from the Republicans: Regarding payments for CIHN's lectures, Melanie S. Gustafson says the Republican Party in 1856 "hired women as speakers, including the well-known temperance and women's rights reformer Clarina Howard Nichols." See *Women and the Republican Party 1854-1924* (Urbana: University of Illinois Press, 2001), p. 20.

129 "I suspicioned then": HWS, v. 1, p. 187.

129 "Free-state army of Kansas": CIHN to Thaddeus Hyatt, October 4, 1856, quoted in KHQ, v. 39, p. 255.

129 "wreck itself on the dark rocks": CIHN to Emma, May 24, 1856, quoted in KHQ, v. 39, p. 252.

129 "viper" and "will strangle it": Ibid., p. 253.

129–130 "I will never desert them": CIHN to Thaddeus Hyatt, October 4, 1856, quoted in KHQ, v. 39, p. 256.

130 "Susan B. Anthony of Rochester has the executive ability": Ibid.

130 "Poor bleeding Kansas — how the soul sickens": SBA to CIHN, September, 1856, quoted in KHQ, v. 39, p. 2, f.n. 69.

130 "Don't ever tell me": Broadside in KSHS.

131 "so poorly clad": New York *Daily Tribune*, November 1, 1856, quoted in KHQ, v. 39, p. 258, f.n. 76.

131 "one of the leading champions of the Emancipation": *New York Tribune*, quoted in *The Liberator*, September 30, 1853.

131 "whose whole souls were in the movement": CIHN to SBA, November 11, 1880, quoted in KHQ, v. 40, p. 452.

132 "And Wisconsin": HWS, v. 1, p. 632.

132 "wretches" and "would come at night": Ibid., p. 643.

132 "died from sheer fright": Ibid.

132 "what woman had done there" Ibid., p. 642.

132 "little men who squeak": Ibid.

132–133 "Are you mothers?": *New York Tribune*, November 8, 1856, quoted in KHQ, v. 39, p. 259.

Chapter 14: Quindaro

Articles about Old Quindaro have appeared in regional newspapers since the early 1900s, but most of these rehash earlier articles and the errors and myths contained therein. The best source of information on early Quindaro is its newspaper of one year, the *Chindowan*, which has been indexed by students at Kansas City Kansas Community College and is available online. It is possible to reconstruct a picture of the town in 1857–58 from *Chindowan* articles, as Alan W. Farley did in "Annals of Quindaro: A Kansas Ghost Town" (KHQ, v. 22, pp. 305–320). CIHN's letters to Susan Wattles also provide contemporaneous descriptions of Quindaro, the integrated school Nichols and her daughter started, and veiled references to the underground railroad. Jeff R. Bremer's "'A Species of Town-Building Madness': Quindaro and Kansas Territory, 1856-1862" (*Kansas History*, Autumn 2003, p. 156–171) denies that Quindaro had an integrated school and disputes its importance as a depot for slaves escaping from Missouri as "mostly mythical," but does not mention either the Wattles correspondence or the Tappan letter, both of which contain contemporaneous references to the fugitive slave network active in Quindaro. (See documentation for Nichols's "starving for our principles" remark later in this chapter and the Samuel F. Tappan letter quoted in Chapter 16.) At this writing, the ruins of Quindaro are being restored through a Save America's Treasures grant under the auspices of the Western University Association of the African Methodist Episcopal Church and its grant partners, the Kansas City Kansas Community College and the Unified Government of Wyandotte County, Kansas.

134–135 "Border ruffians...invaded the neighborhood": *Ho for California!* edited by Sandra L. Myres (San Marino: Henry Huntington Library and Art Gallery, 1980), pp. 95–96.

135 "The violent thunderstorms are enough to wreck the nerves": Ibid., p. 96.

135 "I can bid Kansas goodbye": Ibid.

135 "charity tea": Quindaro *Chindowan*, May 30, 1857.

136 "wrong side out": Wyandotte *Gazette*, December 22, 1882, quoted in KHQ, v. 40, p. 538.

137 "good housewifery": Ibid.

137 "I was always in love with the country": CIHN to Sara T. D. Robinson, September 25, 1882, quoted in KHQ, v. 40, p. 533.

137 "4 base walls": Ibid.

137 "a hundred buildings — many of them of stone": Wyandotte *Gazette*, December 22, 1882, quoted in KHQ, v. 40, p. 539. Nichols's memory may have cast a hazy glow over Quindaro. Another early Kansas immigrant, Jacob Stotler, said Quindaro was more like "a mining camp at the bottom of a canyon" (KHQ, v. 22, p. 308).

138 "the Canada of the escaped slave": CIHN to SBA, n.d., quoted in KHQ, v. 39, p. 427. According to Jeff Bremer, the 1860 census showed Quindaro to have a 10 percent minority population (Indian and black) and more than half the black population in the county (Bremer, p. 169).

138 "Of the many slaves who took the train of freedom": Wyandotte *Gazette*, December 29, 1882, quoted in KHQ, v. 40, p. 541.

139 "All night I crept to and fro" and "I passed a cup of fresh coffee": Ibid., p. 542.

140 "We have concluded, though it looks like [we are] starving for our principles": CIHN to Susan Wattles, May 2, 1859, MWRA.

140–141 "Do our sister citizens know how beautiful": Quindaro *Chindowan*, June 27, 1857.

141–142 "We will tell our readers": Ibid., June 13, 1857.

142 core convictions: In her farewell notice in the *Chindowan*, Nichols writes, "We took the position of Associate Editor conditionally. The conditions requisite to permanency have been wanting" (August 1, 1857). A letter sent to Nichols from Susan Wattles sheds some light on Nichols's abrupt departure from the paper: "I appreciate the obstacles you have met with and sympathize with you in your trials," Wattles wrote. She claimed that had the *Chindowan* been willing to give Nichols what she required — editorial responsibility for a full page "devoted to women's rights" — the newspaper would have gained circulation. Wattles could not see why its editor would resist the economic logic of trying to reach female readers. She had planned to subscribe to the *Chindowan* after seeing an issue with Nichols's name on the masthead, "but after you left I did not want it" (Susan Wattles to CIHN, May 4, 1858, MWRA).

142 "dawn of freedom on her glorious prairies": *Vermont Phoenix*, October 31, 1857, quoted in KHQ, v. 39, p. 410.

143 "Many a brave deed was done there": Wyandotte *Gazette*, June 16, 1882, quoted in KHQ, v. 40, p. 529.

Chapter 15: Woman on a Mission

Before and during the Wyandotte Constitutional Convention, Nichols discussed her strategies, hopes, and fears with Susan B. Anthony and Susan Wattles. She wrote an account for HWS and recounted this period in her life on other occasions. The correspondence with both Susans is especially interesting because it was hurriedly composed and contains none of the complex and stilted syntax that often marks her public writing. Other sources for the chapter are the local and national newspapers that covered the convention extensively.

145 "My blood boils": CIHN to Susan Wattles, March 27, 1859, MWRA.

145 could midwife the birth of woman suffrage: CIHN was not alone in thinking she could make history in Kansas: "It is not at all impossible that Kansas may set a brilliant example to the rest of the world, by ordaining in the Constitution over which it is now incubating, that 'Constitutional distinctions based on differences of sex,' shall never, never be acknowledged within the limits of 'Free Kansas.' Apparently, nothing is needed but a determined prosecution of the campaign, so brilliantly inaugurated, to insure the success of the cause of woman's rights, after the manifold snubbings to which it has been subjected in this older and less gallant portion of our slightly disunited States (*New York Times*, July 22, 1859, quoted in KHQ, v. 39, p. 24).

145 "any constitutional monopoly": CIHN petition to the Wyandotte Constitutional Convention, quoted in KHQ, v. 39, p. 416.

145 "I am forced to the conclusion that it would mar": CIHN to Susan Wattles, May 2, 1859, MWRA.

146 "We are none of us competent to speak": Susan Wattles to CIHN, May 4, 1858, MWRA.

146 "I am ready to act": CIHN to Susan Wattles, March 29, 1859, MWRA.

146 an item in *The Lily*: Susan Wattles to CIHN, April 14, 1859, MWRA. Apparently, the money was being funneled through Susan B. Anthony to her brother Daniel Anthony in Kansas Territory, who was supposed to get the money to Nichols and Wattles. When he failed to do so in a timely manner, and Nichols complained that she was forced to go to Leavenworth and "hunt up your brother," Susan fired off a rebuke to Daniel, who had excused his tardiness by saying he was busy with affairs of the free-state cause. She wrote, "You blunder on this question of woman's rights just where thousands of others do. You believe woman unlike man in her nature; that conditions of life which any man of spirit would sooner die than accept are not only endurable to woman but are needful to her fullest enjoyment. Make her position in church, State, marriage, your own; everywhere your equality ignored, everywhere made

to feel another empowered by law and time honored custom to prescribe the privileges to be enjoyed and the duties to be discharged by you; and then if you can imagine yourself to be content and happy, judge your mother and sisters, and women to be." (SBA to Daniel Anthony, July, 1859, cited in Ida Husted Harper's *The Life and Work of Susan B. Anthony*, v. 1, pp. 169-170.)

146 "There is no man to go with me": CIHN to SBA, June 18, 1859, quoted in KHQ, v. 39, p. 414.

146 "I am in perfect trim": Ibid., p. 415.

147 "So you see I am doing all I can": CIHN to Susan Wattles, July 14, 1859, MWRA.

148 "I felt my wings grow": CIHN to SBA, June 18, 1859, quoted in KHQ, v. 39, p. 415.

149 "womanly" and "My age, my past history": CIHN to Susan Wattles, March 29, 1859, MWRA.

149 "Mrs. Nichols sits at the reporter's desk": *New York Times*, June 22, 1859.

149 "The hospitable tea-table of Mrs. Armstrong": *The Woman's Journal*, August 16, 1879, quoted in KHQ, v. 40, p. 438.

150 "They say I have accomplished": CIHN to SBA, July 21, 1859, quoted in KHQ, v. 39, p. 420.

150 "In this age of intelligence": *Proceedings of the Kansas Constitutional Convention*, Wyandotte, 1859, p. 73.

150 "Her audience was large, promiscuous": *New York Post*, July 25, 1859, quoted in KHQ, v. 39, p. 417, f.n. 61. No copy of CIHN's speech is extant. The Lawrence *Herald of Freedom* was one of the few newspapers that supported her plea for woman suffrage. On July 2, 1859, the *Herald* called for elevating the "intelligent and tax-paying women of Kansas to an equality with the foreigner, who is converted into a voter almost the very moment he lands on our soil."

150 "no Constitutional distinction on account of Sect": CIHN to SBA, July 15, 1859, quoted in KHQ, v. 39, p. 418.

151 "too many old lawyers": HWS, v. 1, p. 194.

151 "I believed then and believe now": Ibid., p. 193.

151 "played upon the old harmonicum": Ibid.

151 the country was not ready: In *Sex And Citizenship in Antebellum America*, Nancy Isenberg argues that the opportunity for constitutional inclusion of woman suffrage was dead by 1859. Despite Nichols's understanding of partisan politics, her local power base, and extensive lobbying, her efforts to secure the franchise failed. Longstanding traditional attitudes could not be overturned even in a place where convention had been turned on its ear: "Neither the existence of two state governments vying for power, armed conflict among its citizens, nor illegal voting deterred

members of the constitutional convention from drafting a conservative document in harmony with 'organic law' and political guidelines found in other states" (p. 193).

152 failed to achieve her most ambitious goal: CIHN was not afraid of "a backward move" when it came to married women's property rights. Other states had adopted such laws by 1859. She warned, however, that women needed to keep a close eye on lawmakers, "as the old abuses will creep in in old or new shapes." As always, she grappled with the finer points of law to a degree most early feminists did not. She was "particularly anxious" about winning equal custody rights for mothers. (She did.) She believed that "In school matters & corporations of all kinds, I feel pretty sure we can get the right of franchise under the laws" (CIHN to Susan Wattles, March 29, 1859, MWRA). The Kansas Constitution reads as follows: "The Legislature shall provide for the protection of the rights of women, in acquiring and possessing property, real, personal, and mixed, separate and apart from the husband; and shall also provide for their equal rights in the possession of their children" (Article XV, Sec. 6).

152 "in all school matters": The University of Kansas was founded in 1866. The University of Iowa admitted women on an equal basis with men beginning in 1860.

152 "extensively denied": CIHN to *Kansas Daily Commonwealth*, November 2, 1869, quoted in KHQ, v. 40, p. 130.

152 "If it be so in Kansas": *The Revolution*, September 2, 1869, quoted in KHQ, v. 40, p. 114, f.n. 52.

152–153 In Atchison, she was invited home: CIHN to Franklin G. Adams, June 12, 1884, quoted in KHQ, v. 40, pp. 559–560.

153 "one of the most thrilling and convincing": Lawrence *Republican*, September 29, 1859.

153–154 "had more real gospel in it": Ibid.

154 "physiologically, intellectually, or morally": Ibid.

154 "We use the pen, the press": Ibid.

154 "as hot a day as ever I experienced": Esther Wattles Memoirs, Linn County Historical Museum, Pleasanton, Kansas.

154 "You must remember that all my life": CIHN to SBA, November 11, 1880, quoted in KHQ, v. 40, p. 452. The quote continues: "only meeting them in a few Conventions & at odd times during the first 4 yrs. from '50 till '54 — till '59, a few times in Kansas in the Wattles family."

155 "block characters" and "negro hating people": CIHN to SBA, July 21, 1859, quoted in KHQ, v. 39, p. 421.

Chapter 16: 'A Vast Army of Widows and Orphans'
Juanita Johnson's records about the Civil War service of her great-grandfather, Chapin Howard Carpenter, helped answer several ques-

tions about Nichols's family during the war. Letters in MWRA vividly describe Nichols's activities during the first year of the war, when she was still living in Quindaro. Unfortunately, none of her Washington correspondence survives. The only glimpse into those years comes from columns collected by Evelyn Leasher in *A Letter from Washington* by Lois Bryan Adams (monograph, Wayne State University Press, 1999), and a tribute to Nichols published in the *Vermont Journal* in 1866.

156–157 "Old John Brown": Abraham Lincoln in *The Collected Works of Abraham Lincoln* (New Brunswick: Rutgers University Press, 1953) by Roy P. Basler, v. 3. p. 502. For an account of Lincoln's five-day trip to Kansas Territory in December 1859 and his first campaign speeches for the Presidency, see *Lincoln and Kansas: Partnership for Freedom* by Carol Dark Ayres (Manhattan: Sunflower University Press, 2001).

157 The streets of Westport: HWS, v. 1, p. 197–198.

157–158 "Missouri wretches": CIHN to Susan Wattles, August 21, 1861, MWRA.

158 "To the hunt!": Lawrence *Republican*, January 26, 1860, quoted in KHQ, v. 39, p. 430.

158 "blessed events": CIHN to Susan Wattles, June 3, 1860, MWRA.

158–159 "Humanity can have railroads": Ibid. On January 24, 1858, Samuel F. Tappan, an early free-state emigrant based in Lawrence, wrote the noted journalist T. W. Higginson, "I am happy to inform you that a certain Rail Road has been and is in full blast. Several persons have taken full advantage of it to visit their friends. Only one or two accidents have happened....If you know of any one desirous of helping the cause, just mention our case to him, and ask him to communicate with Walter Oakley at Topeka, James Blood and myself at Lawrence, or Sam C. Smith at Quindaro." Images of the original letter can be viewed at www.clarinanichols.com.

160 "The State...had paupered the helpless boy": CIHN to SBA, n.d., quoted in KHQ, v. 39, p. 435.

160 "Perhaps no person was ever better": HWS, v. 1, p. 168.

161 "The everlasting Mrs. Nichols": Atchison *Union*, January 22, 1860, quoted in KHQ, v. 39, p. 430.

161 "if he will furnish yarn": Lawrence *Republican*, February 2, 1860, quoted in KHQ, v. 39, p. 431.

161–162 "In 1854...an earnest friend of our cause": *The Woman's Journal*, July 27, 1879, quoted in KHQ, v. 40, p. 438.

162 "I do so long": CIHN to Susan Wattles, April 10, 1861, MWRA.

162 "All over Kansas, were vacant homes, telling of an invader": Testimony to the Memory of Lucy Gaylord Pomeroy, 1863, quoted in

KHQ, v. 39, p. 441.

163 "Three out of four are afflicted with the scurvy": *Chicago Tribune*, March 13, 1861, quoted in KHQ, v. 39, p. 437.

163 "I had become so accustomed — indeed so expectant of loss": Wyandotte *Gazette*, December 22, 1882, quoted in KHQ, v. 40, p. 539.

163 "The 'times' are so hard it is almost impossible to get money": CIHN to Susan Wattles, March 27, 1859, MWRA. Nichols did receive an inheritance from her father but some of it was used during family emergencies. In 1857 Howard fell thirty feet from a building in Quindaro, and during the months that he was unable to work as a carpenter, she paid off his creditors, who were threatening to put his house on the auction block. She also set aside money for educating George and Birsha.

164 "food that went to the hungry spot" and "revived" and "to the former life and to the world": *Vermont Phoenix*, March 6, 1868, quoted in KHQ, v. 39, p. 542.

165 "We expect trouble if the river freezes": CIHN to Susan Wattles, October 21, 1861, MWRA.

165 "My children wander from me": CIHN to Helen and Aurelius Carpenter, July 18, 1869, quoted in KHQ, v. 40, p. 117.

165 "She's no mouse": CIHN to Susan Wattles, October 21, 1861, MWRA.

165 "I think I feel the death of favorite animals": Ibid., March, 1861.

165 "Our people are many": Ibid., October 21, 1861.

166 "I have had several severe cases": Ibid.

166 "She has a fine boy two months old": Ibid.

166 "I have been feeling for months": CIHN to SBA, May 4, 1863, quoted in KHQ, v. 39, p. 442.

166 "Women, equally with men": Ibid.

166 "This war is adding a vast army of widows": Ibid., p. 443.

167 "absolutely necessary": *Letter from Washington, 1863–64* by Lois Bryan Adams, p. 135.

167 "Here Kansas came to the rescue again": Ibid., p. 136.

167 "if their wives, mothers, and sisters could not": Ibid.

168 "chaotic" and "to a most complete": *Vermont Journal*, 1866.

Chapter 17: With Liberty and Suffrage for All

Most accounts of the 1867 Impartial Suffrage Campaign do not mention Nichols, but it is hard to imagine that such a campaign would have arisen in Kansas had it not been for her pioneering work before 1859 and her attempts in the next two legislatures to gain suffrage. Most accounts follow the trail of Lucy Stone, Elizabeth Cady Stanton, and Susan B. Anthony, who were in Kansas for part of 1867. The campaign is covered extensively in HWS (v. 2, pp. 229–268) and in newspaper accounts. See also Ellen Carol DuBois, *Feminism and Suffrage: The Emergence of an Independent Women's Movement in America, 1848–1869* (Ithaca: Cornell University Press, 1978); "With the Help of God and Lucy Stone," KHQ, v. 35, pp. 13–26; and letters received by S. N. Wood, "Campaign of 1867," Woman Suffrage History Collection, KSHS.

170 "The hour of universal freedom is coming": *Vermont Phoenix*, March 8, 1867, quoted in KHQ, v. 39, p. 517.

170 "with a hole in his coat": HWS, v. 2, p. 234.

170 "If I was a negro, I would not want": Ibid.

170 "Mrs Nichols and I came down on him": Ibid.

171 "Everything has conspired to help us": Henry Blackwell to Elizabeth Cady Stanton, April 5, 1867, quoted in HWS, v. 2, p. 233.

171 "O, say what thrilling songs of fairies": lyrics appear on Hutchinson Family website linked at www.clarinanichols.com.

175 "I think it is against the Bible": Maggie Harrington Diary, October 8, 1867 (Lawrence: Douglas County Historical Museum).

175 "There is not one word in the Bible about woman suffrage": PRP, April 9, 1881, quoted in KHQ, v. 40, p. 510.

175 "to abolish the last relic": Wyandotte *Commercial Gazette*, October 26, 1867, quoted in KHQ, v. 39, p. 541.

176 "by my carpenter son": CIHN to Samuel N. Wood, June 19, 1867, quoted in HWS, v. 39, p. 526.

176 "She don't believe in marriage": Emporia *News*, June 7, 1867, quoted in KHQ, v. 39, p. 522 f.n. 16.

176 "a gross slander": Ottawa *Western Home Journal*, June 27, 1867, quoted in KHQ, v. 39, p. 523.

177 "To my thinking men horrified": Ibid., p. 524.

177 "The colored women are proposed": Wyandotte *Commercial Gazette*, June 1, 1867, quoted in KHQ, v. 39, p. 520.

177 "Imagine three or four hundred colored": Ibid., p. 521.

177 "That brat is an armful of reasons": Ibid.

177 "So long as they have no right to the elective": Ibid.

178 wasn't getting enough attention: A thorough examination of Nichols's role in the watershed campaign of 1867 is yet to come.

178 "Now don't talk": CIHN to Samuel N. Wood, June 19, 1867, quoted in KHQ, v. 39, p. 527.

179 "I thought of the novelty of a six-months' journey": *Eighty Years and More* by Elizabeth Cady Stanton, quoted in *Feminism and Suffrage: The Emergence of an Independent Women's Movement in America, 1848–1860* by Ellen Carol Dubois, pp. 83–84.

179–180 "The dirt, the food!!" and "It gave me added self-respect": *In Her Own Right: The Life of Elizabeth Cady Stanton* by Elisabeth Griffith

(New York: Oxford University Press, 1984) p. 128.

180 "mean" and "inasmuch as it is": *The Revolution*, February 3, 1870, quoted in KHQ, v. 40, p. 245.

180–181 "I felt assured we were strong enough": Ibid. See *Doers of the Word: African-American Speakers and Writers in the North, 1830–1880* by Carla L. Peterson (reissued in New Brunswick: Rutgers University Press, 1998) for a study of the lives and racial uplift work of 19th century African American women, including Sojourner Truth and Frances Ellen Watkins Harper.

181 "whenever my breadwinning occupation": CIHN to SBA, April 14, 1868, quoted in KHQ, v. 39, p. 549.

Chapter 18: 'Grant! Grant! Grant!'

Most of the sources for this chapter were family letters and articles by CIHN published in the Wyandotte *Gazette* and *Vermont Phoenix*.

183 "She has got one of the most beautiful": *Wyandotte Commercial Gazette*, February 29, 1868, quoted in KHQ, v. 39, p. 542, f.n. 49.

183 "Oats are harvested and heavy": Wyandotte *Commercial Gazette*, August 1, 1868, quoted in KHQ, v. 39, p. 549.

184 "dearer, sweeter, better self": *Vermont Phoenix*, September 18, 1868, quoted in KHQ, v. 39, p. 559.

184 "I seem to have lost power": CIHN to unknown correspondent, September 30, 1869, quoted in KHQ, v. 40, p. 126.

184 "wept and begged": CIHN to Helen Carpenter, March 26, 1871, KSHS.

184 "She is a natural born thief": Ibid.

185 "so white and pretty"; Ibid. Nichols's statements about Lucy Lincoln are at odds with her many other pronouncements, both public and private, of what was for the time an enlightened view of race. She advocated suffrage for both black males and females, ran an integrated school, denounced attempts to keep free blacks from settling in Kansas, and told Susan Wattles that she would prefer legal unions between black men and white women over the "illegal amalgam" that existed between male slaveowners and female slaves (CIHN to Wattles, March 27, 1859, in MWRA). Nichols believed that many of the differences between the races were due to upbringing and education and wrote that the "perfection" of society depended upon the "practical unity of the sexes — as of the races" (KHQ, v. 40, p. 123), but she was unaware of her own racist attitudes in describing and dealing with Lucy Lincoln.

186 "Grant! Grant! Grant!": Wyandotte *Commercial Gazette*, August 1, 1868, quoted in KHQ, v. 39, p. 550.

186 "General, as one of the mothers of Kansas": Ibid.

186 "You can electioneer for us": Ibid.

186 "Aye, aye. That we can": Ibid.

187 "You were acquainted with him": Ibid.

187 "like an elephant" and "motherly intervention": Ibid.

188 "gassing type": Ibid., p. 551.

188–189 "They were so needy": CIHN to Aurelius and Helen Carpenter, March 6, 1869, quoted in KHQ, v. 40, p. 79.

189 "I am sewing, tending baby": CIHN to Helen Carpenter, n.d. KSHS.

189 "rascality revealed too late": CIHN to Helen Carpenter, March 26, 1871, KSHS.

189 "endurance": Wyandotte *Commercial Gazette*, August 22, 1868, quoted in KHQ, v. 39, p. 553.

189 "Big iron kettles of succotash": Ibid., p. 554.

190 "They moved in a circle": Ibid.

190 "I never can make another home": CIHN to Helen and Aurelius Carpenter, July 18, 1869, quoted in KHQ, v. 40, p. 117.

190 "We can wear our breeches": *Kansas Daily Commonwealth*, October 7, 1869, quoted in KHQ, v. 40, p. 129.

191 "Yes, I am a free lover. I have an inalienable": *New York Herald*, November 21, 1871, cited in *Notorious Victoria: The Life of Victoria Woodhull* by Mary Gabriel (Chapel Hill: Algonquin Books, 1998), p. 148.

191 "fold their hands and starve": *Kansas Daily Commonwealth*, June 23, 1869, quoted in KHQ, v. 40, p. 87.

191 "Poor fellow": Ibid.

191 "both will have bread" and "if they marry": Ibid. A similar article appears as CIHN to "Dear Emma," *Wisconsin Chief*, April 23, 1870.

192 "With a snug little farm": CIHN to SBA, January 1870, quoted in KHQ, v. 40, p. 244.

Chapter 19: Third Class to California

193–194 "I feel so unsettled — homeless": CIHN to Helen Carpenter, March 26, 1871, KSHS.

194 "an eat": CIHN to Helen Carpenter, July 18, 1869, quoted in KHQ, v. 40, p. 116.

194–195 "You may be sure it was a privilege" and "could discuss any topic of general interest" and "with excellent success": Wyandotte *Gazette*, May 30, 1872, quoted in KHQ, v. 40, p. 276.

195 "All together we were a sort of family party": Ibid.

195–196 "I was prepared to like California": Ibid., p. 276–277.

196 "Some of the nicest housekeepers": Ibid., September 12, 1872, quoted in KHQ, v. 40, p. 285.

196 "To the eye of an insider" and "The pine, cedar": Ibid., May 30, 1872, quoted in KHQ, v. 40, p. 277.

197 "durable and beautiful": Ibid., p. 278.

197–198 "And the flowers!": Ibid., p. 279.

198 "'Fower! Fower! Gramma'": Ibid.

198 "The ground has never frozen": Ibid.

198 "the size of the jack rabbits": Ibid., August 15, 1872, quoted in KHQ, v. 40, p. 284.

198 "Poultry raising": Ibid., May 30, 1872, quoted in KHQ, v. 40, p. 281.

199 "The grand old Oak just outside the yard": Ibid., September 12, 1872, quoted in KHQ, v. 40, p. 286.

199 "I miss the cheerful hum": Ibid., p. 284.

200 "tender love from life long acquaintance": CIHN to SBA, August 21, 1881, quoted in KHQ, v. 40, p. 513.

Chapter 20: The Heart of a Loving Woman

The description of the National Woman's Rights Association protest at the centennial celebration is based on the account in HWS, pp. 1-56.

201 "We will not hold ourselves bound": HWS, p. 33.

202 "only officials were invited": Ibid., p. 27.

202–203 "On every side eager hands were stretched": Ibid., p. 30.

203 "I believe my interest in the progress of affairs": CIHN to Franklin Adams, June 12, 1884, quoted in KHQ, v. 40, p. 559.

203–204 "Yes, they must preach" and "Do I charge them": The Woman's Journal, August 4, 1877, quoted in KHQ, v. 40, pp. 424-5.

204 "An Old Friend Returns" and CIHN quotes: PRP, May 8, 1880, v. 19, p. 314. The *Pacific Rural Press* was a substantial (16–24 pages), sophisticated family weekly that covered topics of broad interest. Works by Longfellow, Whittier, Mark Twain, and George Eliot appeared in PRP's "Home Circle," the section that carried CIHN's articles.

204 "a brief exposure to the cold wind": Ibid.

204–205 "I am still confined to bed": Ibid.

205 "The compensations — for I would rather": Ibid.

205 "I know too well the doubt and anxiety": Ibid.

206 In thirty years the movement had grown: Neither Susan B. Anthony nor Elizabeth Cady Stanton attended the First National Woman's Rights Convention in Worcester. At the 20th anniversary of this event, however, they wrote, "The movement in England, as in America, may be dated from the First National Convention held at Worcester, Mass., October 1850" (HWS, v. 2, p. 428). Only in later years did Stanton and Anthony begin dating the movement's birthday from the 1848 Seneca Falls Convention, which Stanton co-organized.

206–207 "The leaders in the Suffrage Movement may all die": CIHN to Worcester Woman Suffrage Convention, November 6, 1880, quoted in KHQ, v. 40, p. 446.

207 "wooden" and "motherly": CIHN to SBA, quoted in KHQ, v. 40, p. 453.

207 "What a book I might have given to my dear children": CIHN, diary extract, quoted in KHQ, v. 40, p. 455.

207 "Your request found me anxious": CIHN to Abby Hemenway, 1881, quoted in KHQ, v. 40, p. 523.

208 "the old haunting fear of seeming": Ibid., p. 524–25. Nichols responsed to the Wyandotte Gazette by writing three long articles on her early pioneer life in Kansas. The articles were published on March 31, June 16, December 22 and 29, 1882 (the third article was published in two parts). In these articles she describes a steamboat excursion on the *Lightfoot* that is interrupted by an explosion (the men run for cover under the tables, while the women rescue the children); the rise and fall of Quindaro and its role in the underground railroad; the "first onslaught of the temperance police"; and the hardships faced by pioneers during an economic downturn.

208 "map out my plan": CIHN to SBA, 1883, quoted in KHQ, v. 40, p. 551.

209 "beyond my comprehension": CIHN diary extract, 1880, quoted in KHQ, v. 40, p. 457.

209 "A Christian government": *Woman's Herald of Industry*, San Francisco, September and October 1881, quoted in KHQ, v. 40, p. 519.

209 "through revolution and reconstruction": Ibid., p. 520.

210 "permeate the masses": Ibid.

210 "With only the right of petition": Ibid., p. 521.

210 "Who can doubt what would have been the influence": Ibid.

210 "To a mother's heart, every mother's baby": Quindaro *Chindowan*, June 6, 1857.

211 "depression of vitality": PRP, January 10, 1885.

211 "I put this and that together": Ibid.

211 "I was often faint in a crowded assembly": Ibid.

211 "I am satisfied from observation": Ibid.

211 "all who value God's breath of life": Ibid.

212 "Dear Susan, I am very sick": CIHN to SBA, January 7, 1885, quoted in KHQ, v. 40, p. 562.

Index

abolitionists, 43, 51, 103, 112, 118, 130, 138, 140, 142, 156, 157. *See also* antislavery movement

Adams, Abigail, 124, 201, 223

Adams, Lois Bryan, 167

ague, 116, 154

alcohol consumption; and divorce, 78; and domestic abuse, 28, 76

American Anti-Slavery Society, 51

American Woman Suffrage Association, 180–181, 228

Amphions (musical group), 76

Anthony, Daniel, 130, 202

Anthony, Susan B., 8, 68, 75, 130, 131, 148, 166, 178–181, 207, 213, 215, 226–227; breaks with Republican Party, 180; CIHN to, 34, 116, 146, 149, 154, 155, 180, 192, 199, 208; "If it be so in Kansas,", 152; meets CIHN, 67–69; protests 1876 centennial, 202

Anti-Female Suffrage Association, 174

Anti-Slavery Bugle (Ohio), 69

antislavery movement, 79, 87, 97. *See also* abolitionists; ties to women's movement, 56, 109

Armstrong, Lucy, 149, 188

Atchison, David Rice, 108

Atchison, Kansas, 118, 152, 162

Atchison *Union*, 161

Baldwin City, Kansas, 165

Baptist Mission (Kansas), 110

Baptists, 25, 140, 174; in New England, 14–15; opposition to alcohol, 27

Barnum, P.T., 76

Barton, Clara, 85

beauty, 23, 39, 65

Bible, 42, 51, 70, 81, 118, 174, 234

"Bible Position of Woman, The," 174, 234

Blachly, Eben (Rev.), 234

Black Jack (Kansas), Battle of, 127, 134

Blackwell, Antoinette Brown, 55, 76, 79–80, 93, 216, 227

Blackwell, Elizabeth, 227

Blackwell, Henry, 170–171, 180

Bloomer, Amelia, 44, 69, 225; CIHN writes to, 12

bloomers, 69–71, 79, 136, 145

Booth, Sherman, 76, 86

Boston, Massachusetts, 40, 100

Brattleboro *Eagle*, 95

Brattleboro, Vermont, 37, 40–41, 41, 48–49, 71–72, 95, 99, 121

Brockport Academy, 26

Brockport Free Press, 29

Brockport, New York, 90, 91; Clarina and Justin Carpenter in, 26; temperance society, 27–29

Brown, Antoinette. *See* Blackwell, Antoinette Brown

Brown, John, 118, 126–127, 150, 156

Brown, Olympia, 171

Brown v. Board of Education, 155

Buchanan, James, 129

Burns, Lucy, 228

Butler, Andrew, 125

California, 190, 194–200, 202; delegate at 1850 convention from, 54; growing season of, 198

Canada, 140, 157

Caroline (fugitive slave), 139

Carpenter, Aurelius Ormando (A.O.), 31, 33, 107, 116, 134, 136, 165, 195, 211, 214; marries Helen McCowen, 135; urges CIHN to move, 190; wounded at Black Jack, 127

Carpenter, Birsha. *See* Davis, Birsha Carpenter

Carpenter, Chapin Howard, 31, 116, 134, 135, 136, 164, 214, 263; in Battle of Black Jack, 127; marries Sarah Jones, 112

Carpenter, Charles, 165

Carpenter, Helen McCowen, 134–135, 184, 189

Carpenter, Irena, 165

Carpenter, Justin, 36, 44; death of, 35; divorce from, 39; marriage to Clarina Howard, 25–32

Carpenter, Sarah Jones, 109, 112, 116, 135, 165

central heating; family life and, 16

Chicago Tribune, 163

cholera, 116

Christianity, 78, 188, 189, 209; and women's rights, 208; slaves and, 43

Civil War, 3, 127, 132, 164–168, 169, 201, 216

Clarina Howard Nichols Center (Morrisville, Vt.), 215

"Cold Water Celebration," 29

colonization, 43

Confederacy, 160, 164, 166

Connecticut, 12, 32, 76

constitution of Kansas, 147–152, 154

conventions, women's. *See* women's rights conventions

co-sovereignty doctrine, 56, 176, 216, 228, 234–235

coverture, 45

Cressy, Timothy, 20, 57

Crystal Palace (New York City), 74–75

custody, 6–7, 56, 62, 63, 66, 77, 78, 91, 95. *See also* divorce; law, 95, 152

Cutler, Hannah Tracy, 159

Davis, Birsha Carpenter, 26, 33, 109, 115, 135, 136, 162, 165, 176, 183–184, 214; starts integrated school, 140

Davis, George Franklin, 184

Davis, J.M., 26, 29

Davis, Paulina Wright, 54, 63, 202, 216, 225

"Declaration of Independence," 29, 53, 124, 201–202, 223

"Declaration of Sentiments," 53

Delavan, Wisconsin, 86

Democratic Party, 98, 123, 148, 150; divided by slavery, 43

Denver, Colorado, 186

Detroit Advertiser and Tribune, 167

Dickinson, Emily, 132

divorce, 6, 39, 63, 78, 95

domestic abuse, 6, 95, 215. *See also* alcohol consumption; *See also* law

Douglas, Kansas Territory, 106

Douglass, Frederick, 56–57, 173,

225–226

Douglas, Stephen A., 97, 106

Eaglewood School, 109
education, 20, 66. *See also* school
  suffrage
elections; Kansas constitution
  (1859), 154; Kansas suffrage
  (1867), 180; Kansas suffrage
  (1912), 151; Kansas territorial
  (1854), 106; Kansas territorial (1855), 111–112; Kansas
  territorial (1857), 142; presidential (1856), 128; presidential
  (1860), 160
Emancipation Proclamation, 166
Emerson, Ralph Waldo, 51
Erie Canal, 25–26, 27, 34
Euripides, 123
Evening Telegraph (Boston), 101

Fifteenth Amendment, 180
Finney, Charles, 27
First National Woman's Rights
  Convention. *See* women's rights
  conventions
Fort Riley, Kansas, 116
Foster, Abby Kelley, 55, 216, 224
Fourth of July, 28–29, 189, 201
Fowler, Lorenzo, 84
Fowler, Lydia, 83–91
free blacks, 43, 154, 157. *See
  also* Fugitive Slave Law
free-soil coalition, 99
free staters, 117, 122–125,
  123–124, 137, 138, 142
Frémont, John C., 128
Fugitive Slave Law, 62, 76; in
  Kansas Territory, 7; inspires
  CIHN poem, 158
Fuller, Margaret, 224

Gage, Frances Dana, 159, 216
Gage, Matilda Joslyn, 207, 216

Garrison, William Lloyd, 51, 224
Georgetown. *See* Washington,
  D.C.
"good time coming," 28, 63, 76
Grace Hudson Museum, 214
Graham, Sylvester, 42
Grant, Ulysses S.; visit to Kansas,
  186–188
Greeley, Horace, 76, 79, 81, 82,
  83, 150–151, 173, 225
Green Corn Festival of 1868,
  189–190
Greenfield Gazette and Courier, 119
Grimké, Angelina, 51, 109, 215,
  223
Grimké, Sarah, 51, 109, 215, 223
Guthrie, Quindaro Brown, 137,
  147

Harper, Frances Watkins, 180
Harpers Ferry, Virginia, 156–157
Hayward (Howard), William, 11
Hemenway, Abby, 207
Herald of Freedom (Lawrence), 122,
  125, 126
Herkimer, New York, 32
Higginson, Thomas Wentworth,
  51, 132, 173
History of Woman Suffrage, 151,
  202, 207
Hopedale, Massachusetts, 55
Howard, Aurelius, 12, 18
Howard, Birsha Smith, 12, 15;
  raising of Clarina, 13, 16, 18
Howard, Chapin, 12, 15, 92, 263;
  as overseer of the poor, 19–20;
  death of, 98
Hudson, Grace Carpenter, 214
Hunt, Harriot, 55
Huron Indians, 189
Hutchinson Family Singers,
  171–172
Hyatt, Thaddeus, 129

Illinois, 97, 131, 159, 160
immigrants, 30, 86, 203
Independence, Missouri, 102, 119
Indiana, 131
Indians, 96, 102, 138; in eastern Kansas, 188–190
Industrial Revolution, 17
Iowa, 98, 128, 142

Jackson, Andrew, 43, 96
Jackson, Mrs., 76
Jones, J. Elizabeth, 159, 160
Jones, Tauy, 114, 254

Kansas. *See also* Kansas Territory; admitted to Union, 161; becomes national rallying cry, 130; drought of 1861, 162; known as Indian Country, 96; popular sovereignty and, 98; suffrage vote of 1867, 180
Kansas City, Kansas, 183
Kansas City, Missouri, 101–103, 110, 112, 150
Kansas Daily Commonwealth (Topeka), 190, 191
Kansas Free State, 126
Kansas Impartial Suffrage Association, 170
Kansas-Nebraska bill, 96–98, 127
Kansas River, 126
Kansas State College, 187
"Kansas Suffrage Song,", 171–172
Kansas Territory, 7, 96, 99, 103, 108, 110; elections in, 106, 111–112; immigration to, 110; land prices in, 163
Kansas Tribune, 115
Kate Swinney (riverboat), 110
Kellogg, John Harvey, 42
Kentucky, 159
Kingman, Samuel, 151
knitting, 6, 12, 16, 93, 96, 149, 161, 164, 184, 207

Ladies National Covenant, 167
Lane Trail, 142
law, 19–20, 62, 66, 73, 91, 144, 161, 216. *See also* custody; *See also* married women's property rights; and domestic abuse, 6, 35; and paupers, 19, 61; and widows, 9, 61, 124; common, 45; disregard for married women's rights, 45; passed by "bogus legislature", 116; unfair to women, 44, 59, 77, 124, 132, 151
Law and Order Party (Kansas), 116
Lawrence, Kansas, 103–106, 104, 112, 118, 124, 126, 127, 138, 153, 158, 161, 163, 175
Lawrence *Republican*, 8, 153, 158, 161
Leavenworth Constitution (1858), 144
Leavenworth, Kansas, 139, 156
Leavenworth Times, 202
Lecompton Constitution (1857), 142, 144
Lecompton, Kansas, 153
Liberator, The, 51, 82, 93
Lily, The, 69, 93, 146, 225
Lincoln, Abraham, 85, 160, 166, 186
Lincoln, Lucy, 184–185
Lincoln, Mary Todd, 214
London, England, 51, 52
Longfellow, Henry Wadsworth and Frances, 42
Louisiana Purchase, 98
lyceum, 93

Madison, Wisconsin, 89
Maine, 131
Manhattan, Kansas, 186
Mann, Horace, 85
married women's property rights,

46–47, 56, 63, 66, 78, 91, 226; in Kansas, 152; in New York, 224; in Ohio, 159, 160; in Vermont, 46–47, 224

Massachusetts, 12, 53, 76, 93, 95, 125, 131, 167, 191, 206, 226; custody law in, 95–96

Massilon, Ohio, 160

May, Samuel, 51

Meriden, Connecticut, 32

Mexico, 157

Michigan, 12, 131, 189, 241

Milwaukee Daily Free Democrat, 76, 86, 87

Milwaukee, Wisconsin, 85, 86, 91

ministers, 42, 51, 81, 89, 93–94, 98, 118, 180, 191. *See also* spheres; and domestic abuse, 34; opposed to woman suffrage, 174–175, 203

Missouri, 76, 98, 101, 119, 157, 159; and Confederacy, 160, 164; slavery in, 164

Missourians, 101, 123, 126, 129; tensions with Kansans, 108–109, 119–120, 132

Missouri Compromise, 98

Missouri River, 99, 110, 118, 128, 137, 138, 142, 143

Moneka Women's Rights Association, 145–146, 153, 176

Montpelier, Vermont, 72

Morrisville, Vermont, 215

Morse, Samuel, 85

Mott, Lucretia, 52, 55, 76, 80, 202, 215, 223, 225

Mudge, Benjamin, 187

National Kansas Committee, 130

National Woman Suffrage Association, 180–181, 202, 203, 212, 228

Nebraska, 96–98

"Negro's hour," 174

New England Emigrant Aid Society, 99, 100

New Hampshire, 40, 102, 110, 113, 131

New Hampshire American News, 112

New Hampshire Sentinel, 118, 127

New Jersey, 213

New York City, 74, 130; Clarina and Justin move to, 30; "mob convention" of 1853, 79–82; women's rights convention of 1856, 131–132

New York Evening Post, 150

New York Herald, 79

New York state, 25–26, 67, 129, 131, 132

New York Temperance Society, 85

New York Times, 75, 76, 149

New York Tribune, 54, 76, 79, 131, 132

Niagara Falls, N.Y., 85

Nichols, Birney, 199, 204, 212

Nichols, Clarina Irene Howard, 13, 21; addresses Vermont legislature, 72–73; appeals to New York women, 132; apple dumplings and, 175; approached by women in distress, 44; as Deborah Van Winkle (pseudonym), 49–52; at Wyandotte Constitutional Convention, 147–152; becomes physician of Quindaro, 165; begins advocating women's rights, 46; begins editing newspaper, 43; breaks with Democrats, 98; "bury myself in Kansas", 161; conducts train rescue, 95–96; dissatisfaction with religion, 140; financial difficulties of, 163–164; first lecture in Kansas, 103–105; first marriage, 25; genealogy of, 236; graduates from Cressy School,

20; Grant (U.S.) and, 186–188; helps fugitive slave, 139; inheritance, 121; in Ohio, 159; lectures in 1856 campaign, 128; lectures in Vermont, 108–109; lectures on boat, 110; Longfellow and, 42–41; makes sketch of Lawrence, 106; matches wits with Col. Scott, 102; minister on Erie Canal and, 34–35; Missourians and, 119; moves to California, 193; moves to Kansas, 109; moves to Washington, D.C., 166; moves to Wyandotte City, 183; on bloomers, 69–71; personal appearance, 22; petition drive in Kansas, 146–147; role in 1867 suffrage campaign, 169–176; second-hand smoke and, 211; settles claim, 113; signs "Declaration of Rights" (1876), 202; speaks at Wisconsin state capital, 89; temperance speech in New York (1853), 77; trains and, 100; vegetarianism and, 42, 105

Nichols, George Bainbridge, 42, 45, 109, 115, 139, 165, 188, 193–194, 197, 198, 214; injured, 115

Nichols, George Washington, 38–40, 45, 62, 72, 83, 98, 114, 214; becomes an invalid, 42; dies, 115

Nichols, Helen, 199

Nichols, Katherine, 199

Nichols, Mary Warpole, 188, 192, 196, 199, 212

Nineteenth Amendment, 213, 228

North Carolina, 125

Notable American Women (1971), 10

Oberlin College, 145

Ohio, 22, 53, 69, 131, 153,
159–160, 189, 225

Oklahoma, 188

Osawatomie, Kansas, 112, 150

Ostrander, Mrs., 87

Ottawa Creek, 113

Ottawa, Kansas, 176

Ottawa Reserve, 114

Pacific Rural Press (San Francisco), 203, 204, 211

Panic of 1837, 32

Parkville, Missouri, 138, 164

Paul, Alice, 213, 228

Peck, divorce case of James and Lydia, 3

Pennsylvania, 129, 131, 185, 241

penny presses, 68

Perth Amboy, New Jersey, 109

Phelps, James, 20

Philadelphia, Pa., 201

Phillips, Wendell, 57, 146, 173

phrenology, 85

Pierce, Franklin, 122

Pierson, Lydia Jane, 44

poetry, 24–25, 32–34, 37–36, 158

Pomeroy, Samuel, 103

Pomo Indians, 214

popular sovereignty, 97

Pottawatomie Massacre, 126–127, 157

Potter Valley, California, 195, 196, 212

Pray, Isaac C., 82

Price, Abby, 55

prostitution, 56

Queen Victoria, 122

Quindaro *Chindowan*, 140–141, 210

Quindaro, Kansas, 5, 7–8, 134–135, 140–142, 143, 163, 164; and underground railroad, 138–139, 158; decline of, 169

railroads, 48, 49, 54, 85, 97, 158,

186, 193, 194, 199; CIHN and, 49

Raritan Bay Union, 109

Republican Party, 148, 150, 173, 180; CIHN campaigns for, 128–129; divided over John Brown, 156

revival meetings, 14

Revolutionary War, 11, 16, 17, 29, 175, 201

Revolution, The, 180, 181, 192

Rhode Island, 12, 93, 131

Ritchie, John, 150

Robinson, Charles, 117, 125

Rochester, New York, 26, 53, 67

Rose, Ernestine, 46, 55, 80, 93, 159, 202, 215, 224

Salem, Ohio, 53, 69

San Francisco, California, 203, 208

Santa Fe Trail, 113

Saturday Visiter, 57

school suffrage, 71, 152, 190, 226

Scott, Col., 102, 157

Second Great Awakening, 26–27

Second Kansas Cavalry, 169

Second National Woman's Rights Convention. *See* women's rights conventions

Semi-Weekly Eagle (Brattleboro, Vt.), 42

Sharps rifles, 118

slavery, 43, 62, 97–98, 102, 108, 117, 125, 129, 139, 144, 154, 157, 166, 203. *See also* abolitionists; *See also* Fugitive Slave Law

slaves, 56, 138, 156, 157, 166

Smith, Harley, 44

Smith, James McCune, 75

South Carolina, 51, 125, 160

Speer, John, 115

spheres, 17, 18, 23, 59, 79, 88. *See*

also ministers; *See also* "true woman"

Springfield *Daily Republican*, 106

Stanton, Elizabeth Cady, 52, 78, 166, 171, 178–181, 202, 207, 215, 225, 227

St. Joseph, Missouri, 102

St. Louis, Missouri, 99, 101, 159

Stone, George, 214

Stone, Lucy, 55, 76, 78, 93, 131, 170–171, 176, 180, 215, 227, 234

"strong-minded women," 68, 79, 123

strong-minded women, 106

suffrage, 66, 145, 150–151, 169, 183, 190, 206, 234. *See also* elections; *See also* school suffrage; black female, 177; black male, 177; various approaches in Kansas, 145, 170; white male, 125

Sumner, Charles, 125, 126, 127

Swisshelm, Jane, 44, 57, 215, 225

Taft, Alphonso, 22, 215

Taft, William Howard, 22, 215

temperance, 27–29, 75–79, 87. *See also* alcohol consumption; in Quindaro, 140; linked to abolition and women's rights, 77; Wisconsin campaign of 1853, 83–91

Templeton, Massachusetts, 95

Texas, 139

Thompson, Daniel, 72

thrift, 13, 30, 137–135, 192

Timothy Cressy's Select School, 37

Topeka Constitution (1855), 117, 124, 144

Topeka, Kansas, 161, 169, 170, 192

Townshend, Vermont, 12, 35, 36, 40, 122

Train, George Francis, 179–178, 180
"true woman," 59, 69, 73, 82. *See also* spheres
Truth, Sojourner, 55, 81, 180, 216, 226
Twain, Mark, 85

Ukiah, California, 195, 214
Una, The, 225
Underground railroad, 8, 138–139, 158–159, 187
Union College (N.Y.), 25
University of Kansas, 152

Van Winkle, Deborah, 50
vegetarian, 42, 105
Vermont, 12, 25, 47, 71, 131, 190, 195, 207; and divorce, 39; called "conservative", 162; CIHN's address to legislature (1852), 72; custody law in, 95; early, 12; passes temperance law, 82; passes women's rights bill, 47
Vermont and Massachusetts Railroad, 48
Vermont Journal, 168
Vermont Phoenix, 37, 38, 108, 114, 170, 234
Visiter, The, 225
voting. *See* suffrage

Warpole, Mary. *See* Nichols, Mary Warpole
Washington, D.C., 50, 125, 166, 184, 187, 212
water cure, 40–41
Wattles, Esther, 145–146, 153, 154
Wattles, John O., 145, 153–154
Wattles, Susan, 145–146, 149, 153, 157, 158, 163, 164
Waukesha, Wisconsin, 90

Weld, Theodore Dwight, 27, 51, 109
Western Home Journal, 176
Western Star, The (Brockport, N.Y.), 30
Westport, Missouri, 102, 157
West Townshend, Vermont, 11, 14, 16, 19, 20, 25, 59
Whittier, John Greenleaf, 100
Whole World's Temperance Convention (1853), 75–78, 86
widows, 60–62, 81, 122, 124. *See also* law
widow's dower, 60, 124
Willard, Frances, 228
Wilson, Woodrow, 213
Windham County Democrat, 43, 49–50, 57, 67, 71, 210, 225; CIHN begins writing for, 38–39; halts publication, 93
Windham County, Vermont, 14, 23
Wisconsin, 82, 83, 86, 92, 126, 131, 132, 160
Wisconsin Temperance League, 86, 89
Wisconsin Women's Temperance Convention, 86–87
Wollstonecraft, Mary, 222, 223
Woman's Herald of Industry (San Francisco), 208
Woman's Journal, 180, 203
Woman's Loyal League, 166
women's rights; and antislavery, 109; and free-soil movement, 124; and the law. *See* law
women's rights conventions; First National (1850), 53, 54–57, 56, 175; "mob convention" (1853), 79–82; Second National (1851), 57; Seneca Falls (1848), 10, 52–53, 225
Woodhull, Victoria, 191
Wood, Sam, 171, 178

Worcester, Massachusetts, 53–54, 66, 206. *See also* women's rights conventions: First National (1850) and Second National (1851)

World Anti-Slavery Convention (1840), 51, 52, 75

World's Fair; of 1853, 74; of 1876, 201; of 1893 (Columbian Exposition), 214

World's Temperance Convention (1853), 75

Wright, Frances, 90, 215, 223

Wright, Martha Coffin, 52, 227

Wyandotte City, Kansas, 143, 144, 147, 149, 163, 183

Wyandotte Commercial Gazette, 163, 175, 177, 183, 189

Wyandotte Constitution (1859), 147–151, 153–154, 190

Wyandotte Gazette, 137, 183, 195–196, 208

Wyandotte Indians, 137, 188–190

About the Author

Diane Eickhoff has taught school in Appalachia and Westchester County, New York, served as director of public relations for a hospital in suburban Chicago, and worked as a senior editor in language arts for a major educational publisher. She conducts living history presentations for the Kansas Humanities Council. A native of Minnesota, Eickhoff lives in Kansas City, Missouri, with her husband, television critic Aaron Barnhart. This is her first biography.